To Da

Keep On Running

A memoir

from

Andy

All the best

Andy Armitage

Keep on Running

Published by The Conrad Press Ltd. in the United Kingdom 2022

Tel: +44(0)1227 472 874

www.theconradpress.com

info@theconradpress.com

ISBN 978-1-914913-65-5

Typesetting and Cover Design by: Charlotte Mouncey, www.bookstyle.co.uk

The Conrad Press logo was designed by Maria Priestley.

Printed and bound in Great Britain by Clays Ltd, Elcograf S.p.A.

For Penny Ovenden
and other grandchildren who may come along

Contents

Chapter 1 – The daffodil competition

The headmistress of the Infants was Miss Sharp.

I was amused that Miss Sharp had very sharp facial features but even more amused by what Miss Sharp would frequently say as we dawdled along the corridor, which I reported to my mother, herself a bit of a linguist: 'Mum – Miss Sharp says "be sharp" all the time.'

It must have been Miss Sharp who had a hand in instigating the Daffodil Competition. So, the teachers gave us daffodil bulbs to take home. Mum placed them in a black plastic bowl and covered them with soil. Then, on a specified day in the spring, we were instructed to bring our daffodils in. I was very proud of mine. The bowls were placed along the corridor on the window sills and then judged. There were first, second and third prizes and, well, no awards for my daffs. I was outraged.

I used this competition, or at least my experience of it, when training teachers some thirty years on, as my first lesson about assessment. Firstly, when we were sent off with our bulbs, we should have been informed about what the judges would be looking for – what makes a good daff? Colour, stature? In other words, what would be the assessment criteria underpinning the judgement? Secondly, the competition didn't seem to involve the deployment of horticultural skills. Mum just put the bulbs in a bowl and they were regularly watered. So why weren't we given guidance about how to grow a good daff? Thirdly, why did the three winners win? Where was the transparency in this competition? And finally, and most importantly, never underestimate the emotional impact assessment can have on individuals: I'm still seething over sixty years later (so much so, I even wrote a book about assessment!)

This experience prefigured many others I was to have in my life. I was to discover that sometimes, however hard you worked and planned, things might not turn out well and success seemed to be a matter of luck. It's as if I was playing a game but the rules were invisible and I didn't know how to win.

I don't know how we afforded it but for a short time we had a cleaner, Mrs Williamson or 'Willie' as she was known. Looking back, it sounds like something from the Royal Household! I remember standing at the bottom of the stairs and, being a child interested in language, I shouted up at Willie, kneeling half way up, cleaning the stair carpet, 'Willie, I can see your willy'. Willie was very good. She came quietly down the stairs and said, 'Andrew, ladies don't have willies – only masters have willies.' My first experience of sex education. My only experience of sex education.

Mum was a creative storyteller and wove her own stories for me about locomotives which she called Puffing Billy and Puffing Billy-ette. I think she must have combined various elements here. Although Puffing Billy was the first actual working locomotive, the tune 'Puffin' Billy', about the locomotive, was the theme tune of *Children's Favourites* on the radio at the time. She might also have been inspired by the Rev Awdry's popular *The Railway Series*. She fielded a small child's difficult questions well. I remember asking her what my belly button was for. She said that when God had finished making me, he pushed his finger in to my tummy to see if I was 'done' and then said, 'You're done.' Although a little disconcerting in retrospect, I was entirely satisfied by this explanation at the time.

'Off to school – the first day'
Clockwise – Baz, his sister Vivien, cousin visiting from Plymouth, me

This is a photo of Baz and I on the first day of school, September 5th 1955 (Mum wrote it on the back), with Baz's older sister Vivian and a cousin visiting from Plymouth standing behind us. We both look happy and even excited about the prospect of school. My memory of that morning is quite sharp. Our parents deposited us at the school entrance and we were then ushered into the hall which had wall bars, a horse (gymnastic) and a large painting *The Adoration of the Magi* by Breughel (I clearly didn't know it was a Breughel at the time. I was a precocious little git but my art history was limited at five. However, I've loved Breughel ever since and was delighted to discover one of the world's best Breughel collections in the

Kunsthistorisches Museum in Vienna, which included *The Adoration of the Magi*). We were then led to our classroom and met our teacher, the kindly Mrs Moore. There was a large picture pinned to the board of a steam training running along by the sea. I remember the picture excited me and I think it was because it was in vivid colours (not much colour in my life in 1955) but more that it hinted there were journeys to exotic places and there were seasides. Sixty years later, on my way to do some work in Plymouth, I was taken aback as my train travelled along the coast between Dawlish and Teignmouth - here was my picture from Mrs Moore's classroom.

That first day was very pleasant: suddenly I was surrounded by nippers my age whom I saw as potential chums. But one poor girl was not too happy. She screamed and wept and wouldn't let go of her mum whom she clung on to. I remember we successfully detached children looked away from the drama: forty-four discreet little folk.

My lifelong tendency to be caught short was established in a traumatic event when I was five. I remember asking to go to the toilet and being turned down by Miss since it wasn't a break time. It finally happened as I stood in front of the nature table. There wasn't much on the nature table – a couple of old damaged pine cones and acorns as I remember, this being Stretford, Manchester, hardly an area of outstanding natural beauty in 1956, a decade before the Clean Air Act. The next thing I knew, I was being rushed home along Victoria Road by an alien dinner lady the teacher had obviously delegated to walk the steaming turd home. And then I'm sitting in Mrs Rose's dining room with Mrs Rose and her children, Philip, Jean and Gillian staring at me in horror from a distance. My mother must have been out shopping and Mrs Rose had kindly taken me in, as you would a parcel, or, as in this case, a bag of shite.

Our only relatives in the Manchester area were Uncle Sam, my dad's younger brother, and Aunty Jenny in Withington. They had an only child, Pam, who must have been twentyish when I was five. I remember they had (and we would reciprocate) Sunday afternoon teas which even in winter were salad affairs – tomato, lettuce, spring onions, Spam and pickled walnuts (I always believed my paternal grandmother, who lived with Sam and Jenny and had died round about this time, had swallowed a pickled walnut but Pam told me only recently that she'd choked on a piece of meat pie. I think it was this made me terrified of choking which I came close to once after swallowing a rather large piece of Chateaubriand in France).

My early memories of 599 Princess Road are all pretty much at or near ground level because that's where I spent most of my time: memories of chair legs, a Bakelite electric fire, shoes and socks, table legs, carpet friezes I ran my dinky toys along. I remember they had a sofa which prickled my short-trouser bare legs. Upstairs, in their toilet, the cistern was on the ceiling and a pipe ran down to the lavatory itself. This pipe had lagging wrapped round it (was it so cold in pre-central heating houses that inside pipes had to be lagged?). I didn't know it was lagging: to me the pipe was a hairy snake which made me too frightened to go to their toilet.

In my teenage years, Dad and I would visit Jenny and Sam on a Saturday afternoon. Jenny was hard of hearing for many years. Dad would tease her by making remarks pitched just below her hearing level which would have her fiddling with her hearing aid, 'I didn't hear that John. What was that?'

Meanwhile, Sam would smile knowingly – it must have been a game they'd played for years – and waggle his finger vigorously in his ear. Like me, Dad was incredibly impatient when visiting people and after an hour at Sam and Jenny's, would start inventing girlfriends for me and ask me what time I was going to meet them.

Pam was my godmother. She married Denis in 1957 and they had their reception at the Deanwater Hotel in Wilmslow (which I see is still billed as Cheshire's premier wedding venue). It was my first ever posh do. As I grew up, Denis was held up to me, by Aunty Jenny particularly, as a role model. And with good reason, I now reflect. As a working-class boy from Rusholme, he'd done well to go to Manchester University in the 1950s to study Engineering. He rose rapidly in ICI and by the mid 60s Pam and Denis were in a beautiful detached house in Thornton Cleveleys, Blackpool (over the years Pam took on a very motherly role and she kindly invited me to revise for my O Levels here after my mum died. I did so and helped myself to Denis's fags piled up in his posh ciggy box). Denis rose to be Head of Engineering for ICI and later Director General of The Engineering Council, which earned him an OBE. But I'm equally proud of Pam. She's always been a bundle of energy and even now, at eighty-five, dashes around the area in Hertfordshire, where they now live. I was delighted when she was awarded an MBE for her work with victim support.

I remember my primary school teachers as if they were sitting next to me. They are, after all, the most important adult role models next to your parents during a very formative period in your life. Miss Carter was the top infants' teacher. She wore a quite striking suit which was bright mustard with large check stripes, had the face of Cruella De Vil and wore her hair in a bun inside a net. All I remember of a year with her is reading a story about a monkey which escaped from a circus. This not a criticism of Miss Carter's teaching but more to do with the impact the monkey's story had on me: it was naughty to escape in the first place – naughtiness being a real draw to a six-year-old – and I remember the thrill of the monkey being free to have adventures.

In the Juniors we had Miss Kyle. It was in her class that I first came across streaming. We were divided into groups, each of which sat round its own table. Of course, everyone knew how bright or not everyone in the class was so it was obvious what the rationale for the grouping was. But this was reinforced by the readers having identical covers except for their differing colours and titles – Book 1, 2, 3, 4 etcetera. Mrs Wilkins was fabulously glamorous in a very 1950s way – heavy make-up, frilly blouses, pencil skirts, seamed stockings and stilettos – very unusual for a schoolteacher in those days. I think it was she who made a vain attempt to teach us elocution – 'Poor tall Paul, all the porters heard him fall'. I knew Mrs Newland didn't like me. She kept me behind one day and threatened that I'd be busted to the B stream if my behaviour didn't improve. I can't now remember what I'd done wrong – probably talking too much, ('Andrew is a chatterbox' she wrote in that term's report) – but looking back, demotion seems an extraordinary behaviour management strategy. Mind you – it obviously worked! Mrs Lewis was very exotic and did exotic things (not that kind of exotic). It was she who showed us in a slide projector, photographs of what was then Ceylon where she'd grown up (she had returned to England with her family after Ceylon's independence in 1948). The image which stuck with me was a shot of the Temple of the Tooth in Kandy. I never then dreamt I'd see it for myself forty years later.

The teacher of the top class was 'Nellie Beckett', beloved by generations of school children. It was also widely known, almost as school lore, that she always cried on the last day of junior school. And Nellie didn't let us down. Now, there was an eleven plus firmly in place at the time (Trafford is still one of the local authorities to have retained selection). However, although we did practice test after practice test, I never remember actually taking an eleven plus test. I can only imagine that one of the 'practice tests' was the real one which, if true, is an interesting educational innovation! I do, however, remember the day we found out who had passed and who had not. The official means of communicating this was via letters to parents. Only, Lancashire Education Committee had not reckoned with the Royal Mail and these letters arrived on different days for different children. When this came to light, Miss Beckett, obviously thinking it unfair that some kids knew and others didn't, pointed at each child saying 'Yes' or 'No'. I think she was right to do this but what a graphic demonstration of the unfairness of selection it was and I'm sure my lifelong abhorrence of selective education was born at that point and reinforced by then attending a grammar school myself.

Interesting sidebar - a close mate in the Sixth Form was Tony Lloyd, now Labour MP for Rochdale and a former minister of state in Tony Blair's government and Opposition spokesman in Corbyn's Shadow Cabinet. When Stretford Boys Grammar School merged with Stretford Girls Grammar in 1986, the school had a multi-year reunion at the school on Great Stone Road before closing. Both Tony and I attended and, several beers in, we got to arguing about selective education – Tony does good argument. Although we generally associate the Labour Party with supporting comprehensive education because of its social cohesiveness, there is a quite widely held view among Labour supporters, of which Tony is one (or at least was in 1986), that grammar schools are important levers of social mobility for working class children. My argument was that he and I had succeeded in spite of the school we went to, not because of it. (At the same reunion, the former headmaster - whom I had already based a character on in the BBC's *Keep On Running* - sidled up to me. He hadn't seen me in eighteen years. I had one hand in my pocket and held a pint in the other. 'Ah – Armitage. Still playing with yourself I see.' Wish I'd got that line into the TV play, two years earlier!)

Our desks at primary school were integrated units - two desks, one seat. There was an ink well in the top corner of each desk which had a sliding metal cover (this, I recall was made in West Bromwich which, at the time, sounded very exotic. I was in West Bromwich relatively recently and, no offence to its burghers, 'exotic' it is not). Now the desks had ink wells because we wrote with pens which had scratchy nibs and wooden handles. Being ink monitor was a much sought-after role. At the time of the incident I was sharing a desk seat with John Gabbay. We were very good friends – I went to play at his house, he at mine. I don't recall what sparked it but we had a disagreement which ended up in an ink fight which involved flicking ink at one another's exercise books. Cut to after school. The entire class has adjourned to Victoria Park to see the Armitage v Gabbay bout, the boxing ring formed of coats and jumpers. The fight was quite evenly balanced when two men came over and broke it up. John and I were separated in class and I don't remember ever speaking to him again. He went on to qualify as a doctor and had a very eminent career in public health and the last I heard was Emeritus Professor of Public Health at the University of Southampton. I've always felt terrible guilt about that fight and I'm still not sure why, whether it was because it was I who had challenged him to the fight or that we hurt each other – we were both a bit bruised and bloody – or whether it was about the loss of a friend. So – sorry John, 60 years on.

Five boys from my school, Vicky Park, were selected to apply to the major direct grant grammar schools in Manchester. I've always wondered whether I was selected because 'Pop' Wardle, the headmaster, was a drinking buddy of my dad's at the Conservative Club. They fell out later because, according to Dad, Harry Wardle would always ask for 'a pint and whiskey chaser, thanks very much, Jack'. Dad changed his drinking allegiance to the Trades and Labour Club. Dad was a Tory but was never fussed where he drank.

The Manchester Grammar School entrance test was a game of two halves. The first was a test of Maths and English. I got stuck on the decoding questions. You were given a series of number sequences which, if decoded, spelt words. Couldn't crack it however much I tried. I think they were looking for budding Alan Turings or recruiting early for MI5. Years later, a teaching colleague of mine at the University told me that, earlier in his career, he'd taught maths at MGS and, when the entrance exam took place, one of the teachers would take the test papers up to the staffroom whereupon the teachers would attempt the papers and all fail miserably. The letter from Lord

James of Rusholme, the High Master, telling me I'd failed, arrived on a Saturday morning, Dad bringing the letter upstairs to show Mum and have a hushed conversation with her before they gave me the bad news, which I knew anyway.

The two boys from Vicky Park who did get places at MGS were both sons of teachers and it was years later, when I was in the education business and knew a bit about assessment, that I wondered whether that had something to do with their success through their being able to practise on past papers or, at least being schooled by their parents. But this may be sour grapes at my failing: educational failure leaves long and deep scars.

Ironically, my first BBC drama, *Keep on Running*, was set in a northern grammar school and the director, Paul Seed, himself an MGS product, cast his former MGS English teacher, Bert Parnaby, as the headteacher. Bert had taken up acting after retiring from being a Her Majesty's Inspector. In this role he had run a wonderful course for Further Education teachers of English I'd attended at St Anne's College, Oxford a decade before. Strange connections.

The two other schools I'd applied to were William Hulme's Grammar School and Chetham's Hospital School. The latter was the school which had child abuse scandals relating to the 1980s when it was a specialist music school. At the time, however, it was a general academic school and took Manchester Cathedral Choristers. I remember very little about the William Hulme's entrance exam, except that it had (and still does have!) very impressive buildings in Whalley Range. However, I vividly remember part of the Chetham's test which was my first experience of cultural bias in assessment. I had to read a passage out loud to a teacher who then asked me questions about it. One involved reference to a housewife who put newspaper over her carpets in the summer. 'So why would she do that Andrew?' Because she's insane? I didn't have a clue. The right answer was to stop the sun from discolouring her carpets. What? We only had two partially carpeted areas in our house – most of our floors were covered in lino. In spite of this, I was offered a place at Chetham's. However, there was a catch. I was the accomplished head chorister at my local church at the time and the offer was conditional on my transferring to the Manchester Cathedral Choir, a bit like Denis Law crossing from Man City to Man U, which he did round about this time (via Torino of course, soccer history buffs). I was very happy at St Matthews; it had one of the best church choirs in the North West. So, I turned Chetham's down. I was also offered a place at William Hulme's, which I also turned down. At the time, I told my parents that I wanted to stay with my chums and go to our local grammar school. Which was true. However, I wonder in retrospect that I sensed I might have been out of my depth in the more challenging environment of a direct grant grammar.

Baz and I had a blissful childhood. Baz lived next door. His family had moved up from Plymouth about 1954/5. Baz's dad worked at Glovers Cables so the emigration was clearly about work in the middle of the austere 1950s. At the time, Trafford Park, around a mile from where we lived, was one of the largest industrial areas in Europe. When my sister left home, I moved into the box room which was the other side of the wall from Baz's room and we used to tap out messages like prisoners in adjacent cells. One time, we thought we could communicate directly between these bedrooms with two tin cans with string stuck through the holes in the bottom of them. However, we weren't aware that if anything touched the string it would block the sound waves.

Usually, Baz and I played together but sometimes – and particularly in the evenings – we would join around fifteen to twenty kids who lived around the back alleyway between Mitford Street and Jackson Street where Baz and I lived. It was kind of mass play but sometimes small groups of girls would break off and have self-contained skipping games or hopscotch. I think they felt safer and less threatened in these single sex groups but it would always piss us boys off and we'd look at each other, tut and tilt our heads, 'Girls'. Ticky was the most common game as well as Hide and Seek but the most popular were games like Ralley Vo and Please Mr Crocodile Can I Cross Your Golden River? In the former, two teams would be formed - the stalkers and the prey. The prey would go off and hide and the stalkers would go after them. If you caught and tagged prey they would have to stand inside a chalked enclosure unless freed by other prey who had evaded the guard and tagged you. The game was over when all prey were inside the enclosure. Please Mr Crocodile would involve Mr Crocodile usually facing a wall while the other kids massed behind him. He would issue a condition usually referring to those who were wearing a particular colour and they would be able to move forward. However, Mr Crocodile would suddenly swivel round and if he caught you moving, you were out. The object was to reach Mr Crocodile safely, tag him and become the next Mr Crocodile. These games were the most popular with us, I think, because they were communal and involved team membership.

Bonfire Night was a big deal in 1960. This was partly because there were so many sites for them, most of them crofts. These were bomb sites which, even fifteen years after the end of WW2, had yet to be rebuilt on. We had such a site not far from us on the corner of Barton Road and what was then King Street (it subsequently had flats built on it called 'Pinfold Court'. In the days when this area was agricultural, there was a pinfold or pen here for runaway sheep). During the half term week's break, which always seemed to precede Bonfire Night, or 'Bongy Night' as we called it, Baz and I would collect wood and any other flammable material and drag it back to our bongy which would grow to a considerable height over the week. At the same time, we would squat on King Street in the early evening, our badly made guy sitting in a push chair between us, asking for a penny for the guy. Most people passing avoided having to give us anything saying, 'You're too early, lads, far too early'. One evening, my Dad was coming down from the Conservative Club with a couple of friends after an early evening drink and Baz and I didn't manage to get away in time. I got it in the neck when I got home. 'Begging…in the street…my son!' Whack. One year, the rumour was that Johnny Oil, a big lad, was coming round bongies and setting them alight on November 4th. So, Baz and I stood guard over our bongy on the night of November 4th until nine o' clock, which was quite late for ten-year-olds. Oil never showed.

When the director Adrian Shergold became artistic director of the Soho Poly, a premier writers' theatre, he intended to continue the tradition of lunchtime shows as well as full-length evening plays. He asked me to come up with some ideas. I did.

Two or three times a week. His responses were always negative. Then one day I called him and said 'It's 1960. Two ten-year-olds are guarding their bonfire because it's rumoured that a big lad is going to turn up the day before bonfire night to set their bonfire alight. And he turns up. It's a sort of *Waiting for Godot* but, this time, Godot arrives.' 'Great said Adrian. It's commissioned.'

The play opens with Alan and Baz sciss-pat-bricking while waiting for Johnny Oil, imagining what they would do if Oil turns up. Their promised responses show bravado. And then, Oil does turn up. He humiliates the two, nicks their penny for the guy money, steals their cigs but flings them to the ground when he sees they are five Park Drive tipped, preferring the Passing Clouds he nicks from his dad. Alan goes off to look for help. Meanwhile, Baz and Oil's exchanges indicate that Oil's bullying conceals a rather sad soul looking for friendship. He then reveals that the reason he torches bonfires on November 4th is that, as a young Catholic boy, he'd learned that bonfires were anti-Catholic celebrations which he was desperate to prevent. As Alan returns, Oil quickly dons the guy's clothes, intending to ambush him. But Baz tips Alan off and they both jump Oil and tie him up. Having turned the tables, they then proceed to humiliate Oil. Baz thinks they've gone too far and wants to release the captive. Alan has other ideas and intensifies the humiliation, even suggesting they hurl Oil onto the bonfire and set it alight. We don't know if he's serious. Alan and Baz fight and Oil is released and leaves. It is clear Alan and Baz's falling out cuts deep and their friendship won't be the same again. Shortly, Baz will be going to secondary modern and Alan to the grammar, to be a 'grammar bug':

ALAN: Right – well – see you about.

BAZ: Right. I'll tell you one thing. Don't let us see you wearing your uniform anywhere near our house when you go to the grammar.

ALAN: I won't – don't you worry.

BAZ: You'll have to wear that stupid cap. And all the first years' caps are too big for them, 'cause their mams buy big sizes so when their heads grow they don't have to have new ones.

ALAN: You're just jealous, you.

BAZ: Jealous – me? I'm glad I'm going to Gorse Park. At least I won't be a snob like you. We don't need to wear caps.

ALAN: I bet you…

BAZ: Shut your head, grammar bug.

ALAN: Dimbo.

BAZ: Grammar bug.

ALAN: Dimbo.

BAZ: Grammar bug.

ALAN: Dimbo.

BAZ: Come here and say that…

ALAN: Get lost.

BAZ: I will – don't you worry. Enjoy your sparklers, grammar bug.

ALAN: I will – don't you worry.

'BAZ exits. FADE to BLACKOUT apart from a spot centre stage. ALAN pushes the pram with the guy into the spot which then fades slowly as there are sounds of excited children's voices, a crackling bonfire and exploding fireworks.'

At the time of the incident, I thought Johnny Oil's arson was just a vandal's desire to spoil other people's pleasure (Johnny Oil might well have been John Hoyle I realised when I was writing the play. But *Johnny Oil* was such a good title!). When I came to write the play, I thought having a religious/cultural motive would make him a much more sympathetic character. Although Baz and I did go to two separate schools shortly after this event, I actually don't believe this led to the end of our friendship. Indeed, we went on holiday to Jersey together six years later. However, a looming post eleven plus separation between the characters gave their falling out at the end of the play a real poignance.

The play opened as a lunch-time production in November 1982 with the brilliant Phil Daniels as Oil, with Nick Conway and Stuart Wilde in support. Nick was to go on to play the lead in my first BBC drama, *Keep on Running,* two years later. The play was well received: the Sunday Times called it 'a nostalgic, amusing and at times edgily disturbing drama', while for The Stage it was 'rough, raw and menacingly funny'. Time Out thought it '100% magic' and it even got a long review in the New Musical Express, '*Johnny Oil* is well worth shelling out for. Go see it.'

Baz moved with his family to Wrexham around 1970 and we lost touch. I would love to have invited him to London to see the play but there was no way I could have found him. In the 90s, at the height of the Friends Reunited craze, I did try to see if he'd registered with his old school but he hadn't. During the internet years I entered his name into Google – I was sure I'd get a hit. 'Tredgidgo' is an unusual Channel Islands name. But all I got was a naval engineer in Australia. Then, a couple of years ago, I entered his full name. Barry's middle name was 'Malcolm', his father's first name. The hair on the back of my neck stood on end. There was a photograph of a grave. 'A loving husband and father who passed away 12 May 1998. Gone but not forgotten.' He'd died at the ridiculously young age of forty-seven. This was my Baz. The Billion Graves information had him born December 1950 in Plymouth. The grave was in the Eaton Socon Cemetery in St Neots, Cambridgeshire. I did Google 'Tregidgo - St Neots' and got hits which were possibly remaining members of Baz's family. I considered contacting them but thought better of it. I didn't want to re-ignite any grief.

Each evening, the hooter at Metrovicks in Trafford Park went at five o' clock and within half an hour, buses, nose to tail, trundled down Barton Road at the end of my street, the main southern artery out of the Park. Each bus was full of men. Each man wore the same uniform: brown, belted mac, flat cap and brown army style lunch box. The bus procession went on for up to an hour. One winter's evening I was walking down our street towards Barton Road but there was something not quite right about the men in the buses. As I got closer I realized that most of the men hung their heads. Some were openly weeping, which startled me because you never saw an adult cry.

What they knew and I was soon to find out was that earlier that afternoon, 6th February 1958, BEA Flight 609 had crashed on its third attempt to take off from a slush-covered runway at Munich Airport. On the plane was the Manchester United Football team, the Busby Babes, along with supporters and journalists. Twenty of the forty-four on the aircraft died at the scene. The injured, some unconscious, were taken to hospital where three more died, resulting in twenty-three fatalities with twenty-one survivors. The team was returning from a European

Cup match having knocked out Red Star Belgrade to reach the semi-finals of the competition. United were a phenomenal post war success story. They were attempting to become the third club to win three successive English league titles; they were six points behind League leaders, Wolves, with fourteen games to go. They also held the Charity Shield and had just reached their second successive European Cup semi-finals. The team had not been beaten for eleven matches. But it was not just their footballing excellence that endeared them to the men on those buses: The Busby Babes carried the hopes for the future out of the austere 1950s of these men themselves. United *were* Manchester, were them. The same love has been passed down to today's Mancunians, with 'Flowers of Manchester' banners waved at home matches. It snowed in Manchester that evening, almost as if the snow was in sympathy, a pathetic fallacy.

BAZ: *It was the only time I've seen my dad cry.*
ALAN: *It's horrible when your mam and dad cry. I hate it.*
BAZ: *He heard about it at work.*
ALAN: *What?*
BAZ: *The Munich Disaster.*
ALAN: *Oh aye.*
BAZ: *We both cried.*
ALAN: *I felt lousy all day.*
BAZ: *All day? I still feel lousy. Did you ever see Duncan Edwards play?*
ALAN: *No – my dad said he would have been the best player in the world. Better even than Puskas or Di Stefano. And he should know, my Dad.*

(Johnny Oil)

I had joined St Matthew's church choir around seven years of age at my mum's suggestion. In those days, you had to audition. The choirmaster was one Bertram Rowley, a very grim-looking guy who frightened the life out of me. But I got through the audition and joined up. Mr Rowley was soon succeeded by Ronald Frost, a wonderful man in his twenties who took the choir to unforeseen heights. Selected choir members were on the interview panel for his role – very contemporary. Mr Frost would go on to have a distinguished career as Chorus Master and Principal Organist of the Halle Choir as well as Director of Music at St Anne's Church in Manchester.

My feeling about singing then was the same as when I'm immersed in a good piece of fiction now: nothing else exists – you are in the world of the book as I was in the music then. The University I taught at has done a lot of interesting research on the health benefits of singing and I am sure I was conscious of this as a child. Singing made me feel good.

The schedule was demanding: choir practice Tuesdays and Fridays, Matins and Evensong Sundays. You then had weddings on Saturdays, with up to three or four a day at the height of the summer season. Now these were good little earners: half a crown for weddings and five bob for the odd funeral (£3 and £6 in today's money). None of us had any idea what we were singing about but it didn't seem to matter. We all waited until potentially dirty words cropped up and giggled when they did. 'God is gone up with a merry *trump*' 'As *pants* the heart for cooling streams' (my italics).

At choir practice, our principal aim was to provoke Mr Cordingly, a tenor who taught English at Sale Grammar School, using bad, disruptive behaviour to bait him. He was wonderfully, predictably responsive. His head would shake, his face would redden and he would suddenly explode, 'Can these boys *not* destroy our choir practice please!' His syntax gave away the problem he was having. In his day job he was used to full control of the situation. But as a mere choir member he had to defer to Mr Frost. And he was actually saying – 'Please control these choirboys because I can't!' But we all knew this, which it was why it was so exquisite to provoke him. We had the instinctive insight of a social psychologist.

At one practice, Mr Frost gave us some exciting news – St Matthews was one of only fifteen to twenty churches nationally to be invited to send a chorister to make up the Royal School of Church Music Choir which would sing at the World Anglican Congress in Toronto and then tour eastern Canada. But who would be the lucky chorister? A problem for Mr Frost. But he solved it brilliantly by taking three of us over to Heaton Moor Parish Church, another invited church, where Mr Gerald Barber, the organist and choirmaster, auditioned us and made the final decision. I got the gig! I had to go down for rehearsals the Easter before the summer trip to the RSCM's then Headquarters at Addington Palace near Croydon. I went with Angus, the boy from the Heaton Moor choir. Quite how we navigated the national rail system and got across London aged twelve, I'll never know. It would have been a safeguarding issue now. Not in 1963. I had never seen such opulence as there was at Addington Palace, a Palladian mansion which had been for many years the summer residence of the Archbishops of Canterbury.

The lads in the choir, from all over the country, got on well and played football in the Capability Brown landscaped gardens when not rehearsing. I made friends with a Lancashire lad whom we called 'Grandad' because he was a bit older than the rest and wore Grandad glasses. The poor guy's voice had completely broken by the time we got to Canada in the summer and he had to mime throughout the tour. There are newspaper photos of the choir in the Toronto Public Library Archive, one of which shows the front row of the choir and there is Grandad on the left of shot.

Catching the rays – British High Commission, Ottawa, August 1963

Sadly, Angus missed the summer tour. He had a terrible accident on a scout trip and lost the sight of one eye. When I returned, I went over to see him and showed him all the photos I'd taken with my Brownie 127. We flew the Atlantic in a BOAC turbo prop airliner. It was my first ever flight and I made the mistake of taking my shoes off. I couldn't get them on again when we arrived in Toronto and I had to cross the tarmac in my socks. It was a very exciting trip. We sang in all the eastern Canadian cities – Montreal, Ottawa, Toronto and visited Niagara Falls. Everything about Canada was better than home – the countryside, the food, the climate. I was particularly struck by the air quality coming as I did from the land of pea soupers (I'm sure it was this trip which led to my considering a doctorate at the Ontario Institute for Educational Studies in Toronto in my twenties).

I was on my way to evensong one Sunday and had dismounted from my bike to walk it the final fifty yards or so when I passed two lads I knew as Billy Boot and Sean Gaffney. One of them, I forgot which, shouted the classic, 'Were you looking at me?' line, the ultimate rhetorical question. Before I had the chance to say I wasn't, Gaffney punched me in the face. I went down, my drop handle-barred tangerine Sun Super Snipe clattering on top of me. I can still remember that punch: not painful but numbing. I can't remember the exact sequence of events, but the police shadowed me on the journey home. Even I thought this was overkill. I didn't want grassing the lads up to invite a further attack. I'm recalling this event partly because it was traumatic but also because it was an interesting example of how social divisions can breed such resentment and anger at such an early age. The lads recognised me as a 'grammar bug' – both were at the local secondary school. Plus, I was on my way into church to sing in the choir: a cultural world away from theirs.

Some years ago, my nephew Paul came to stay. We were discussing members of our family and I mentioned I had photos of them. He asked to see them. So, I took out the three plastic wallets I kept the photos in. Paul was aghast. How could I treat this precious record of my life and his family with such apparent lack of care? Shamed by his reaction, I dutifully went out and bought photo albums and over several months – getting the photos to fit (and stay) in those four small envelopes is a tedious and, for someone with my lack of dexterity, difficult business – arranged the photos carefully in them. Well, I managed to complete two of the three before running out of patience and stuffing the remaining photos in the front page of the third. I've kept these albums on my desk and it's really helped having them to dip into while writing. However, the photo on top of the pile is a class photo of 1Y at Stretford Grammar School in 1962. I am on the back row, furthest right and I noticed I had a pen in my top blazer pocket: surely a sign that I was going to be a writer! The only boy with a pen in his pocket.

Form 1Y, Stretford Grammar School for Boys, April 1962.
The only boy with a pen in his pocket

And it was around this time that my literary flair was falsely recognised. Our English teacher, Mr Hayes, had set us a very challenging task for homework. We were to write a poem with the line 'These I have loved' at the end of each verse. Unfortunately, I was uninspired and after some time head scratching, Mum stepped in. I reckon she was a frustrated writer and here was an opportunity. I only remember one verse:

> 'The aroma of freshly baked bread,
> The pillow where I lay my head,
> The books that I have often read,
> These I have loved.'

When Mum and Dad returned from the next parents' evening, they were glowing. 'That Mr Hayes,' said Dad. 'He thinks you're a genius. It was the poem you wrote.' Mum smiled. It remained our secret.

In the first year at Stretford Grammar School, we were in unstreamed classes 1W, 1X, 1Y, 1Z. By the time we got into the second year we were streamed in the strangest of ways: two upper classes and two lower classes. The former were 2L and 2G, in which pupils learned French and Latin or French and German. The latter were 2F1 and 2F2, in which pupils learned only French. Philip E. Vernon's work on ability would have been widely known in 1961. And in his hierarchy of abilities, verbal educability (VEd) was nearly at the top. But that doesn't mean someone with higher VEd had the ability to learn two foreign languages rather than one! Bonkers. My first teaching job was at a school in Huyton, Merseyside. There were three streams of two classes: the HU stream, then YT and finally ON. And, of course, I was given 4N to teach last thing Friday afternoon. It wasn't long before they said, 'Ey sir, we may be the divvies but we're not that divvy. We know how to spell H-U-Y-T-O-N.'

I've often thought funny people were often generally very clever people and I remember some delightful moments at school. In one lesson Sir was demonstrating diffusion. (Why – I'll never know. Like most things, in most subjects, we got taught stuff which had no obvious purpose. Why diffusion? Why balance chemical equations? What was a Wheatstone Bridge?). Sir poured the blue solution into a gas jar full of water. Then disappeared until it diffused. Probably off to the staffroom for a fag. Very popular activity. Mind you – I was to develop it as a teacher. In his absence, Mike Porter decided to give the diffusion a helping hand and emptied a bottle of Quink into it. 'Good grief,' exclaimed Sir on his return, 'never known it that quick before.'

In the chemistry lab, a favourite trick was to place one of the smaller boys in the fume cupboard to see how long it would be before Sir noticed. There were two gloriously eccentric friends, Jim and Gis, who got up to all sorts of strange things. We were doing social and economic history and the teacher was explaining the industrial revolution and the importance of the canal system, particularly James Brindley's Bridgewater Canal which ran very close to the school. The teacher claimed that the canal was nine feet deep, whereupon Jim stuck his hand up. 'It's not, sir. It's only six. Me and Gis measured it.' I remember this as the first demonstration I'd witnessed of the superiority of practical learning by doing over academic learning.

I was lucky enough to go with the school on two educational cruises, which generations of schoolkids have enjoyed. The

MS Dunera and Devonia were two wartime troop ships that were re-equipped as floating classrooms. But it was hardly the learning opportunities we lads were interested in, nor the exotic ports we docked in: La Coruna, Lisbon, Palermo, Tunis. It was the girls – hundreds of them from all over the country. I have a photograph of we boys about to weigh anchor on the Dunera and I've just spotted in it a face which was to become famous. This was Peter Noone, later to become Herman of the Hermits (not much later: this was 1962 and the Hermits' first hit was *I'm into Something Good* in 1964).

All aboard the MS Dunera. I am anxious in the duffel coat left.
Pete Noone is in the middle

Pete Noone was to become a folk hero of the school and there were a number of (apochryphal, I think) stories about him. One is that he said to his maths teacher 'For all the maths you've taught me this year I couldn't stand on my hands and fart out the two times table', whereupon he was sent to the head who promptly expelled him. I don't think that was the end of his school career because his biography has him at St Bede's in Manchester. Another story has him returning in a white roller after the Hermits' success, buying an ice cream from F.Mattiusi, whose van sat outside the school during lunch and breaks in the summer, and eating it leaning against his car. It's great to hear current Man U fans singing *I'm into Something Good* at home matches.

My mother was born in 1906 so was forty-four when she gave birth to me. My sister Heather claims I was an accident – probably true – and that Mum drank all sorts of potions to get rid of me. Probably not true – Heather's wishful thinking. I have photos of her aged eight in the Braunton Operatic Society's production of The Mikado (drama's in the blood dahling) and aged fourteen at the Barnstaple Grammar School Sports Day. Mum was a very academic woman. The kids around us in Stretford would bring their homework round to ours. I was a bit jealous of the attention they were getting but proud of her reputation. She apparently had a place at Cambridge, quite something in 1924 but the family couldn't afford to support her. I have a copy of Chaucer's General Prologue to the Canterbury Tales which she annotated. The annotations were excellent and I used the copy when I taught A Level English myself. I gave it to my own step-daughter, Lauren, when she qualified as an English teacher. Instead of university, Mum joined the civil service and here she is, Amy Helen Bawden, having passed her Clerical Officer, Ministry of Labour exam listed in the London Gazette 4th September

1925. She did well in the civil service and we see her again in the London Gazette 7th December 1934, having passed her Executive Officer exam. This meant a move to Manchester where she became the first woman manager of a labour exchange in the country. Quite a feat. And where she met my father, Jack Armitage.

The Mikado, Braunton Operatic Society 1914.
Mum, front row, standing 2nd right with wand

Dad had run off to the First World War, like many other boys, under age at fourteen. He seems to have spent time both as a messenger and medical orderly. (He kept up an interest in medicine throughout his life, saying he would have liked to have qualified as a doctor if he'd had his life over. I discovered that, in his 50s and 60s, he'd often volunteered in local hospitals, which he'd kept quiet about.) Like many who had lived through the horrors of war, he wouldn't talk about it but spun amusing, obviously invented, anecdotes. One was that, carrying a message close to enemy lines, with the Germans firing mortars at him, he suddenly needed to pee. He nipped into a nearby copse to do his business. The Germans gave him respite while he was in there but resumed mortaring him when he ran off again. On another occasion, he captured fifteen German soldiers, single-handed. He brought them back along the trenches to the sergeant-major. He told Dad to take them back again. They had a shortage of food and wouldn't be able to feed the captives. 'Take them back, Armitage,' he said. 'Take them back where you found them.' I have his war medals in front of me on the desk: The British War Medal (he managed to blag two of those) and The Victory Medal. He also brought back a German helmet with a spike on top, which I used to parade around in as a young boy – not very wise in post WW2 Manchester!

Mum and Dad, Biarritz, 1937

Mum and Dad had a very glamorous life in the late 1930s. Dad made a lot of money in the furniture business and they had smart addresses in the posh Cheshire suburbs of Bramhall and Gatley. (Dad was an absolutely brilliant salesman. In the 1950s, he'd work Saturdays in a Manchester furniture store and sometimes took me in with him. I was astounded by his capacity to sell anything to anybody. One of his tricks was to mutter inaudibly the price of something when customers asked, on the grounds that the actual price might put them off.) I have photographs of Mum and Dad in Biarritz with their friends, Mum in a very smart box jacket with two tone shoes, Dad in a startling broad black and white striped jacket.

WW2 destroyed the furniture business and post war, Dad joined the civil service in the role of technical officer for the Ministry of Works. He was on a modest income and 1948 has them moving into a rented property, 103 Jackson Street, Stretford. 103 and 105 (where Baz lived) were new in 1948: the only two houses on our side of the street to be bombed and rebuilt. It must have been a real come down for them after the glamour of the 30s. It could have been this misfortune had something to do with his terrible mismanagement of money: it's an affliction I've inherited, I'm afraid. Dad was always robbing Peter to pay Paul. On one occasion, he borrowed money from my sister, Hilary and her new husband, Jack, money which they as newlyweds could ill afford. When it came for them to be repaid, they were startled when a Ministry of Works lorry turned up with piles of carpet, no doubt taken out of a decommissioned prefab. Dad's repayment.

I have two older sisters, Hilary and Heather. As a seven-year-old, I was very jealous of anyone who showed an interest in them. Teenagers didn't really have anywhere to meet in the fifties and Sunday morning church seemed to be a popular pick up event. After church, couples could be seen strolling through the town, chatting. I had tracked Hilary and Heather who seemed to have a double date with Graham and his gormless brother, Alan from St Matthews, down King Street. The foursome stood, chatting, at the junction of King Street and Barton Road. I had gathered my small gang and we hid behind bushes on the croft (to be made famous in my play *Johnny Oil*) and pelted the four with stones. I think I got away with it. But, looking back, I am surprised at my capacity for violence at such a young age. Alan and Graham make an appearance in *Picture Friend* (see below) when they come to take the girls to the pictures. 'What are you going to see?' asks the mother in the awkward silence as they wait for the girls to come down. '*The Ten Commandments,*' replies Alan (in what I believe was a first TV appearance for David Thewlis), 'wait till you see the Red Sea part,' he gasps, 'it's fantastic!'

As a boy, I got on well with Hilary – she almost played the role of a surrogate mum. Heather was another matter. We fought like cat and dog. I have painful memories of her sitting on me to pin me down, her large blue school knickers smothering me. I wonder what trauma that has caused me in later life! I asked her recently (she just turned seventy-nine) why she was so aggressive towards me. She said she just found me irritating. I think it might be something to do with middle child syndrome: she was no longer the baby of the family when I came along. In fact, my parents re-used the pram Heather had been in eight years previously and when I was first taken out in it, the eight-year-old stood by the gate scowling as it passed and said, 'Not fair, my pram.' In 1984, the BBC producer, Brenda Reid, rang me up and asked me if I wanted to contribute to a Screenplay series she was commissioning for BBC2. Did I? Come the day, I went in to the BBC to discuss what I wanted to do. I didn't have a clue. I've always been someone who has reacted to deadlines at the last minute and I was on the Central Line approaching White City when I suddenly thought that since my family was interesting to me, it might be for viewers. Brenda commissioned *Picture Friend*. In it, June Ritchie played my sister and Jim Broadbent my father. More about that in Chapter 4.

Me, Hilary, Paul, Richard, Jonathan, Simon – mid 1970s

Hilary and Jack had four boys, in quick succession: Paul, Simon, Jonathan and Richard. I was very close to the boys, particularly in my twenties. Initially, when I was at Liverpool, I would visit them in Lymm, the other side of Warrington. The family lived in a bungalow with a loft bedroom up a ladder, where I slept. I liked my lie-ins at that stage in my life but it was not to be at Lymm. The boys rigged a dart board up on the other side of my bedroom door and would play darts, hurling the arrows hard into the board at ungodly hours of the morning to get me up.

Jack was a talented turbine designer but the increasingly unstable nature of the manufacturing industries in the 1970s has them relocating to the East Midlands and they settled in Market Harborough. There were memorable events there. My favourite related to 'indoor fireworks'. The print on the side of the packet promised safety indoors. But the result was a major fireworks display which burned several surfaces in the house. The boys loved it. Jack went ape-shit.

Fearful of Jack's future in Thatcher's unstable Britain, the family emigrated to Calgary in 1983. Paul stayed behind, having started an architecture course at Nottingham. Simon became a key player in the extraction of oil from the tar sands in Alberta. Jonathan has his own company which works internationally and which, I believe, specialises in locating oil reserves and Richard, now retired, worked as a water engineer at Fort McMurray in the Athabasca Oil Sands in Alberta. It's obviously been difficult over the years to maintain relationships with the boys and their families given the distance between us.

It was a sunny June day in 1964 when Heather took me aside. I remember exactly where we were – to the left-hand side of the front bay window. She told me that Mum had a terminal illness, had six months to live and there was nothing anyone could do about it. In shock, I muttered something entirely inappropriate, 'Well, that's spoilt my day.' 'No,' she said, 'I think it'll spoil your life.' She was spot on.

What subsequently happened was quite bizarre and I still don't understand the reasoning behind it. Although we siblings knew, as did Dad, Mum was not told. So, we spent the next, very painful six months keeping the awful secret from her. We went on a last family holiday to Blackpool that summer. Much of the holiday is a blur but I couldn't handle sitting with the rest of the family on the beach and disappeared to the local pool at every opportunity, diving continually off the high board, a coping mechanism. Peter and Gordon's hit *World Without Love* was top of the charts that summer and it was played endlessly at the pool.

That autumn I joined the Stretford Children's Theatre, partly as a distraction but partly because I fancied myself as an actor. It was a delusion I had for the next fourteen years until I dried up on the stage of the Vanbrugh Theatre during a RADA audition at the age of twenty-eight and I finally realised I didn't have what it takes. Stretford Children's Theatre was founded by local teacher, Bertram H. Holland and became a power house of talent producing the actors such as June Ritchie and David Schofield. Its story is told in Bertram Holland's 1968 publication *Beginners on Stage*, which I thought was a very clever title. My first part was small – no infinitesimal. I was to play Sir William Catesby in *Richard III*. He only has one line after possibly the most famous line in the play:

RICHARD: *A horse, a horse – my kingdom for a horse!*
CATESBY: *I'll get you to a horse, my liege.*

The play has a large cast and by the time wardrobe got around to the bit parters like me, they were running out of costumes. The tights they offered me were pink. Pink tights for a fourteen-year-old boy! Word got around at school and my mates turned up in force. When I came on with the horse offer, they cheered and stamped their feet, a response out of proportion with my role. Richard was played by a young man called Andrew Winton. I marvelled at his capacity to learn so many lines, let alone speak them so effectively. The play ran for six nights. One night, something bizarre happened. The cast accidently began Act 5 instead of Act 4 after Act 3. So, we had the Battle of Bosworth Field accompanied by Holst's Planet Suite, the climactic event of the play. Then the lights went up for Act 4, the night before the Battle. Surreal. I'm not sure the audience noticed but the cast performed Act 4 like zombies, not quite knowing what had hit them.

Mum's condition deteriorated that autumn and she was taken into Park Hospital (where the NHS had been launched in 1948 and I'd been launched two years later) a number of times. She had acute nephritis, which was end stage kidney disease in the 1960s. She was too old for a transplant at fifty-nine and dialysis wouldn't have worked. She was finally taken into hospital one night in early January 1965. I lay in the adjacent room as she was carried down the stairs on a stretcher screaming, 'I don't want to die'. I thrust my fingers hard into my ears.

I must have gone down well as Catesby because I got the lead in the next production, Nicholas Stuart Grey's *The Imperial Nightingale*. I was to play Bamboo, The Fisherman. I remember absolutely nothing about the play except the physical challenge of the role. This was as follows. Bamboo enters and exits on a low punt-like boat at the back of the stage. There is a bank which conceals the bottom half of the boat and the wheels underneath it. Behind the bank, ropes are attached to each end of the punt and it is then pulled off stage left or right by the stage crew while I mime punting/rowing. Now, stage crew are easily bored, having nothing much to do during scenes. My punt pullers decided to yank the rope, making me sway and have to steady myself on the pole. And they did it at different stages in the scenes, never on the same lines, to surprise me. This got laughs from the audience during romantic, lyrical scenes which were not supposed to be funny at all.

The Imperial Nightingale opened on January 27th 1965 for a five-night run. The first night went well and after the curtain at the Civic Theatre, I turned right at the post office and picked Dad up from the Conservative Club. I did the same the following night. This time Dad burst into tears when he got out of the club. Mum had died earlier that evening. Dad must have driven to the club straight from the hospital because we climbed into his Austin England, parked around the corner. He drove it down the back alleyway behind the house, not wanting to bump into any neighbours. I continued as Bamboo the night after and two nights after that. Later, Bertram Holland would write to Dad praising me for being a wonderful trooper. I wasn't. I was just grateful to have the distraction during a terrible time.

We went as a family to the funeral parlour on a Sunday afternoon. We all filed inside and stared at Mum's body in an open coffin. Dad kissed her forehead. I couldn't. I felt guilty about that. But I couldn't. Dad and I fell out over my hair. He wanted it cut for the funeral. I couldn't understand how unfashionably short hair would show respect for my dead mother. Dad won. I got it cut.

The funeral was at St Matthew's Church where I'd been a happy head chorister for six years. As we entered the front pew, the metal grill at the side of the pew gave way and Dad's left leg went down the gap. Hilarity being so close to hysteria on such occasions, I had a fit of giggles.

We drove to Southern Cemetery for the interment. All I remember is passing Chorlton Bus Station. I think I recall that because I was envious of ordinary people doing normal, mundane things like catching buses while I sat in this grey pall of grief. That memory brings Auden's poem *Musee Des Beaux Arts* to mind:

> 'About suffering they were never wrong,
> The Old Masters: how well they understood
> Its human position: how it takes place
> While someone else is eating or opening a window
> or just walking dully along.'

Dad took good care of me after Mum's death. The Essoldo cinema had a rather posh café' on the first floor and he arranged for me to have a daily lunch there. I only went once. As a four-teen-year old boy on his own, I was conspicuous and therefore uncomfortable and, anyway, preferred to get fish and chips at The Quadrant with my mates, then sit and eat them in Gorse Park. But Dad and I did go out for meals in the evening which I enjoyed. Our favourite was a Chinese restaurant, a novelty in 1965. I would always have a wonderful prawn curry. At the end of the meal – I never remember anyone else being in there – Dad would share tips with the waiters who were keen racing fans.

One evening, I went to rehearsals at Stretford Children's Theatre but they had been cancelled so I came straight home. There was a lady with Dad in the front room. They were both embarrassed – I think they thought I might have disapproved of their relationship so soon after Mum's death. I was delighted there was someone to bring Dad some comfort. Gladys was to become my stepmother some six years later. She was so different from my mother. Eccles born and bred, she had been in the typing pool in the office where my dad worked. She was very funny in a particularly cutting Mancunian way which Tony Warren caught so well in the early days of *Coronation Street* and she and Dad were a great double act.

I did go off the rails at school over the next couple of years – just in time for my O Levels. I didn't do badly in the end, passing six out of seven, enough to get me into the 6th Form. The seventh was Art, which I failed twice, once in the summer, then again at the following January retake. This was embarrassing as Heather was a talented artist later lecturing at Coventry and Hornsey Colleges of Art. The grades then were the complete reverse of today's GCSEs – 1-6 was a pass, with 7-9, three degrees of failure. Even though there were twenty questions on the paper, Mr Bunce only gave us the resources for one question – draw a plant in a vase. He'd obviously got a job lot of teasels because we were given one of these each to draw. The stem of my teasel had broken, however, and I had to hold it erect with my left hand while drawing it with my right. Someone with a keener artistic sensibility might have considered a broken teasel a more poignant image, but, no, my teasel was going to be erect like everyone else's. Grade 8, Fail. For the January exam, I opted for a seascape. Which I finished early. So, to pass the time, I built the paint up on my cliffs with a palette knife. When Mr Bunce came to collect our efforts, we picked up my seascape but the thickly overpainted cliffs stayed on the table. Mr Bunce and I managed to tape the cliffs back into the hole in the painting. The examiner must have pissed themselves when my 'seascape with tape' thudded through the letterbox. Fail, Grade 9.

That summer, Baz and I went to stay with his relatives in Jersey. They ran a general store in Grouville and we found ourselves helping to decorate the Grouville float, the parish's entry in the Battle of Flowers. Our co-workers were two sisters, Annette and Susan. I fell straightaway for the beautiful Annette and she for me. Unfortunately, Baz and Susan didn't feel this way about each other, so they spent our holiday as gooseberries while Annette and I acted out our passionate love affair. All a bit awkward.

The girls were the daughters of a wealthy tomato farmer and the family had a very smart cruiser moored in Gorey Harbour. Happy days were spent on the cruiser consuming the father's Canadian Club Whisky. I think their Mum and Dad thought things were getting out of hand between Annette and I (they were) because one day the cruiser was moored at Gorey no longer. Dad had cruised the family off to France to get the girls away from these two highly suspect Mancunians. I came down to the harbour every day but no cruiser (strings accompaniment here). Baz and I got painfully sunburnt in the meantime. I remember our watching the 1966 World Cup Final, two bright red lads shouting and cheering. Eventually, the family did return and Annette and I resumed our love affair for the last couple of days of our holiday. I was heartbroken when I left. We pledged to carry on the relationship, Annette moving to Manchester to train as a nurse. But, of course, it all fizzled out. The Beatles' *Revolver* came out that summer and I played it compulsively. When I hear tracks from it, I always think of Annette.

Baz and I in Jersey posing in our hipster trousers, 1966

My sister, Heather – one of Hugh Heffner's first bunnies
at The Bunny Club, Park Lane, 1966

I began in the sixth form studying French, German and
Russian A Level. I had started Russian the year before – the
idea being that we did O Level in eighteen months and then A
Level eighteen months later. We were taught Russian by Billy
Russell, an ex-Sheffield United player. We were also taught

German by Gerry Knox, a Lancashire cricket player who taught out of season. He would pace the classroom floor as summer approached, looking across the playing field towards Old Trafford Cricket Ground. 'I'm like a caged beast,' he would say. Strange connection between sport, modern languages and teaching here. Russian defeated me. Unlike Romance or Germanic languages, Slavic languages have no connection with English, or none that I could see. Russian is also a highly inflected language (like Latin) with meaning changed by modification of the words themselves rather than by word order, which makes it hard to learn. I switched to English from Russian, a move I think that would define my future. I flourished at English. I'd worked hard at understanding Gerard Manley Hopkins, a poet I still venerate, and, in the end, Frank Smith, our English teacher, had asked me to conduct the teaching sessions. Which I did – and enjoyed.

My friend Ian, who became the brother I never had, lived on the other side of Barton Road, about two minutes away. We had a lot in common. Our fathers were drinking mates at the Conservative Club and our mothers died pretty much at the same time. In fact, I remember my dad getting hold of a top of the range wheelchair for his mum who had MS.

Ian was to be best man at both my weddings, in 1973 and 2007 (conducting the service of blessing this time, having been ordained in between). Ian had come to Stretford Grammar at 13+. Now what did the school do with Ian and the other thirty lads who had come from surrounding secondary modern schools? Yes – instead of integrating them, it put them all in their own class and called it the X class – 3X, 4X, 5X! Ian left after the fifth form and worked as a quantity surveyor. He soon got fed up with this and went to Stretford Technical College to do A Levels. It turned out that we therefore did our A Levels at the same and became study buddies – our only leisure going two or three nights a week to the Horse and Jockey in Chorlton – now a very trendy pub in a trendy area.

Watching *Keep On Running* again, my first TV drama, loosely based on my sixth form experience at Stretford Grammar, I was struck by one central theme being the conflict between the teachers and the boys, particularly in the sixth form. The head-teacher, in his sermon to Alan, argues that education merely standardizes people like him and that the lad needed to go off and create something individual, personalised to himself rather than go to university. It's OK for the head, Alan argues, he's already benefitted from education. Then there's the violent deputy head. I was struck, in the 90s, by how so many SGS boys who were there around the same time, suffered trauma from the violence of the teachers and reported it on Friends Re-united. Indeed, plimsoll- and baseball boot-wielding teachers were a common sight. One of them, Thomas, had allegedly taught at a borstal and wacking boys seemed a full-time occupation for him. Mr Neafsy, who later became Chief Education Officer for Knowsley (sic), would insist you looked directly ahead during his history lessons and gave you the slipper if you moved your head to one side or the other. The violence was I think so widespread because of the testosterone swirling round an all-boys school. I'm not sure if I knew it at the time, but I clearly did when I wrote *Keep On Running* in my 30s, there were a lot of damaged people teaching in the 60s. These men, if they were in say their mid 40s when teaching us in the 60s, would have been born around 1920 and were possibly combatants in but certainly lived through The War. They must have resented what they had sacrificed for boys who had benefitted from the NHS, who were now in the vanguard of the challenge to authority, about to get access to the plethora of new universities established in the mid 60s following the Robbins report.

The 60s were alleged to be the decade of the sexual revolution. Not round our way. All of us were far too scared of the consequences of sexual intercourse. Young unmarried women weren't to have access to the pill until 1974. Condoms were almost entirely inaccessible to lads. The only place you could get them was the barber's, an all-male environment. And no self-respecting barber would say 'Anything for the weekend, sir?' to a mere teenager.

So, we were confined to light and heavy petting. It was compulsory to report the previous night's sexual adventure at school. The knowledge of who was going out with whom was worthy of social media today – encyclopaedic. The prompt question would be, 'What did you get?'. You needed to lie to save face whatever had happened but the sexual adventure would be divided into stages. There was 'a bit of outside'. This meant you had squeezed one or more breasts from the outside. This was not in any way erotic since most girls had rigid, some-times conical bras which were rock hard. The next stage was 'a bit of inside', which is self-explanatory. We then move to the lower part of the body. Success here resulted in 'a bit of finger'. I don't remember any of this being remotely enjoyable, for anyone! I didn't enjoy sex until I got into my twenties. And I didn't learn about the clitoris until later. No-one said. However, most sexual adventure reports usually concluded with 'Yeah

- then, well we went all the way.' The climax, as it were, of the process. This was a highly structured procedure. My favourite scouse joke recognises this: a lad and girl drive out into the country side. They pull up in a remote spot and climb into the back of the car. He puts his hand up her skirt. She stops him and says, 'Ey, where's your fucking manners? Tits first!'

I decided I wanted to go to university to do English and Drama. Going to university was not an automatic expectation. Only around 10% of school leavers went to university at the time. There was quite full employment and the majority of my peers left after the fifth form aged sixteen to take up jobs as bank clerks or in insurance or similar. My head teacher laughed at me. 'You wouldn't be able to get into a Christmas club with your grades, Armitage, never mind university.' This incensed me (as I think it was supposed to) so I began to work furiously hard and continued to the exams the following June. In the mean time I worked most Saturdays as an assistant salesman for Corona Soft Drinks Ltd. My driver and I would go from road to road, street to street. Most people had pop each week so you would knock on the door, collect any returned empty bottles and fetch whatever bottles they wanted that week. What fascinated me was, as each door opened, you were looking into a particular family's world, with its tears, its laughter, pain and pleasures and smells! It was a curiosity about people I've always had which was partly to lead to me being a writer. The highlight of the day was sit-down fish and chips at a chippy in Urmston – the best I've ever had. I think the taste was intensified by the energy you needed to take on board for the afternoon. When you applied to university then, you applied through the Universities' Central Council for Admissions (UCCA), now UCAS and you had six choices. The letters from universities always seemed to arrive on Saturday. So, I would crawl in Saturday night, Gladys and Dad always there, knackered from the drinks round and there would be a brown envelope. The letter inside the envelope would have a dot, the colour depending on the university's decision and you could always see this through the envelope window before you opened it: green for an offer, red for rejection and blue for waiting list. My school must have expressed low grade expectations for me because I had five reds on five consecutive Saturday nights: I began to dread coming home.

Not confident about the outcome of my A Levels, I decided, as insurance, to apply for the one-year pre-entry course run by the National Council for the Training of Journalists at Darlington and Harlow Colleges and Highbury College, Portsmouth. I was quite keen on a career in journalism at the time. Selection involved a trip to London, an exam and an interview. This was the only exam I've ever sat with an ashtray in the corner of the desk and we were permitted to smoke throughout! The exam involved two tasks: the first was to write a news story about a hotel fire. You were given a range of press releases and had to base your story on these. I noticed in the interview notes relating to one guest that a young man who had helped guests escape from the flames had disappeared afterwards and was clearly not a guest himself. This became 'Search for Hero Passer By' or some such. You were then given a wad of council minutes and asked to find a story. Somewhere in the dense, turgid text was a claim made by one of the councillors that the council was in breach of the recently passed Caravan Sites Act through failing to provide sites for travellers. It was a belter. At the interview in the afternoon, the panel were full of praise for my pieces, said I was a natural journalist but that, if I had the opportunity, I should go to university. It was an important filip in my life. I'd performed modestly in my O Levels, been marked as unfit to go to university by my school. Here were professionals saying I was worthy of joining their ranks. I was well chuffed!

It was a tradition for departing sixth formers to enter the school the night before the last day and 'decorate' it. No vandalism this, just effigies of the headteacher on a scaffold, streamers in the staff room and such. This we did but to get out of the back of the school afterwards involved scaling a twelve-foot fence. I jumped off half way down, but not realising I wouldn't be able to see the upcoming ground in the dark, fell badly. I was unable to walk the following day and missed the last, glorious day of term.

That summer, Ross Thackrey and myself plodded the streets of Manchester, looking for holiday work. We struck it lucky at the department store Lewis's in Piccadilly Gardens. 'Got just the thing for you lads,' said the grinning personnel officer. Cut to the Toy Department. Ross and I were dressed as Ice Warriors. The store had acquired the costumes from the BBC: ugly papier-mache heads, bulbous bodies and reptilian rubber legs. The idea was to walk across the floor to a makeshift cage, frightening the children as we did so. Neither of us had seen this particular Dr Who series so we didn't know what noises the Ice Warriors made, so we kind of half growled and half hissed at the kids. As we stood in the cage, some of the kids started to laugh and pointed at Ross's leg. We hadn't realised that one of Ross's rubber legs had become unfastened and dropped, revealing his wiry white human leg, which rather undermined his ferocity. When the Ice Warrior job finished, we became stage hands for the children's variety show Lewis's put on in the theatre on the top of the building. It was a good summer.

When the A Level results came out, I did better than I thought with four decent passes. I phoned my dad up. 'Dad, Dad, I got four A Levels.' 'Why didn't you get five?' Such a dad response. 'Because I only took four, Dad!' I went into clearing and got three offers: English at Edinburgh and St David's College, Lampeter and English/Philosophy at Liverpool. I chose Liverpool – far enough away to be away, close enough to pop back and Liverpool was a happening place to be in 1968.

Chapter 2 – The 18 to (almost) 30 adventures

I arrived at my new digs in Garston, Liverpool on the Saturday before term started on the Monday. All the halls of residence places had long gone by the time I applied through clearing. I was desperately homesick as soon as Dad drove off in his Austin England but also excited as a new chapter was starting in my life.

In Canterbury, where I now live and worked, I have, over the years, watched the procession of cars entering the City every September weekend before the start of term at the City's universities (until 2020, of course), each car with a duvet rolled up in the window, and understand exactly how those new students feel. In Liverpool, two returning 2nd year law students took pity on me and took the new boy over to the pub with them. Then my ten fellow digs partners arrived in dribs and drabs on the Sunday. We were crammed in a bit: I shared a room with Martin, a psychology student whom I was destined to share flats with for the next two years.

Martin was a slowly spoken but devastatingly funny man from Bradford. I was also to be his best man when he married Margaret several years later. At that wedding, I recalled a number of memorable anecdotes about our flat-share. My favourite was when Martin returned from the students' union bar one evening extremely drunk. He'd bought himself fish and chips on the way home. But he was having difficulty eating them. So, he tied his university scarf to his right wrist, looped it round his neck and pulled it down with his left hand, the chips and pieces of fish rising effortlessly to his mouth. This didn't go down well with the audience of Lancashire Catholics and Yorkshire Methodists.

I only recognised the dualism in my life relatively recently and first spoke of it at my 'do' when I left my university post seven years ago. My entire life has swung between Apollo and Dionysus. On the one hand, I am a highly rational person, enjoying precision and calculation. Alison laughs at me as I add up columns in my cash book instead of using Excel to do it for me. I have worked as an Ofsted inspector, which involved making complex judgements quickly based on data and experience and against tight criteria. On the other hand, I can be anarchic and feel the romantic conception of creativity to be the right one – artists being seized by ideas and emotions. Tony Lloyd told me he thought I was a pretentious prat in the 6th Form, always going on about Pinter and Becket and Theatre of the Absurd (I was to perform in a great absurdist drama, Fernando Arrabal's *Condemned Man's Bicycle* as Liverpool's entry to the NUS Drama Festival). So, I think choosing English *and* Philosophy suited both dimensions of my identity. The philosophy practised in British universities in the sixties and seventies (in fact across the English-speaking world – I was taught by an Australian and an American) was very much in the linguistic tradition, closely allied to Maths and Logic, the philosophy of Oxbridge. There was absolutely no mention of any continental or Eastern philosophy anywhere on the syllabus. Rational argument was at the heart of this tradition. So, philosophy appealed very much to my Apollonian side. On the other hand, literature appealed to my Dionysian side. I gradually became more interested in philosophy, I think, because literature courses in universities were actually courses in literary criticism – they were about a second-hand appreciation of literature, not doing it, not writing. I would ultimately fulfil that Dionysian need by becoming a writer myself.

Every Saturday night, there would be a band at the University. These were weird events. The band would do a set but there were no seats and people would dance in the main area so, it was a sort of gig-dance. One Saturday night, Trevor and I went in his open topped Austin 7, which he'd driven all the way up from Plymouth (we all told him what a stupid idea that was – an Austin 7, in Liverpool!). Marmalade were playing and they struck up 'Ob-la-di, Ob-la-da' (which was to top the charts the following January). Trevor and I went on to the dance floor. Women really did dance round their handbags in those days. And there she was - a vision, Mary, the most beautiful young woman I had ever seen and whom I would go on to marry five years later, dancing with her cousin.

Mary was still at school, in the upper sixth, about to take her A Levels the following summer at her convent school. Mary's Catholicism was never a problem, never a barrier. Later I would go to mass with her regularly. I really liked the mass, feeling it mysterious and ritualistic, properly religious in contrast with the pusillanimous CofE services I had been used to. I fell in love with Mary straight away and she with me. I knew at the time that this had a lot to do with my need for emotional stability and support after my mum's death only four years before – I was waiting to be loved.

Mary's parents, Robert and Jane, ran a newsagent's on Smithdown Road, with a very nice house off leafy Ullet Road (unfortunately, they were to fall on hard times a couple of years later and had to sell the house and move into a flat above the shop). Robert was a lovely man, clever, funny, artistic. Like his daughter was about to do, he had attended Liverpool College of Art. Jane was another matter. She despised me as soon as she clapped eyes on me. I could never work out why. She used to go on about me being from Lancashire like her father. He lived in their house, confining himself to one room. Did I remind her of her hated father? Was it the danger she saw in me, a non-Catholic, marrying her daughter? Whatever it was, I reciprocated the antagonism and we were never to have a decent relationship, even after Mary and I were married.

I was disappointed in my study of English at Liverpool. I simply didn't enjoy it as much as I'd enjoyed A Level. I suppose this was partly because most of the teaching took place in large lecture theatres with hundreds of students – battery farming. And, however engaging, listening to lectures was passive learning and I'm not very good at that. I don't remember much tutorial work either. And the curriculum was very unimaginative. Apart from the Chaucer and Shakespeare courses, the courses focussed on historical periods. I did 1660 to 1790 and 1790 to 1902 (why 1902?). So, the emphasis seemed to be on vast swathes of texts and writers, a cook's tour of English Literature, rather than close study of individual texts. Even a genre-based course would have been more enjoyable.

In contrast, there were never more than fourteen or fifteen in the philosophy group. The lectures were interactive, really engaging, with combative intellectual jousting. I loved it. And the lecturers were funny, eccentric, dramatic. Raymond Frey, who had this lilting New England drawl, closed a lecture on

British empiricism thus: 'So – will we see Berkeley lift Locke's veil of ideas? We'll find out next week'. And with that, he swept out.

The head of department, A.C.Lloyd, was eccentric – he was everything you would want in a professor of philosophy. One of us asked what happened to our papers after the exams. 'I was on a train just after The War,' he said. 'We got to the Swiss border and gendarmes got on the train. Immigration forms were distributed to each carriage. We were required to complete them there and then. The batches of forms were passed up the train. But, after we set off, a sea of paper passed our carriage window. We looked out and there, at the front of the train, was a gendarme tearing up the immigration forms and flinging them into the air.'

There were stories, apocryphal, of Lloyd hanging out in gambling clubs in Toxteth. Lovely idea of a professor using his knowledge of probability and number theory in gambling, 'The Prof', a Graham Greene character. What was true was that a small group of students who took his political philosophy option would be sitting on the floor outside his room before the sessions would take place. All of them were Trots or Maoists, wearing their parka or donkey jacket uniform. They worshipped him. I learned only recently that he came from a very political background. His parents were Fabians and would holiday with George Bernard Shaw and the Webbs. He is described in Richard Sorabji's British Academy tribute as a 'Labour Party Lenninist in the mould of the Webbs.'

I've never been one for getting up, nor has my sister, Heather. My father, in contrast, was a habitual early riser and would engage in the challenge of getting us both up from 7am onwards. So, it was not malice or lack of interest which made me miss Mr Williamson's logic classes, optimistically timed at 9am on Monday morning. When it came to the Logic and Philosophy of Language exam at the end of the year, one of the questions on the paper asked you to determine the validity of an argument. Now – I knew that I'd need to use truth tables for this. But I'd only ever handled arguments with three variables and this argument had hundreds. It went something like: 'If the Romans come over the hills they will not use chariots. If they do not use chariots they will be armed. If they are armed…..' and so on. And on. I began in earnest, and continued, and continued. The exam ended and I had only half answered one Logic question out of the four I needed to.

When Mr Williamson told me I'd failed, I was certain I could detect a wry smile on his face. He told me that, using the truth table method, it would have taken me several years at that exam desk to complete the question. But had I attended his classes I would have been familiar with R.C.Church's book on symbolic logic which describes a negation method of determining validity which would have taken me a quarter of an hour. I would need to retake the paper in September. I went to see Professor Lloyd to appeal but he wasn't impressed. 'What happens if I fail the retake?' I asked. 'You'll have to leave the University, won't you?' said he matter-of-factly. No counselling off courses in those days!

That summer there was no vacation. There was frenzied logic revision. I got a job at Ingersoll-Rand in Trafford Park which made compressors and I still don't know what they are. My job was as a stock records clerk. Every time a work-man came for a part – I knew what parts were called and where to find them – I would hand it over and make a note of it in the files so we knew what stock we had left and when to re-order. I would need to work every vacation for the rest of my degree. I had a full grant but this was not enough to live on. Plus, if I was at home, I was subject to Dad Tax. However, the other reason I worked every vacation was the curiosity I would later display as a writer. I was interested in other people's worlds. And, particularly, other people's working worlds. Some of the most effective drama has been set in people's working worlds from John Byrne's *Slab Boys* to the numerous hospital dramas, from *Boys from The Black Stuff* to *Auf Wiedersehen Pet*. I will say later that, for me, the research for a drama would always be as interesting as writing it. It appealed to my active, social side.

The summer drew on – me with my head in R.C.Church's tome and handing out compressor parts. Then a phone call from Mary. She'd done badly in her A Levels, with two EEs and was in a state. I took the day off from compressors and dashed over to Liverpool. Jane was impressed that I'd shown such concern for Mary and thanked me. I think it was the last nice thing she ever said to me. I spent the day comforting Mary whose plans to read art history at Edinburgh, Newcastle, Leeds or Manchester were now in tatters. Truth be told, I was secretly relieved she'd be staying with me in Liverpool and going to Liverpool College of Art.

For the following two years, because of the relationship with Mary, I tended to get vacation jobs in Liverpool. Retail jobs in department stores were normally easier to get because the pay was crap, the jobs were crap and there was a high turnover. One vac, I landed a job in Lewis's in Liverpool, the sister store of the one in Manchester I'd worked in during my A level summer. But this wasn't a sales job. I was given a large wooden box on wheels. Starting in the basement, my job was to ascend the store collecting empty cardboard boxes. When I got down to my lair in the basement, I would punch the bottom of each box and then flatten it. As I proceeded through the store pushing my box on wheels, I would shout, 'Mind your backs, ladies and gentleman, please! Mind your backs.' Eventually, I used to say outrageous things instead with the same intonation: 'You're all twats ladies and gentlemen please.' 'Great rack ladies and gentlemen please.' This was very childish but it relieved the tedium and gave the job some risk in case there was a complaint. I'd already prepared a defence. 'Said what? Outrageous. That customer must have something wrong with his hearing, sir'.

In another store, which I won't name because it was a hive of criminal activity on the part of the sales staff, I was sequestered to the tiling department. It was on the regular salesman's day off that I discovered what he was up to. A succession of tradesmen came in and when I told them what the charge was for their goods, each said, 'Yeah – and the discount?' The regular guy was charging them a fraction of the retail price, effectively operating his own trade business at the expense of the store. He'd ring up the discounted price so his till was fine at the end of each day. Presumably, he was collecting backhanders on his time off. I didn't dob him in but promptly left.

In the second year, Martin and I rented a flat in Wavertree, well, more of a bedsit than a flat. It was a large room with two beds and a couch with a curtained off kitchen area. Sounds like the set of an early Pinter play. I was very proud of it – my first flat. We soon realised that it was plagued with mice. They tended to come out at night. I was terrified of them. If I arrived home before Martin, I would sit in the bathroom next door for hours before eventually plucking up the courage to enter the bedsit. I would then cross the room walking across the furniture to avoid the vermin.

I decided I needed to broaden my experience of university beyond academic work so I joined Dramsoc. I had the lead in Fernando Arrabal's *Condemned Man's Bicycle*, which Liverpool entered for the NUS/Sunday Times Drama Festival. I don't remember much about it, except that I spent much of the performance seated at a piano going up and down the scales while Irene Whitehead sort of danced in a see-through blouse across the stage. Bizarre stuff. I didn't know what it was about, although my friend Julie, who was in the audience, said it moved her to tears. Then we did *Oliver* as a pantomime for the local schoolkids. But it all came to a standstill with a production of Jean Genet's *The Balcony*. At one point, my fellow performer and I thought we should have the same line, 'Well – go on, then'. We both said it to each other a number of times, hoping that the other would use it as a cue for further lines. But we didn't. We ended up just looking at each other hopelessly and walked off stage. This experience left me mortified and I vowed never to tread the boards again.

Other extra-mural activities included writing for the Guild Gazette, the university newspaper, as well as the Sphinx, the university magazine (one issue of which I co-edited with the poet Adrian Henri). I also tried my hand at arts administration, helping with the direction of the Liverpool Festival. For some reason, university accounts were frozen at the time and all payments to artistes were in cash. I remember wandering around with £800 (£12,000 in today's money) in my pocket to pay The Nice, headlining the Liverpool Festival, which I handed to Keith Emerson at the end.

During my first year in the Garston digs, I would often sit at the back of the 86 bus with a pleasant, well-spoken student who always wore a sheepskin three- quarter length. He was I think in Carnatic Halls of Residence so would get off at Mossley Hill. In the Spring of 1970, students occupied Senate House over the University's investments in South Africa. This was in the middle of the Liverpool Festival and, with a large number of our audience in Senate House, we decided to take events in there. I think we were despised as bourgeois, particularly me with the director of Bristol's Arnolfini Gallery trailing behind me. As a result of the sit-in, the ten-person organising committee was either expelled or suspended. I recognised one of these: my sheepskin coated bus companion. I would later realise that this was Jon Snow, of Channel 4 News. Ian Williams, one of the suspended, writes about a fortieth anniversary event in The Guardian:

'Last weekend, some sixty survivors gathered to celebrate the fortieth anniversary of the occupation of Liverpool University senate house in 1970 to protest the university's investments in South Africa and the views of the then chancellor, Lord Salisbury. His lordship's family name had been given to the capital of Southern Rhodesia, and he was a supporter of apartheid and holder of racist views so extreme that Cameron's Conservative party would not now countenance them (or at least their public expression).

One of the most galling things for the reactionaries of the university was that we raised a red flag, which flapped provocatively for two weeks, on the pole above the senate house. The university, egged on by baying Tory backbenchers, was vindictive in its response. It held a kangaroo court to try the ten members of the committee elected to run the occupation. The court expelled one, and suspended seven, including me, for two years and two for one year – probably the harshest treatment meted out during the wave of student protests. The Economic League promptly put all ten on their infamous blacklist of people not to be employed.

For example, Jon Snow, suspended for one year, never returned and thanks the university for diverting him from a likely legal career to one in broadcasting, while my own suspension led me to China during the cultural revolution and a chequered career in politics and writing on subjects ranging from railways to rum and the UN.'

(Guardian 24.3.2010)

In the summer of 1970, Mary and I decided to go on a working holiday to Spain. Her parents were OK with this because we would sleep in separate male and female dormitories. We flew out to Malaga on a Comet aircraft arriving quite late at night. There were a crowd of students on that flight and we all made our way to the Malaga youth hostel. There was room for the women but not the men. An elderly lady appeared and beckoned the ten or so men. She had three bunks. The first three lads grabbed them and the rest were shown out in the back yard. So, we faced a night sleeping under the Spanish stars.

When I went to pick Mary up in the morning she appeared to be ill. They wouldn't let me into the women's dorm to see her. They had called a doctor so I mooched round all day. I remember having lunch in the youth hostel refectory and I was staggered when I tasted the soup: it wasn't just stone cold - it was chilled. Horrible! It was called 'gazpacho'. The British diet was hardly international in the early 70s, although I had discovered Chilli Con Carne in the university student union. Mary eventually recovered - she'd had sickness and diarrhoea. It was only in later years when other partners got sick when travelling with me that I realized that I was causing the illness because I'm so awful to travel with. I panic at the slightest problem. My wife compares me to the Catherine Tate character who screams at nothing. I'm particularly bad driving into cities. Memorable panicked arrivals have been in Madrid, Paris, Olbia, Milan, Santander, Rome, Bologna, Los Angeles.

The Campo de Trabajo, the work camp, was in a small mountain village, Cortes de La Frontera, south west of Ronda. We had to get the Osuna train up to Bobadilla and then the Algeciras train at Bobadilla. The line ran along the valley bottom and we eventually arrived at Cortes. We were picked up in a van which then climbed to the village, high up in the mountains. The Campo was international and we joined around twenty other students from Spain, Sweden, Italy, France, The Netherlands. Everyone pitched in to prepare meals and I was delighted to sit down to our first – fish and chips. That's more like it. The delight was short-lived. The fish were whitebait – which to the Mancunian student were disgusting little fish with their heads and tails still on! Even worse, the chips were cooked in olive oil. Our accommodation was rudimentary – well the male dorm was more rudimentary than the female dorm which at least had doors and windows. We had neither so that before lights out, swarms of exotic insects would gather on the ceiling. One morning, we all sat up with alarm: Swedish Peter said in a Swedish monotone, 'There is a pig in the room.' A wild boar had wandered in and, fortunately for us, had wandered out again.

El Campo de Trabajo – levelling football pitches, Andalucia 1970

This was still Franco's Spain and the Guardia Civil would patrol our work site every day. The Spanish students would provocatively sing Communist working songs as they did. Cortes was a very poor village and our task was to level the ground between two football pitches. However, I think those running the camp had underestimated how hard it would be for us to work in thirty-five degrees, with pickaxes and shovels, with no shade. I acted as shop steward and got the working day down to a couple of hours – we were volunteering after all! The rest of the day we'd spend sleeping or repair to the village café where Bernabe, the cheerful waiter, would serve us with ice cold beer, Coke or fruit juice - sumo de frutta.

Narcissus prae cacti – Andalucia, 1970

In 1996, nearly thirty years later, I was on holiday in Nerja, east of Malaga and decided to visit Cortes de la Frontera, the poor mountain village. Poor mountain village no longer. It is very accessible from Malaga via a new main road and is now full of swanky second homes. Bernabe's café had gone as had the village square with the bullet holes in the walls from the Civil War. Only the bandstand had lasted. Leave the past to the past.

I was now in my final year. I couldn't be arsed reading all the books on the literature courses – there were too many of them. So, I charmed a number of women into lending me their notes, which worked a treat. However, I decided I wanted to excel in philosophy so I began to work very hard.

At one point, I turned nocturnal – working by night, sleeping by day. When the exams arrived, I was ready. Every paper I took was the same. The topics which came up were those I'd revised. It was like a Zen experience every time. I was flying. I had a stroke of luck with my dissertation. I'd argued that Immanuel Kant's refutation of Anselm's Ontological Argument for the existence of God was decisive. The external examiner was J.L.Mackie, an eminent philosopher who specialised in Ethics and the Philosophy of Religion. He was famous for his defence of atheism.

I got a 2:1 but it wasn't until I received the letter from A.C.Lloyd, that I'd realised how close I'd got to a first. I knew exactly where I'd screwed up. There was a question on the Advanced Ethics paper which I was unprepared for. It was, basically, 'Should you shop your brother for a crime he'd committed?' I'd anticipated all the questions on the other papers and had prepared answers but this one caught me out. We had been advised that the exam room was not the place to think an issue through. There wasn't time. What I should have done was consider how those holding particular ethical theories would have responded to the question. I was grateful in the end not to get a first. I would probably have done an Oxbridge B.Phil or D.Phil and gone completely insane. Less of the contemplative man for the time being. I had a place at Oxford to take a PGCE course, teaching English in secondary schools and further education.

Dad and I, graduation, July 1971. Shame about the sale board but it does authenticate the setting!

1971. At the end of my post-graduation round-Europe hitching tour, I called in on Pam, Denis and the children in Den Haag, where Denis had been posted with ICI. Pam pulled the hippy in quickly off the street before the neighbours saw. The jacket is brown and yellow velvet.

I arrived in Oxford on a cold October Saturday before the course started (I make a habit of doing this). I felt a bit over-awed, like Jude The Obscure arriving in Christminster. I had digs out at Five Mile Drive, north of the city. The digs were with a retired couple with an enormous alsatian. There were a couple of other post grad students there: one I never saw and another, a scientist who kept strange hours. As well as being taught in The Department of Educational Studies in Norham Gardens, you were made a member of a college. Mine was Jesus, alma mater of Harold Wilson and T.E Lawrence.

To be admitted to the university you had to matriculate. This involved attendance at a grand event in the Sheldonian Theatre. The vice-chancellor, who was then the historian, Alan Bullock, said a lot of stuff in Latin and that was it. You were in. Because my digs didn't offer evening meals, being a member of Jesus meant I could eat in college each night. It was also good that you paid battels, college charges payable on a termly basis. I did alternate with the local Wimpy. One night in the Wimpy, I met the Professor of Anti Poetry at the Anti University of London. One of his recent poems joined London and Brighton, which involved him driving between the two cities, stopping off every five miles or so and chalking a word by the roadside. Those were the days!

There were around two hundred on the PGCE course and every week we crowded into the main lecture theatre for lectures on educational theory: History, Psychology and Sociology. I wasn't too fond of these for two reasons: I don't get on with passive learning, listening to someone drone on and taking notes you can't decipher at the end; and I couldn't at the time understand how theory could help me become a good teacher. I make an exception for a series of brilliant lectures by the sociologist A.H.Halsey, who was Anthony Crosland's adviser. However, my disenchantment with theory lectures led to me lying in when they were happening, a la Liverpool Logic Monday mornings. And I did get caught out. The Director of the Department was A.D.C.Petersen, one of the founders of the International Baccalaureate. As I was arriving at the Department, late, Petersen was leaving, having given his lecture. 'Ah,' he said. 'So, what did you think of my lecture – do you agree with me?' Wily old fox knew I'd skipped it, and was enjoying my faltering response. Much more useful than the theory lectures were the English method sessions, which I remember being very active and led by a young, passionate teacher called Alice Wakefield.

I also met Vanessa. She'd read Theology at Bristol and was training as an RE teacher (you had to have a second subject and mine was RE). Vanessa and I became good friends. The relationship was platonic: Vanessa had just married Chris and they had a small house in Jericho. The albums of the year were Carol King's *Tapestry* and James Taylor's *Sweet Baby James* and Vanessa and I spent a lot of time listening to them. One of the PGCE students who'd graduated from Oxford was a big player in OUDS (Oxford University Dramatic Society) and I did join this crowd but only socially. The Oxford course was a kind of sandwich course: Michaelmas Term in Oxford, Lent Term on block teaching practice and Hilary Term back in Oxford. I wonder if my life would have led to me entering the media in a different way if I'd been in Oxford longer, say as a post-graduate student, a la Rowan Atkinson.

Dad and Gladys, Wedding Day, Eccles 1971

There were too many students for us all to be placed in Oxfordshire schools, so volunteers were asked for to be placed elsewhere in the country. I reckoned experience in a London school would be good for the future so volunteered. My sister, Heather, was now living with her husband, Brian and three of his children in Chelsea. She offered me a bed for the term. I was placed at Ravensbourne School for Boys in Bromley. This was ideal. Every morning, after a short walk up the Kings Road, I would hop on the Tube at Sloane Square for one stop to Victoria. The trip to Bromley South was fifteen minutes and the walk to the school ten minutes. This trip was against the incoming tide of commuters to Victoria.

Ravensbourne School was in its first year as a comprehensive school having previously been Bromley Grammar School for Boys. I don't think anyone had told the staff who swanned around in gowns. The staff room had a championship- sized snooker table which didn't leave much room for anything else. The boys were pretty well behaved and the practice was relatively easy. I did get put in detention by the head. I was standing outside a classroom waiting for latecomers but he thought I'd been thrown out of a class. I found I was quite an innovative teacher from the start and ran a project with the third years, thirteen-year-olds, to produce a newspaper. (In my teacher training days, when I was trying to place my PGCE students in FE colleges, principals would say 'I don't want to risk inexperienced students with my exam classes.' I'd respond, 'I think you'll find that what they lack in experience, they will have oodles of in creativity, enthusiasm and innovation which some of your more experienced teachers may be lacking in'.)

What was good about being in London was that my tutor, Alice Wakefield, had to plan ahead to visit me and observe a lesson, which gave me a chance to perfect it. For her first visit, I taught a dream of a lesson. I took out a box of matches (impossible now) and asked the boys to instruct me how to light a match, assuming that I'd never done it before. When they gave me an instruction, I'd deliberately misunderstand it so they had to be more and more explicit and exact. It was a brilliant lesson which I used for years after, teaching English Language.

I came unstuck on Alice Wakefield's second visit. I'd decided to do a drama lesson around heavy metal bands that the boys were keen on as a variation on the previous class-room-based lesson to show my versatility. So, I rehearsed it several times. Alice arrived and took her place at the back of the hall. I explained what I was going to do. Whereupon the boys exclaimed as one, 'Not again, sir!' They stitched me up like a kipper, they did. Alice did giggle, to give her her due.

The summer term was idyllic. We post grads, who only had two terms in the city, needed to cram all the Oxford experience into one eight-week term. So, it was punting on the Isis, it was getting up to hear the choir on the top of Magdalene Tower sing May Day in at dawn, followed by a champagne breakfast, it was the Exeter College May Ball.

I also made several trips up to Liverpool for job interviews. Mary had a final year of her degree to complete. I was very keen to teach in FE and had a number of FE interviews. But it was a very crowded job market and teaching in FE then was a highly desirable job for graduates. And the conditions of service and pay were far better than in schools. (The reverse is the case these days). I also ballsed up spectacularly. I stupidly walked into one interview with a Guardian under my arm. A Daily Telegraph was sitting on the Head of English's desk. Didn't get the job. So, I began to apply for school jobs. I struck lucky at a school in Huyton. I think it was because I noticed a bridge game going on in the staffroom. 'Oh, do you play bridge?' asked the head of English. 'Yes – love it', I lied, having learned my lesson. However, the following year was spent running out of reasons for not being able to join the staffroom bridge games!

My starting salary was £1600 per year (about £21,000 now). I couldn't afford to buy a jacket outright but bought one on HP from Burtons. Teaching in Huyton was very different from teaching in Bromley. When I arrived at the school on the first day of term, I found a lad wandering down the corridor. My understanding was that no pupils were allowed in school until the first bell. I told him to leave. I was astonished when he looked over at me and replied, almost casually, 'Oh – fuck off, sir'. I was amused by the contempt for authority the 'fuck off' represented, with the vestigial respect the added 'sir' implied. The deputy head pulled me aside one day. 'Two pieces of advice. Go into the first classroom you see, hit the first kid you see and say, "That's for notten. Wait till you do something". And always wash your hands *before* you go for a slash. Otherwise you'll get chalk on your flies and the kids'll say, "We know what you've been doing."' I came across some unconventional approaches to behaviour management. I was walking along the corridor with the deputy head of English one day when he went over to a line of kids waiting to go into a classroom. He shouted at them and pulled faces. As we carried on, I asked him what that had been about. 'I do it regularly,' he replied. 'If they think you're a loony, you become unpredictable and the kids are wary of you and behave.'

Teaching English on Merseyside was challenging. For example, scousers pronounce 'were' W-H-E-R-E and 'where' W-E-R-E, so teaching spelling became complicated. One of my favourite pupils was Squirrel. Every time he saw me he'd say, in this very high squeaky voice, 'Ey – sir - gis a ciggy'. I was attempting to teach Squirrel's class about newspaper bias one day and it was very hard work. So, I gave up. They had all been asked to bring in newspapers so I said, 'Look – just cut a picture out of your paper, stick it in your book and write a story underneath.' When I came to mark this work, I got to Squirrel's book. He had stuck a photo of the tallest man in England standing next to the shortest man in England in his book. But there were bits of words sticking out both sides of this photo. When I gave Squirrel his book back, I asked him for an explanation. 'Ar – ey, sir,' he said. 'You said "stick the photo in your book and write a story underneath." Well, I couldn't do it in that order so I wrote the story first and stuck the photo on top.' Note to future teacher trainees, always be precise when setting tasks and ensure your learners fully understand what you want them to do. Early in the year I made a classic error. I said to my English class, 'During break, I want you to find something to write about.' 'Like what, sir?' 'Oh – anything you find that interests you,' said I, naively. At the time, I was unaware of the geography of the school grounds. Back in the classroom after break, my class began to return. With half trees, frogspawn, frogs, newts, a gate. All this had been brought through the school from the large pond in the grounds, which I didn't know existed and the corridors were strewn with weeds and branches discarded on the way. I got the very worst of bollockings from the deputy head.

I was taken aback by the extraordinary lives a lot of the kids lived: lives of deprivation, of violence. But, this being Liverpool, there was laughter as well. Danny told me about his dad, who was one of Liverpool's premier lead thieves. He needed to get his lead to a fence on the other side of Liverpool so he compressed it into a lump that would fit into a duffel bag. His family lifted the duffel bag on to his back and off he went on his moped. But he took the Rocket roundabout too quickly and he came off the moped. However, the duffel bag pinned him to the road. Police cars were called across the city to come and witness the spectacle.

This year being Mary's last, there were plans to be made. Mary's friends and cousins had colonized Richmond and Twickenham. They were all enrolled on teacher training courses at colleges in the area and we'd been down to visit them. We both fancied a move to London. I wanted to do a part-time MA in Philosophy of Education at the Institute of Education, while Mary intended do a PGCE in Art Teaching at the same institution. Mary applied and got a place. In those days, places on MAs at The Institute were very competitive and I was to take a qualifying exam to get on my MA in the autumn before it started.

I went for a number of jobs that summer: the job I favoured was at Orpington College of Further Education. As I arrived at the College for the interview, I knew this was where I wanted to be. That year, the College's second, it had moved into a purpose-built building in The Walnuts, the central shopping area. Everything about the place was spanking new and I remember this real sense of new beginnings when I arrived that September, when a good three quarters of the staff were new. The Head of General Studies was the charismatic Pat Saunders and it must have helped that, among the many experiences he had had, he'd lived on a long boat on the Bridgewater Canal in Stretford. That helped me get the job.

But that summer, disaster struck. We were watching a play at the Everyman Theatre and one of Mary's tutors from the College of Art took her aside at the interval. He gave her the heads up that she'd failed her final degree show and would need to repeat the year. I was angry that she'd found this out in this way but I suppose the tutor thought he was doing her a favour by tipping her off. So, our plans for the future were in complete disarray.

We decided that I would go ahead with my Orpington job and MA plans. If Mary was going to make a serious fist of her resit, she'd have to work very hard and she wouldn't have much time for the relationship that year. My childhood friend, Ian, had landed a teaching job in Lewisham so we decided to look for a flat together mid-way between Orpington and Lewisham, somewhere Bromley way. The plan was that Mary, who now had a deferred place at The Institute for the following year, would visit at weekends that year and then, once she'd done her PGCE, we'd look for a place together.

Mary was happy to visit but, if we were married, it would be OK with her mum and dad. I was content with this. I thought marriage was where we were heading anyway. So, from a standing start, we managed to organise a wedding in a fortnight – which is how it should be done – no Save The Day notifications a year in advance in those days. Since we were to be married in a Catholic Church and I was a non-Catholic, we needed to attend instruction by the priest who was to marry us. We managed to get this down to one session because of the short period of time before the wedding. We went to the Presbytery on a Friday evening and the priest got down to business. When he learned I'd studied philosophy, including Scholasticism and Thomas Aquinas, I was given accreditation of prior learning. The priest then began to tell us about the persecution of the Lancashire Catholics. I must have started to drift away because he suddenly asked me what he clearly regarded as a crunch question, 'If you came home after work and your wife refused to fulfil her marital function, what would you do?' By now it was dinner time and I was hungry so my interpretation of his question was – I come home and Mary refuses to cook dinner, what would I do? I thought I was being compliant when I answered him confidently, 'No problem, father, I'd go off and do it myself.' He gave me a very strange look, which he was to repeat when he married us a week or so later.

The wedding took place at St Clare's Church, Arundel Avenue on a gorgeous August Day, 1973. Mary looked radiantly beautiful in an antiquey lace dress. I didn't do as well. Money was short so I had on a brown brushed denim suit with very thick platform soles and high heels which meant that I kind of tootled down the aisle at the end. The priest of the strange look actually did a wonderful homily in which he talked of the symbol of the ring as representing eternal love. Mary's Uncle Paul lent us his rather nice house and garden in North Liverpool for the reception. I remember being utterly exhausted during the day and managed to sneak upstairs for a sleep.

That night, Mary and I stayed at the Adelphi Hotel in Liverpool, where my mum and dad had spent many happy times in the 1930s. I remember Mary developed lockjaw - nervous exhaustion, I think. The next day, my Huyton mate, Jeff Letts and his wife gave us a lift to our first honeymoon destination, Ross-On-Wye, on their way to Devon. Why Ross-On-Wye? No idea. The next stop was to be Braunton, in Devon, where my mum had been brought up. I had decided to surprise my Aunty Audrey, whom I found on her knees gardening. Her first response was indeed surprise and she then grudgingly invited us in for tea. I had no better luck with her daughters who'd promised to see us off at Barnstaple station but never showed. I can only imagine there'd been a serious rift in the family. Heather muttered once about the Devon brigade regarding Dad as a city slicker. And I have a vague memory of someone suggesting Dad had borrowed money from them which was not repaid. This would have been completely in character. It was curious that we went down to Devon every year but that had stopped when I was nine or ten and we were never to go again. Family rifts are extraordinary things. They often seem to be caused by trivial events but these conceal deeper divisions which no-one ever discusses.

A fond memory of trips to Devon was going for the day to Saunton Sands, which was and is the finest beach I've been to in the UK. You parked at the top, shepherded by walnut-brown-faced men in white coats (interestingly, this same car park featured in a recent TV news clip about post Lockdown beach madness). Towering regally above the beach is the shimmering, white art deco Saunton Sands Hotel. I marvelled at the Bentleys and Rollers arriving and leaving. I told my dad, I was about eight, that one day I was going to stay there. And I did – it only took me sixty years. I went on a spring mini break a couple of years ago. And I wasn't disappointed. The restaurant particularly is first class.

Ian and I had found a very comfortable four-bedroomed flat in Beckenham. We took on the lease and let the other two bedrooms to Brian and Paul, two teachers from Ian's school in Lewisham. With Mary visiting only at weekends, life reverted to a student existence with four bachelors. We had rotas for everything: shopping, cooking, cleaning. We even had our own milk bottles in the fridge, the latest levels marker penned. Although I missed Mary, life with the lads was fun.

One night the doorbell rang and there stood a giant of a man who asked for one of our four, who happened to be out. When we asked what it was about he growled, 'It's a personal matter.' When our flatmate returned, we told him breathlessly about the visitor. He wasn't at all fazed. We managed to wheedle out of him that the guy had been a hair weaving clinic rep. Our flatmate was indeed, in his mid-twenties, very thin on top. When the rep was due to return, the three of us soaked our hair, combed it over and started watching TV in the main room the rep had to pass through to get to our flatmate's room. He eyed us eagerly as he passed through – three more potential weavees.

So, I began eleven very happy years at Orpington College. Initially, I taught a range of programmes – A Level and what was still then O Level. Best of all was the Civil Service Clerical Officer's exam group. These were all clerical assistants approaching retirement who were desperate to get on to a higher grade to enhance their pensions. I was twenty-three – with a whole group of uncles and aunties. What I enjoyed about the teaching was the range of students you came into contact with. What many of them had in common was that they were getting a second chance, a fresh start. And they needed this chance for different reasons. Some were straight out of secondary schools which didn't do A levels. Others were very bright direct grammar or public-school students who'd not fancied their school sixth forms. Yet others were adult students who'd had unhappy school experiences years before. Whatever the reason, they all wanted to be at the college. FE colleges still have this fresh start, second chance role, although post Raising of The Participation Age, there isn't much choice about continued learning after turning sixteen!

Some of the Orpington students stick in the mind. One A level English student in my first year was serious and quietly spoken. I knew there was more to him because he was the first of his contemporaries to dye his hair. I shared a train journey with him to college once or twice. He was moaning about his dad going on at him for staying out weekday nights. He explained he had to because he was in a band. They had their next gig at the Greyhound in Croydon – did I want to come? I never made it but, had I done, I would have seen the vocalist who metamorphosed into Billy Idol with his then band Generation X. Bill Broad, as he was then, became a member of what an NME journalist called the Bromley Contingent. It included Siouxsie Sioux (also an Orpington College student) and other early punk rock artistes. In fact, the Bromley area was positively oozing creative talent. David Bowie and Peter Frampton hailed from Beckenham while the writer Hanif Kureshi was from Bromley.

I also fondly remember the Bermondsey Boys. These were seven or eight lads from Bermondsey who crossed the river, believing the colleges in the leafy burbs would be of higher quality. They all followed a Pathway course which was a grouping of, then, O Levels roughly allied to an occupational area. I taught the Bermondsey Boys English and General Studies. They were a bunch of lovable rogues who regularly stitched me up. We had a weekly spelling test and one week, one of the lads said, very seriously, 'Sir,' they insisted on this formality even though no other students did, 'Sir – it'd be much better if you wrote the words on the board.' I was half way through writing up the first word on the board when I realised. Ron, the course director of General Studies, had asked me to whizz through the history of western philosophy and religion in about four lessons. The Bermondsey Boys turned out to be acute thinkers. They refuted Anselm's ontological argument in one, arguing that you couldn't treat existence as a predicate – not in those words of course! However, I wasn't convinced by their refutation of Bishop Berkeley's theory of perception which held that objects couldn't be said to exist if they weren't observed, 'Sir, you could look through the key hole and the objects wouldn't know they were being seen.'

I thought it would be good for the Bermondsey Boys to see some contemporary theatre. So, I booked tickets for Nigel Williams' cracking play *Class Enemy* at the Royal Court. None of them had been to the theatre before and they assumed it was something posh so they turned up, to a man, in three-piece suits. *Class Enemy* was essentially *Lord of the Flies* in a London classroom. Phil Daniels, who I never realised at the time would play my Johnny Oil in a decade's time, played the scorching central role of Iron. Now, the Bermondsey Boys, unfamiliar with theatrical convention, could not see that these were actors playing roles; they assumed what was happening in front of them was real. So, they began to shout in support of some characters and barrack others. This continued in the pub next door where the actors had retired after the curtain.

Early that autumn, on the 10th of September in fact, I took the qualifying exam for the MA. One paper in the morning, one in the afternoon. The exam hall was close to the Euston Road so, at lunch time, I went over to the snack bar on the outside of the station, bought a sandwich and coffee and went to sit down. I didn't get to the table. There was an enormous explosion in the station bar next door – I remember it echoing in the main concourse like someone had smashed a giant drum. I instinctively did an Olympic leap over a table and chairs and ran. The IRA were later to claim responsibility for it as well as a second bomb at Kings Cross. I was hardly in a state to write philosophy essays in the afternoon but I battled through the paper. I did put something like 'I was in a bomb incident at lunch time' in the hope that this would mitigate my poor performance, but it was no good. I failed. One of the Philosophy of Education department at the Institute, Pat White, kindly offered to set and mark essays through the year to give me a better chance the following year. It did. I began the MA the following September.

I was to develop very warm relationships with many of my colleagues at the college, some of whom were very entertaining. A small group of union committee members would go to the pub every Friday lunchtime. Often the worse for wear, they would return in the afternoon and make loud insolent anti-management remarks aimed at the nearby management corridor. They wouldn't have got away with that in today's managerialist FE!

Then there was the very eccentric Jilly. I don't know if she came from a very posh background but she sounded like she did. She'd run off with one of her A level students when he went to university and they lived in a caravan while he did his degree. They now lived with their four children down the road from me in Beckenham in what was a very eccentric household. We would often drive one another to work. I never knew what to expect when I called for her. One day, there was a large iguana staring at me from the middle of the sitting room carpet. On another occasion, their two ferrets got out and attacked an elderly lady around the corner. Jilly and I ran a theatre-in-education group during recreational activities on Wednesday afternoons. One Wednesday, I had an important phone call just before the class started and Jilly offered to go down and get it going. When I went to the drama room, there was Jilly sitting in front of the students sobbing and saying she thought her world had ended. I knew she was in an emotionally febrile state because of marriage difficulties and I walked towards her, put my arm round her and suggested we go up to the staff room. She angrily threw it off. 'For fuck's sake, Andy,' she yelled, 'can't you see – I'm improvising!' Pam, an English lecturer, was queen of the back-handed compliments: 'Oh Norma, so good to see you in a coat that fits at last'.

I had a phone call in November. It was poor Gladys. Dad had died of a heart attack that afternoon, aged seventy-three. They'd only been married two years. Gladys had set out to visit him in hospital – he was already there for a stomach complaint – but when she arrived the bed was bare. This was long before mobiles so he must have died after she set out. I was very proud of what the doctors told her – that, as they tried to revive him, he thought he was in a fight and rained punches on them all. The former army boxer and professional referee had gone out fighting. *'Do not go gentle into that good night, Rage, rage against the dying of the light.'*

The following January, Monica, a new Sociology lecturer, had arrived in the staffroom like an explosion. A big afro haircut, denim dungarees, a red fist sewn onto them, she was an almost stereotypical feminist-sociologist. Mind you, we were all a bit stereotypical in the 70s. I was the proud owner of grey, elephant cord dungarees, which I wore with a collarless shirt, red neckerchief and red kicker boots! At first, I didn't take much notice of Monica, just acknowledging her comings and goings, but I did this with all staff because I had the desk next to the staffroom door. All this was to change.

So, second time around, Mary was successful in her finals and got a good 2.1. She moved into the Beckenham flat and began her PGCE. I remember a dreadful Easter break to Cornwall with a fellow student and her husband. This woman was foul to me as we were leaving London, her husband aiding and abetting her foulness and I remember being on the verge of demanding the car be stopped to let me out. I couldn't envisage a journey to Cornwall with Cruella de Vil and Dracula (mixed genres, sorry), let alone four days in Cornwall. The cottage was pretty, in Marazion facing St Michael's Mount, but the company was poisonous. Mary took some black and white photos of me in the cottage – lying on a chaise longue, with fag in hand, dark and brooding. I really didn't have a clue what was going on with these maniacs. More seriously, I wondered about Mary's strange choice in friends.

Brooding in Cornwall. 'L'existentialisme est un humanisme'

It happened suddenly and surprisingly. Monica and I fell for each other. I suppose she was everything Mary wasn't: highly political, opinionated, tomboyish, intellectual, loud. But falling for Monica didn't mean falling out of love with Mary. For the first of three times in my life, I was in love with two women at the same time and didn't know what to do about it. It was a form of torture which eventually became a kind of madness. And that was just me! (My wife, Alison, has a rather different perspective, suggesting I have a propensity to want my cake and eat it as well as wallowing in the drama of these situations). I told Mary very quickly – I didn't want deception to be added to the list of crimes. The situation was complicated – Monica herself had a serious on/off relationship with Rees, a teacher and budding writer, so we formed a kind of love quadrangle. There was no way I wanted to leave Mary but life between us was clearly fraught. I tried to end the relationship with Monica a number of times.

Mary got a job teaching art at a local school and things seemed to settle down. But my feelings for Monica grew. In the boiling summer of 1976, Monica and I went on holiday together to the West Country. Mary had had enough. She moved over to Twickenham to stay with her cousins, commuting round the South Circular, poor thing, to complete her teaching year in Beckenham. As soon as this happened, Monica announced she was going on holiday to France with Rees and his friends. So, the two women I loved had both gone!

Ian and I decided we needed to get away. I had become the proud owner of a white Triumph Spitfire and we motored down to the South of France. Ian was (and remains) no linguist so the holiday was spent with him urging me to ask this or find out if they've got any of that. The only French he knew, which he kept repeating was 'il resolure' which wasn't French at all. We lived in a two-man tent – which was sweltering in the hot Riviera summer. Ian promptly had a bout of gastro-enteritis. When we got home, there was a letter from Monica telling me how much she'd missed me and could we try again.

We did try again but it wasn't long before she returned to Rees. Mary had by now gone back to stay with her parents in Liverpool and I decided to make one last effort to rescue our relationship. I drove overnight to Liverpool, arriving at five in the morning. I had a couple of hours kip in my car, parked up in Sefton Park before eventually turning up at Mary's. The red carpet wasn't exactly rolled out. For Mary, it was too late. She'd had enough. She wasn't interested.

In the autumn, Monica had changed her mind about Rees and said she wanted us to live together. I moved into her flat in Beckenham but it wasn't long before we both realised it wasn't going to work. I moved back into the flat with the lads.

The following year, I had a call from Mary. She had met someone over in West London. He was also an artist and they were going to begin a new life together in his native Yorkshire. They came to pick her stuff up and I reckoned it would be awkward and painful all round if I watched them do this so disappeared to the pub. Some years on, I saw the two of them had developed a very successful wall hanging business with individual and corporate clients all over the world.

That summer, Ian and I went on holiday to Devon and Cornwall. For me, it was a nostalgia trip to some of the places I'd been with Monica the summer before. We stayed in some not very salubrious B and Bs. Shortly after getting back, I got very itchy pubes. I examined the area and saw things the size of pinheads…moving! I caught a couple of them, put them in a plastic case and went to the doctor. He was an old buffer with a handlebar moustache. 'Good God,' he cried. 'pubic lice! Haven't seen those in Beckenham since The War'. He prescribed a lotion which I duly applied. That night, I walked into the pub and my friends at the bar pointed at me and shouted, as one, 'pubic lice!' The lotion was very pungent. They all insisted I must have got it through sex. But, as I hadn't had sex for some time, this was impossible. I concluded that one of the B and Bs we had stayed in hadn't changed the sheets between guests.

I don't know how, but over that emotionally turbulent summer of 1976, I managed to complete my MA dissertation. My tutor on the course had been Professor R.S. Peters, one of the giants of British Philosophy of Education of the 20th century whose private tutor had been George Orwell. After the course ended, I went to pick up my dissertation from his room. I have used what happened next with generations of trainee teachers, as a lesson in how not to assess. Peters took the dissertation from his bookshelf and gave it to me. I looked inside to see what the assessment sheet said. (One of Monica's friends was an examiner for my course so I knew already I'd been scored as B+ across the board.) There was no assessment sheet. There was no annotation of the text. Nothing. I asked Peters, 'So – er – what did you think of it?' 'Thin,' he replied. Thin? 25,000 words of blood, sweat and tears. Thin. I guess like a lot of intellectuals he was not very emotionally intelligent but 'thin'? Fuck me.

Undeterred by this experience, I signed up for a PhD at the Institute of Education which would focus on teacher language in the classroom. I lasted a matter of weeks. I remember sitting in a carrel in Senate House library on my tod, surrounded by books and wondering how I had ended up there. I had begun my education surrounded by forty-four classmates twenty years before and was completing it alone in a cell. The British Education system gradually strips you of learning companions. I had signed up for the ultimate Apollonian trip but this was no way to spend your best years! I was to audition for RADA shortly after. (I managed to avoid doing a PhD throughout my career. It got tricky in the Noughties when universities began to encourage and then demand their staff had doctorates. The crunch points for me were the annual appraisals with my dean. At one, she asked me why I hadn't done a PhD. I told her the Senate House story claiming that I was, in the end, a social learner. 'That's all right,' she said, 'why not do an EdD, the bulk of that is taught, perfect for a social learner like you.' I managed to prevaricate until the next appraisal. This time I tried to sidestep her by claiming that I preferred to put my writing energies into publications about practice, rather than research. 'That's all right,' she said, 'why not do a PhD through publications.' I managed to prevaricate again and by the time my next appraisal became due, she'd moved on!)

Ian and Brian, another flat-mate, decided they needed to get on the housing ladder. Ian bought a place on the Croydon side of Beckenham and I followed – I had nowhere else to go. I wasn't aware at the time but I was at a bit of a crossroads in my life. Personally – I had two broken relationships behind me. Professionally, although I still enjoyed teaching, I wondered whether this was it. And, psychologically, I developed hypochondria – which has been a lifetime affliction. Physically, I began to be regularly plagued by boils and this went on for some time. And then I went to the doctor complaining of a pain in my upper torso. He wrote a letter of referral which he sealed and gave to me. That's how it worked in pre-digital days. Of course, I steamed it open and read that I was suffering '…a pain in the hypochondrium.' I wasn't sure if this was secret code for the gastro-intestinal consultant at Bromley Hospital, who certainly ordered a battery of tests.

The barium meal was bearable. But I didn't anticipate the trauma of the barium enema. It was the first time I'd had a tube up my bum and I didn't like it. My colon was pumped full of barium. Photographs were taken and I was asked to get rid of the barium in the loo. I sat on the loo relieved as gallons of barium poured out of me. I was on my way to get dressed when the nurse beckoned me and asked me to get on the trolley again. A tube was promptly pushed up my bum once more and then I was inflated, like a balloon. Photographs were taken again. The drive back to Beckenham was difficult. I had an old Beetle at the time, with very high pedals but I was continually emitting long, powerful, painful farts, so using the pedals was hard work. As soon as I got home, I whipped out a cassette tape recorder to record the farts because I thought no-one would believe me. The longest was fifty-five seconds – nearly a minute of gas.

At work, I got close to one of the drama lecturers, Liz. She was very witty, clever, talented and good fun. She'd not long been married and I drove her over to Eltham to sign the contract for a house purchase in Sidcup, not knowing at the time that this was the house I'd be moving into in a couple of years' time.

Meanwhile, I decided I needed to address my ambition to be an actor before it was too late and I applied for RADA.

Liz helped me prepare for my audition. For my Shakespeare, Liz reckoned I should do the Bastard from *King John*. It was a bit different from the many Hamlets she thought I would be competing against. And it was a bitter, cynical speech. For my modern, I chose deluded revolutionary Malcolm Scrawdyke from David Halliwell's hilarious *Little Malcolm and His Struggle Against the Eunuchs*.

Come the day, around thirty of us sat round the edge of a room and the Principal of RADA, then Hugh Cruttwell, went around the room asking us which audition pieces we were going to undertake. Liz had been right: Hamlet, Hamlet, Hamlet, Ophelia, Hamlet, Ophelia… We were then ushered up to a common room to wait to be called for our audition. When it was my turn, I entered the room, which was bare apart from two chairs on which a portly young man and attractive woman were seated (when Mel Smith became famous, he looked familiar to me. I read in his biog that he had indeed taught at RADA in the late 70s. He was the portly man). The room overlooked Gower Street and traffic roared by. I'm sure they deliberately chose these rooms to test your nerve. I didn't know how the pieces went down but I did get a few belly laughs from Mel during the Halliwell speech. After the audition, you returned to the common room and waited to see if you'd got through to the second auditions which were to take place in the Vanbrugh Theatre that afternoon. One by one we were called to one of the two phones in the common room and were told either to wait around for the pm audition or asked to leave. The process was all a bit brutal. One poor woman who'd flown in from New York that morning especially for the auditions fled in tears after her phone call.

The afternoon auditions were to take place on the Vanbrugh Stage with the selection panel in the darkness at the back. I think I was overawed by the occasion because I dried during the Shakespeare speech. I was asked some rudimentary questions by the panel and that was it. When I opened the letter from RADA some days later, I kind of knew, rather like Manchester Grammar School nearly twenty years before, that I was unsuccessful. RADA did me a favour. Once I'd got inside the business, I realised how shitty life is for most actors most of the time and I know I didn't have the psychological resources to deal with that life. But if I can't act roles, why can't I create them for actors to perform. Why not write?

The relationship between Liz and I got stronger; we were attracted to each other but we were such good mates and enjoyed one another's company enormously. But, then, Liz's relationship with her husband deteriorated drastically. He was to move out and Liz invited me to live with her. I bought her husband out and took over his share of the mortgage and, in late 1979, moved to sunny Sidcup. I'd only hitherto known it as the place where Pinter's tramp in *The Caretaker* needed to go to get his papers. I would later be branded the 'Sidcup Comedy Playwright' in the local press, a soubriquet I did not think was cool!

Chapter 3 – Around the Fringe with Adrian

They say every teacher has a play about education in them. I first wrote *Marking Time* as a one-act play. The reason was because in the late 1970s London had a very active lunch-time fringe and I reckoned this was the best market for it. I still have the list of theatres I sent this to and it reads like a roll-call of the Fringe: Almost Free, Head Theatre, Putney, White Lion, Soho Poly, ICA Theatre, Croydon Warehouse, Pentameters, Lamb and Flag, Young Vic Studio, Theatre Royal, Stratford East. I have the script report from Stratford East written by the playwright, David Cregan:

'Marvellous dialogue, really very, very good indeed. The girl is not well drawn but his may be because she is part of the plot and the plot is rather thin. But the insights and balances of discussion and above all the marvellous rhythms of dry, witty speech are excellent.'

The Croydon Warehouse got back to me very quickly. They loved the play but (ironically) they were about to launch a season of full-length plays as evening productions. Could I turn it into a full-length play? Yes – I could. The Croydon Warehouse was a ten-minute drive away. It was run by three actors: Richard Ireson, Sam Kelly, who would go on to achieve fame and praise for parts in *Porridge*, *Allo, Allo* and a number of Mike Leigh films and Adrian Shergold, who would become an eminent and successful theatre, TV and film director and with whom I would have a fruitful professional relationship for the next fifteen years.

Marking Time is set in the marking room of a London comprehensive where Frank is marking English exercise books. His mate, Alan, a PE teacher, keeps interrupting him: he is ostensibly there to keep an eye on his athletics prodigy, Tony Watson, training out on the school field but, as soon becomes clear, he is hanging around to meet Jenny, the new Social Studies probationary teacher. The relationship between Frank (Francis) and Alan is at the centre of the play. Frank is nicely settled with Jackie but the single Alan scoffs at their lifestyle:

ALAN: *Look, as long as I've got a bed, a chair and a Baby*
        Belling, I'm happy. I don't need to surround myself
        with....what is it, your wallpaper stuff...?

FRANK: *Hessian.*

ALAN: *Yeah, that's it - Hessian...bloody sacking...and those*
        Habitat spotlights...I don't have to surround myself
        with them to make me think I've done well for myself.
        You'd buy coal from Habitat, if they sold it. Maisonette
        mind you've got.

On re-reading the play for the first time for forty years, I was suddenly reminded of the relationship between Bob and Terry in *The Likely Lads*. In fact, I just discovered a script report from Manchester Library Theatre which said exactly this. But I don't remember any conscious influence at the time I wrote the play. Both Mancunians, my Frank and Alan, who it's clear grew up together, appear to be loosely based on myself and my lifelong friend, Ian. There are some similarities: I am something of a cultural snob and I regard Ian as a bit of a philistine; I was in relationships for a long time when Ian wasn't; we both began teaching in South London at the same time but Ian taught RE in a comprehensive school and I taught English in FE. There the similarity ends.

What did intrigue me was the relationship seems to pre-figure two other relationships which would feature in future work: Alan and Baz in *Johnny Oil* and Alan and Frank in *Keep On Running* (interestingly, these two Alans are based on me - Dad's middle name was 'Alan' - whereas it is the *Marking Time* Frank who is based on myself). I don't know why I switched. But what is very clear is that each of the characters based on me represents the moral nadir of the plays. Mine is the character who is conventional, conservative, hypocritical, cruel and insensitive, snobbish. Now, I kind of knew this but had never thought why I subjected myself to this self-flagellation. I think I now have a clue. I have always felt guilt about my mother's death. She was in hospital for three weeks before she died and I didn't visit her once. I couldn't. My fourteen-year-old self just couldn't hack it. This guilt was compounded by what I heard the night after the funeral. I had gone to bed early but Heather and Dad sat up talking. Of course, I was hanging over the bannister earwigging. They both agreed that Mum getting up to make sandwiches for me and my girlfriend, Jane, for a Children's Theatre hike in Derbyshire had been the trigger for her downturn and final admission to hospital. I don't pretend to understand this perception unless there was some projection of their own guilt onto me. But it stuck. And I reckon my literary self-lacerations were attempts to assuage that guilt, acts of expiation.

Jenny is the plot driver of the play. She's been trying out a sex education project with Frank's class. He discloses that he's received letters of complaint which he's had to pass onto the head. It's clear that Jenny's project has challenged in many ways what is still a very conventional school. Alone with Jenny, Alan asks her out. She would but it turns out she's seeing Alan's protégé, Tony. She is summoned to the head who wonders what she's done to invoke enough meanness in Alan to get him to dob her in. She realises that she is too innovatory for the school. Alan, in spite of his rebuff, takes her side and he leaves with her to work in an alternative education project.

Underpinning the play is a debate about education. The 1970s had been a decade of debates about education, the Prime Minister James Callaghan setting the tone in a speech in 1976 at Ruskin College, Oxford and initiating The Great Debate. Jenny is a progressive educator. In her approach to sex education, she is all for honesty and openness, for adults setting an example to kids not adding to their fear and guilt. Frank is more of a traditionalist:

FRANK: *Because that's what everything's become now, hasn't it? The instant package, the skills pack, the life kit. Follow the instructions and assemble the kit – it's easy – no problem.'*

(Ironically – two years after I wrote these words, my first educational textbook was published, a resource book for FE students, *Do It Yourself – A Guide to Social and Life Skills.)*

Alan is a more complex character. You get the impression he was disaffected at school and chose a non-academic career path and believes the emotional, personal and physical dimensions of education are as important, if not more important, than the academic dimension. He is complimentary about Jenny's sex education project and it comes as no surprise when he goes to join her at the alternative curriculum project at the end.

Norman is the old lag, the classroom cynic:

NORMAN: *Mind you, if I had my time over I wouldn't go
               into teaching.*
ALAN: *You enjoy it really, Norman.*
NORMAN: *'It were better to perish than to continue
               schoolmastering.'*
FRANK: *Shaw?*
NORMAN: *Carlyle. It's a mug's game. The pay's piss poor and
               you've no more status than a prison warder, because
               that's basically what you are. And it's always been like
               that outside the grammar schools. Nothing's bloody
               changed. I've always had to do a second job. I only
               recently gave that up.*

Marking Time opened on 26th June 1979 and had fifteen performances. There was a cracking cast which included Stephen Whittaker, Marion Bailey and James Garbutt. It was generally very well received with most commentators praising my gift for dialogue. Here, Alan responds to Frank's pedantry with ridicule:

ALAN: *You want to eat some real food. (Points to his sandwich)
           Like this – real food. An entire meal in every
           centimetre of this. Tyrolean mountaineers live on this.
           It's all they live on. Know how to eat, do the Germans.*
FRANK: *Tyroleans aren't German. They're Austrian.*
ALAN: *How do you know?*

FRANK: I've been there. I've had a Tyrolean holiday.

ALAN: Not that holiday when you got stranded?

FRANK: (Aggravated) Yes.

ALAN: When you booked with that shady firm in Soho and the airline went into liquidation while you were away?

FRANK: The very same

ALAN: ....and Jackie wouldn't let you buy an English newspaper because they were too expensive, so you only found out about it when you got to the airport, where you spent four nights in arctic conditions but eventually got a ride with another airline, which took you to East Midlands instead of Gatwick? And you had to get the overnight mail train to Kings Cross, where you found you only had Austrian Schillings which the taxi driver wouldn't accept so you had to wait till the tubes started. And you both went down with flu when you got home? That holiday?

FRANK: That holiday.

But there were faults with this first play. Julia Pascal in Time Out: 'Unfortunately, the device of an interspersed variety act weakens the play's structure, as does the undeveloped theme of sex between teacher and pupil'. And Anne Morley-Priestman in The Stage, 'Armitage has a gift for dialogue but he overstates a little and has been allowed to get away with it by the director, Warren Hooper; also, he has not yet learned to break down his chunks of rhetoric and conversation into manageable slabs.' The play was very wordy and a lot of the dialogue was unnecessary and indulgent. I learned a lot from this first play about dialogue, about structure and characterisation. In fact, having a play produced is the very best way to learn this by attending rehearsals and gauging audience reactions at performances.

That autumn, Adrian asked me to co-write a play we devised together, *Houdini – My Father Shook His Hand* which was to receive a lunch-time production. Albert Coles and his daughter Dawn, aka The Great Marengo and his ravishing assistant Natasha, arrive at a cabaret club in Openshaw, Manchester to rehearse their act for that evening's performance. The Great Marengo is an illusionist and wants to try out a new trick 'Escape from The Grave'. Dawn wants to sing as part of the act, particularly as talent scouts are due at the club that night but Albert isn't having any of it on the grounds that her singing will slow the act down and, anyway, she 'has a voice like a barrel of gravel'. They are met by general factotum Les who is on a six months Job Creation Scheme at the club. Albert is not impressed by Les's lack of professionalism:

ALBERT:*We'll need drums. We have to have a drum roll. It's germane.*
LES: *I can play the organ. A bit. Well, I can knock out a tune. Sort of. I can do the Boys' Brigade drum solo.*

For his part, Les is not impressed with what he's seen of showbiz.

LES: *All the conjurors I've seen here have been crap. We had a bloke here last week. He did that trick where you produce a fan of cards from nowhere, throw them into a hat and then produce another fan and throw them into a hat…and so on. You know how it's done?*

ALBERT: Yes – Leslie – I am a member of the Greater
Manchester Branch of the Magic Circle.

LES: Well – instead of just pretending to throw them in the
hat and slipping them behind his hand again – the
daft bugger actually threw them into the hat. So –
when he came to produce the second fan of cards, he
couldn't!

But Albert is defensive about his profession:

ALBERT: Don't scoff son! Don't you bloody scoff! That's easily
done. What lay men like you don't realise is that an
illusionist is taking chances all the time. One wrong
movement of the hand – one fraction of a second out
with his timing – his career's in ribbons. Who else
takes chances like that these days – eh? No bugger does.
That's who. Everybody's a machine minder – from top
to bottom. A nation of minders. No wonder they're not
interested in craftsmen. Real craftsmen.

When Albert goes off for some kit, Dawn tells Les what she
wants him to do. The dress rehearsal begins:

ALBERT: Right – drum roll. (Assumes Hungarian accent)
Ladies and gentlemen. Tonight, for the first time in
your wonderful country, I shall attempt a trick only
performed by the Egyptian mystic, Rahman Boy and
the great Harry Houdini. I shall, with the assistance of
the beautiful Natasha, cheat death. I shall, Ladies and
Gentlemen, escape from the grave.

(The drum roll begins. DAWN bolts down the coffin as in the first run-through. But once DAWN has drawn the curtains round her, she quickly re-emerges and, accompanied by LES, belts out 'Help Me Make It Through the Night.' ALBERT shouts and bangs on the coffin lid throughout the rendition but finally falls silent. DAWN and LES open the coffin. DAWN had tampered with the interior locks so that ALBERT couldn't undo them from inside. But LES is horrified. ALBERT has not escaped from the grave or cheated death. He lies there, deceased.)

The joy of rehearsals was waiting for Sam Kelly to corpse. He always went on the line, 'Do you remember Daredevil Dave the one-legged high diver? He used to dive off the edge of Shanklin Pier – well, hop, really.'

Houdini – My Father Shook His Hand opened on November 13th 1979 with the wonderful Sam Kelly as Albert, Shelagh Stephenson (subsequently a successful playwright herself) as Dawn and Stuart Wild as Les. It didn't do too well audience-wise. Lunch-time in Dingwall Road, East Croydon isn't exactly the West End. One lunch-time we had no audience at all and had to resort to giving free tickets to the gang digging the road up outside. However, it was well received. 'Sam Kelly is particularly good as Albert with Stuart Wilde properly moronic as Les. Shelagh Stephenson is both gritty and blousy as Dawn,' said The Stage. Jim Hiley was very complimentary in Time Out: the play was 'model lunchtime entertainment….well observed and jam packed with witty lines. Sam Kelly's performance as the mad prestidigitator is, right down to his string vest and orange socks, a lovingly detailed gem'.

The economic recession really began to bite in 1979 and my college was challenged with responding to youth unemployment by providing life skills and vocational preparation programmes. I was promoted to Senior Lecturer in charge of these programmes. Although many were critical of these programmes, I was very positive about this work from a teaching point of view. By now, I had been teaching English for nearly a decade. My view was that anyone could teach A Level English well to motivated students but that it took special skills and a special approach to meet the challenge of the students on these programmes.

Although I was attracted to vocational teaching, I did question whether work related education was what many of the students I taught needed. Many had learning needs which would have been better met in a more protected environment than the workplace. Work experience was an element of all courses. We placed Tim in a warehouse and by the first lunchtime I received a panicked phone call from the supervisor asking us to take him back. The supervisor had given Tim a stock-taking task. It was a five-minute job. He needed to walk along the edge of the piles of pallets and record the number on the sides of each pile. When Tim didn't return after two hours, the supervisor went in search of him. He found him on top of a pile of pallets. He was opening each box of goods and counting the contents - a task which would have taken him several years to complete! We relocated Tim to the college drama department where he was given the task of alphabetically filing playscripts. The drama teacher asked me to come down and look at Tim's handiwork. In one file drawer, all the scripts had been placed in one bulging hanging file under 'T': 'The Alchemist', 'The Cherry Orchard', 'The Tempest'…and so on.

Students were required to complete a weekly record of achievement. Tracy's was quite brief. 'Monday – we done Communications. It was boring. Tuesday – we done Numeracy. That was boring too. Wednesday – we done Leisure Activities, which was boring'…and so on through the week. When I had a tutorial with her, I tried to explain what was required. 'So, Tracy, the idea is that you describe in more detail what you've learned in each session. Otherwise, you'll forget what you have learned. And, Tracy, a bored person is a boring person… ' Tracy's response was priceless. I came to sit down with her at the tutorial the following week. 'Monday – we done Communications. It was not boring. Tuesday – we done Numeracy. That was not boring neither. Wednesday – we done Leisure Activities, which was not boring.'

I was lucky enough to be awarded an Arts Council Buying Time Award on the basis of my first two plays. It allowed me to take six months unpaid leave from college during 1980 and I was not required to produce anything. But without the possibility of production, I found it hard to motivate myself. This was not helped by the six months coinciding with the couple next door deciding to renovate their house so it was like writing in a building site. I will say again later that the research for a piece was more enjoyable than writing a piece. And one incident I remember well. I had decided to write a play based on a holiday to Tenerife I'd taken a couple of years before. It was called *Too Much in the Sun* (never got produced but did get a rehearsed reading at the Half Moon Theatre in the East End). One of my characters wore a hair piece and, as someone who prizes veracity in writing, I needed to know how a hairpiece would behave in hot summer sun. How to find out? I picked up the yellow pages (no Google then) and looked under 'Hair'. The first on the list was 'Croydon Hair Clinic'. I began to laugh as I was dialling as the absurdity of my enquiry struck me:

Receptionist: Hello – Croydon Hair Clinic.
Me: Yes – er – it's about a toupee…
Receptionist: Oh – she doesn't get in until eleven. You better call
*   back then.*

I think what made me laugh so much and for so long was the casual mention of 'she', as if the receptionist fielded queries like this every day and it was always for 'her', the fact that she rolled in at eleven, that there was a toupee specialist at all and that I was laughing on my own. I duly rang back after eleven – following a number of attempts when I started giggling as soon as I lifted the receiver. I was put through to She:

Me: Hello – it's about toupees…
She: Well I hope it's not a complaint…
Me: How d'you mean?
She: I've been inundated… (This was July) …I always
*   stress that the All European Hairpiece is the only one*
*   guaranteed not to discolour in extreme weather. You*
*   take your chances with the acrylic ones – some do, some*
*   don't. One gentleman tried to blame us when his wig*
*   floated out to sea while he was swimming. I suggested*
*   he'd not put enough two-sided tape on it…*

I have never been a practical person, which my double failure in Art O Level testifies to. But our house in Sidcup was to be the scene for three of my DIY spectaculars. The renovator next door offered to fit a new bathroom for us, which he did, leaving only the Habitat ceiling light for me to fit. Up the steps I went to screw the light into place on the pine ceiling. Spotting the three electric wires, I came down again and decided to turn off the electricity. Up the steps I went again with electric drill in hand. But the drill wouldn't work. Down I came. I replaced the fuse in the drill's plug. No – still the drill wouldn't work. I scratched my head. It was some time before I twigged. The drill wouldn't work......because you've turned the electricity off! The second spectacular was to occur in the same bathroom. Liz and I felt it would be nice to have mirror tiles up one wall of the room. Finally, the bathroom was finished. Liz was the first to take a bath in it. Not long into Liz's bath, there were piercing screams. I ran to the bathroom. Liz was fending off mirror tiles which, one by one, were peeling off the wall and falling onto her in the bath. I had not read the warning on the packets that these mirror tiles were unsuitable for bath-rooms because the steam from a bath renders the adhesive on the two-sided tape which holds them in place ineffective. My third blunder, and the one of which I am most ashamed, happened in the freezing winter of 1980-81. Before we flew off to Morocco at Christmas, Liz asked me to put up in the kitchen a Habitat shelf to hold her grandmother's treasured crockery. Liz should've known really. She was living with man who had no idea about which rawl plugs were appropriate for different walls nor how the size of screw relates to the weight of wall furniture. On our return from Morocco, Charlie from two doors down who had been looking after the house got to us before we went in. 'Something terrible, terrible….' he muttered under his Scottish doom-laden breath. The shelf had come off the wall. Liz's grandmother's crockery was in a thousand pieces. I never forgave myself. And I don't think Liz ever forgave me.

This ineptitude with my hands is only part of the discomfort I have felt generally with the physical world, what someone once referred to as 'the innate hostility of inanimate objects' or 'resistentialism'. The most dramatic example of this I can remember is when I once stopped off at Cite Europe in Calais on my way back from a trip to France. This was a Sunday and I wasn't sure whether Cite Europe was open so I went through the heavy revolving door and just stood there trying to ascertain whether the shops were open. Then, 'bang', the still revolving revolving door hit me and flung me to the ground. As I began to get up, still stunned, the revolving door hit me again, knocking me over once more.

Liz took a year out from teaching and went off to do a full-time MA in Drama at the University of Essex. I took over some of her teaching and particularly enjoyed the A Level Theatre Studies teaching which was right up my street. The plague of boils, which had been arriving continually since the late 70s, returned relentlessly. Most of them congregated round my scrotum which was horrendously painful, hindered walking and made sexual activity impossible. I was hospitalised on one occasion. I lay on a bed in one of those embarrassing gowns which is open at the back and doesn't cover your arse however much you re-arrange it. Screens were placed round the bed and, suddenly, James Robertson-Justice arrived with a posse of eager medical students. 'Lift the gown,' he said imperiously. I did so.

'So, what would you do with that?' he asked the posse. 'Put a poultice on it?' risked one feeble student. 'Exactly,' said he and they moved on. A poultice was duly applied. But whereas an ambulance had brought me on account of my not being able to walk, I was abandoned at the hospital and had to endure a very painful, jolting bus ride home.

At this point, I also developed full-on Obsessive Compulsive Disorder. I'd always been mildly afflicted – I remember when I was in the Beckenham flat having to pile my coins up from the largest up to the smallest before going to sleep and then go through the process again if they fell over! But this was the Real McCoy. Experts have identified four strains of OCD. The first produces a fear of contamination and can involve endless hand washing. The second induces a fear of accidental harm. The third involves unacceptable taboo thoughts and mental rituals and the fourth, the Just Right OCD, involves symmetry, arranging and counting. I had a little bit of Number 3 (I had to mentally recite all the stations from Victoria to Orpington and had to start all over again if I got them in the wrong order. I can still do it: Brixton, Herne Hill, West Dulwich, Sydenham Hill, Penge East, Kent House, Beckenham Junction, Shortlands, Bromley South, Bickley, Petts Wood and Orpington). But I suffered mainly from the Just Right OCD. The Just Right OCD was the most time consuming. It mainly hit when I was leaving or entering the house. Before leaving, I had to insert each plug round the ground floor, some an even number of times, some an odd number of times. When I returned, I needed to park the car exactly three inches from the kerb – no more no less. And I had to manoeuvre the car until it was in the right place and at right angles to the kerb. I could see curtains and blinds twitching with neighbours wondering what the maniac at thirty-nine was doing. My worst symptom appeared when I was doing my accounts. If I made a mistake I couldn't cross it out. I had to tear the sheet up and start again on a new sheet. The problem with all this was it was so bloody time consuming you were unable to actually live your life. This all happened when Liz was in Essex and I felt alone in making sure life worked. I believe OCD is an attempt to control your life. In performing the rituals, I felt I was placating powerful forces which threatened my existence. This extreme OCD didn't last beyond a year. There have been vestigial tics all my life. I always have to check doors are locked, sometimes more than once and have been known to re-enter the house more than once to check the gas taps are off!

In 1983, the Soho Poly wanted to take a play up to the Edinburgh Festival. After the success of *Johnny Oil* in 1982, Adrian Shergold proposed that I write a sequel to *Johnny Oil* which would stand alone as a play at the Festival but could then return to the Soho Poly and become the second act of a full-length evening production. So *Oil Strikes Back* was born. The conceit was that, eight years on, Johnny Oil is now a Corona soft drinks driver and Alan, Baz's friend from the bonfire, now at university, would take a vacation job as his assistant. In Edinburgh, the play had a prime venue in the Assembly Rooms. It didn't do well. There was too much an audience needed to know from the original *Johnny Oil* play, to be able to appreciate this sequel. In September the two plays were remounted at The Soho Poly as one full-length play and the evening worked well. What I most liked was that the gulf between Johnny Oil and Alan, nascent in the first act, had really grown over the decade.

Johnny wonders why Alan's doing the job. Alan tells him he's a student and that this is the summer vacation:

JO: I thought you were. You can tell students.
ALAN: How?
JO: They're polite all the time. Eh – have you been on University Challenge?
ALAN: I tried for our team but I didn't get on.
JO: I bet you have to be really clever. Me and Verna watch it. Verna can answer some of the questions. I don't even understand them. I don't like that bloke though.
ALAN: Bamber Gascoyne?
JO: He smiles all the time. He talks to you like you're a turd. Then he laughs when you get it wrong as if he knew the answers all along without looking at the card. Eh – is that what it's like at university? D'you have to sit at one of them counters while some bollock asks questions.
ALAN: No – that's just the programme.
JO: What are you 'reading'?
ALAN: Philosophy.
JO: You want to talk to Verna's grandad. He does that.
ALAN: Really?
JO: I wouldn't fancy it. It's mainly old people he sees. And when he gets home he stinks of feet. It gets into his clothes.
ALAN: You're thinking of chiropody.
JO: Are you taking the piss, son? Eh?
ALAN: No – philosophy's different.
JO: What is it then?

ALAN: Well – 'philo' means 'love of', 'sophos' knowledge.
        Philosophos – love of knowledge.
JO: What d'you learn then?
ALAN: It's not a subject like all the others. You – well –
        examine fundamental questions.
JO: Like what?
ALAN: What is truth? And – er – what is knowledge? Can
        miracles happen? Do we really see what we seem to see?
JO: How long have you been doing that, then?
ALAN: A year.
JO: Have you got any answers yet?
ALAN: Well – no…
JO: I'd jack it in then, son.
ALAN: That's not the point.
JO: 'Do we really see what we seem to see?' Fucking hell. I
        bet some comedian's making money out of that an' all.
        Your professors, eh?

I mentioned earlier that characters in *Marking Time*, *Johnny Oil* and *Keep on Running* based on me marked the moral nadir of the plays and related this to guilt about my mother's death. I think something different is going on here. In allowing Oil to mount a common-sense attack on philosophy and thereby the whole academic world was a way of dealing with the cultural tension caused by my transition to a world of education and literature from the world of Baz, bonfires and Oil himself. This transition had started at grammar school and had accelerated through university and moving to live in the South of England.

The play opened to very good reviews. Steve Grant in Time Out praised 'The excellent Phil Daniels [who] plays Oil with some good support from Tilly Vosburgh and Nick Conway.' 'Adrian Shergold's production…coaxes all the nuances and atmospheres from the script and Phil Daniels as the rough savage Oil makes him bristle with bewildered aggression,' thought Nicholas De Jongh in The Guardian. Irving Wardle in The Times had admiration for 'two electrifying performances.' The Sunday Telegraph felt it was 'a strong play', while Michael Coveney in the Financial Times thought 'the writing is like a happy amalgam of Barrie Keefe and John Byrne – (a) lovely evening – well directed by Adrian Shergold and ingeniously designed by David Rogers.'

When Adrian Shergold moved to the Theatre Royal, Stratford East (Sam Kelly once called it a pub which happened to have a theatre in one corner) to be Phillip Hedley's associate director, he took me with him. Or, rather, I followed. Adrian and I ran a youth theatre project over the summer for Newham young people which culminated in a performance at Stratford East's new studio theatre, 'The Square Thing'. In the autumn, I ran writers' workshops. The first stage was to invite successful writers to talk to aspirant ones: Henry Livings, Barrie Keefe, Mustapha Matura and Mike Leigh went down particularly well. The second stage was to encourage the writers to come up with miniplays which would then get a rehearsed reading. One of the plays was written by someone who clearly had a mental health problem. I couldn't understand a word of what he submitted. He threatened to kill me if I didn't give it a rehearsed reading. It got a rehearsed reading although no-one, including the actors, understood a word. I don't remember any talent emerging from those rehearsed readings. The irony is that a 19-year-old from Wapping called Tony Marchant walked in with a full length play already completed. Tony would go on to be one of our best British screen writers, eventually winning the BAFTA Dennis Potter Award. I've been in two minds about the value of creative writing workshops as a means of finding writing talent ever since!

At the end of April 1980, six armed men entered the Iranian Embassy in Princes Gate and took the twenty-six people inside hostage, demanding the release of Arab prisoners in the Iranian state of Khuzestan. On the sixth day, a bank holiday, one of the hostages was killed and the body thrown into the street. In response, the SAS stormed the building rescuing all but one of the hostages and killing five hostage takers. This all took place live on TV. The Snooker Championship was also live on TV that day. And I remember switching over to the snooker until something happened at the Embassy. It was a bizarre TV event, unprecedented and nothing like it has occurred since. This was the first time the SAS had come to prominence. And the dramatic outcome was a huge filip for the Thatcher Government.

What interested me was that, shortly after the siege, the SAS advertised for people to join the SAS Territorial regiments with the slogan *Fit, Keen and Over 17?* and the queue to join, made up mainly of young people, stretched from the Chelsea Barracks down the Kings Road. What intrigued me was that only the summer before, there had been riots by mainly young people across the country and particularly in Toxteth and Brixton which were partly caused by distrust of the police and authority. And yet, here we were, barely a year later, with young people identifying with an ultimate symbol of authority. Theatre Venture Commissioned *Fit, Keen and Over 17?* from me following a group of young recruits on an SAS selection weekend. It's worth quoting the review in The Guardian by Nicholas De Jongh who got it in one:

'There comes a sudden chilling moment at the close of Andy Armitage's jovial view of a weekend initiative course for territorial recruits when the mood darkens. And the play's whole focus darkens sharply.

Until then, *Fit, Keen and Over 17* has concentrated upon the possible tests and trials for a young quartet of teenagers eager to join the SAS volunteer reserve.

Belief is suspended and licence taken because two of the four are girls: Armitage deals with future and imagined circumstances when feminism is so rampant within the military that women become possible recruits. Though this is a subsidiary issue, his licence is finally justified.

The four are typical products of the East End – a traditional recruiting place for the army – and all in search of antidotes to boredom and incentives for excitement. The boys are sharply distinguished – Terry, a swaggering, loud-mouthed gardener who teems with military dreams and Roy, a sharp quiet boy. The girls, Denise and Dawn, are closer to sterotype.

The circumstances in which they find themselves, with a staff sergeant looking for 'artists in warfare', involve initial blindfolding, humiliation and insult. But the main action centres on a battle of the sexes as each pair is dropped from a helicopter, instructed to find the way to base 20 miles away and at night. Only one of the four will be selected.

This scheme makes for a rather exciting, well-observed clash of wills, character and the sexes….and when the four finally reach their destination to find themselves in another tense dilemma, only one of the four has the sort of dangerous courage to make him a natural candidate for the SAS.

It is at this point that we discover Armitage's scaring, plausible hypothesis: a future in which the army will be trained to fight [in a] civil war in England.

There is no attempt to caricature the army officers who emerge with sense and sympathy, as does the staff sergeant who finally dismisses himself in disgust…the well-acted occasion is trenchant and appealing in drama and argument.'

As the captain, seconded for the selection process from a new MOD/Home Office Unit tells the SAS sergeant:

HAWKINS: *You are right in a sense, Sykes. All wars are the same. The fact that your wars have so far taken place under a tropical sun shouldn't deceive you into thinking that war on the streets of this country between its inhabitants would be any different. After all, the enemy hasn't changed. Malaya, Oman, Borneo, Aden – in each case you were fighting the same force – that of chaos and disorder. And he's here now, Sykes. He's already invaded. He's in our streets, our schools. He echoes through our shopping malls, enters our homes through the TV screen, vandalizes our housing estates. We need an army recruited from the battlefield he's chosen to fight on. That army is to be the territorial army. And this regiment will be its vanguard.*

The play was well-reviewed across the board. '[The] up and at'em production is a triumph..and Theatre Venture's young performers acquit themselves well', said Ann McFerran in Time

Out. Lyn Gardner in City Limits found the play 'full of crude energy and humour.'

Two amazing things happened as a result of the *Johnny Oil* productions. I got a new agent, then Lemon, Unna and Durbridge (now The Agency (London) Ltd), one of the foremost agencies for theatre, TV and film writers in the country. One of their first acts was to call me with an invitation. A BBC producer, Brenda Reid, had seen *Johnny Oil*. She was producing plays by writers new to television on BBC2. Did I want to be one of them? Yes – I did.

Chapter 4 – Keep On Running

In the 1980s, aspirant Further Education managers were sent by their colleges to the Further Education Staff College, a rather clubby kind of country house near Blagden, Bristol. There were three courses: Head of Department 1, 2 and 3. As soon as I arrived for the first, I looked around and knew I didn't fit in. There was something all these people had in common. They were driven in a way I was not. My suspicions were confirmed when I took a test. Apparently, I was too people-rather than task-oriented – not a good omen for an FE manager, apparently. So, I didn't make Head of Department 2 and 3 and I began to look around for an alternative to FE management. (Interestingly, I would later become a Head of Department in Higher Education for ten years and became rather good at it, my department gaining an Ofsted Outstanding grade the year before I retired.) At this stage, my first TV play hadn't been transmitted so making a living from my writing didn't seem feasible. I began to look at teacher training jobs in higher education – something I'd always fancied doing.

At the same time, Liz was getting itchy feet. There wasn't much chance of advancing her career at the college. The facilities weren't very good – there was a drama room but that was it. We both decided to fire off applications, agreeing that we would stay in the South of England. Liz was the first to score a bull's eye. Hampshire had a tertiary college system – all post 16 education took place in these institutions, further, adult and higher education. Not only had Liz landed the Head of Drama role, the college had a fully equipped professional theatre which she was to be the artistic director of.

My turn came later in the year. This was 1984 and the Thatcher Government's Education Reforms were in full swing. Essentially, they were delivering the reforms that Callaghan had suggested nearly a decade before in his Ruskin College, Oxford speech. The year before, the Government had launched the Technical and Vocational Education Initiative (TVEI). This was the largest curriculum intervention ever by a government. It was a broad, experimental scheme aimed at preparing 14-18-year-olds for the world of work and developing personal qualities such as enterprise and problem-solving skills. My new role at what would become Canterbury Christ Church University would be to help new and existing teachers to deliver this pre-vocational education.

So, it was a summer of upheavals. We bade our farewells to Orpington FE College where we'd both spent the best part of a decade. We put our house on the market. This was not a good time to sell and buy houses: the market had not yet recovered from the recession of the late 70s. Originally, when we first landed the two jobs, we agreed it would be best if we moved to somewhere between Canterbury and Hampshire, like Reigate. However, it transpired that Liz's job was going to involve weekend work as well as weekday work so we agreed to buy somewhere near the college in Hampshire.

The summer was spent looking at properties in Hampshire villages. I'm not very good at instability and with work, home and relationships all up in the air, I threw a bit of a wobbler which manifested itself in paranoia. For some reason, I thought our local dry cleaners were out get us. I don't know why I chose them. Since my job was more flexible and, since we still had to sell the Sidcup property, we agreed Liz would get digs in Hampshire in the short term and I would commute down to Canterbury from Sidcup, forty-five minutes' drive. We had found a very nice detached property with a 100-foot garden near the town station in Hampshire but we obviously had to sell the Sidcup house first. So, for two months, Liz would come home most weekends. Sundays were very sad. We would have Sunday lunch together listening to *Gardeners' Question Time* before Liz would climb into her car for the trip back to Hampshire, which was quite arduous. The south western corner of the M25 had not yet been finished. You had to come off at Reigate, detour through Dorking and Guildford before picking up the M3. I still get very sad when I accidentally switch *Gardeners' Question Time* on.

Once the Sidcup house was sold in November 1984, I would spend weekends in Hampshire and rented a small flat at the college during the week. I remember moving in one dark Sunday night. As I was collecting my stuff from the car, I was accosted by my next-door neighbour, an elderly music lecturer. 'Don't worry if you see me walking naked round my flat. I often do it', she warned me. 'Oh – and no solids after 11pm. The pipes go right across my ceiling and it's very noisy.' Where had I come to?

The mid 80s was a time when TV drama was moving from the studio to film. My first two BBC plays were made mostly in the studio but with some scenes on single video camera. These were shot at exterior locations but with one video camera, not on multiple cameras as in the studio, nor on film cameras. My three other BBC dramas were films. Studio drama is a very good intermediate medium for the writer making the transition from theatre to film. As in the theatre, there is extensive rehearsal before the shoot itself. For *Keep on Running*, I would travel up to the North Acton rehearsal rooms and work with the director and actors and there was time to redraft the script before the final recording script was drawn up. This was very similar to preparation for a theatre play. Also, the writer has a birds-eye view of the action up in the gallery, watching the unfolding of the studio play, whereas the writer is mostly not very welcome on film sets because everyone is terrified that they might want to change things and interfere with the tightly packed schedule of very long days that they are going to have to stick to.

Keep on Running was shot in the BBC studios at Llandaff, Cardiff. Even back in the 80s, the Beeb was very conscious of being London-centric. This was confirmed by one of the technicians in the gallery. When I told him we all felt we'd had such a warm welcome, he replied, 'You will have done, mate. All we get here is Singer of The fucking World'. Mind you, this devolution didn't come without its problems: all the extras came from Llandaff High School so we had to ask them to rhubarb, rhubarb quietly as they passed through, in case the viewer wondered why a school in a play set in Manchester was entirely populated with Welsh boys. It was thrilling to sit in the gallery and watch the play being put together. What most impressed me, and still does, is the sheer professionalism of everyone involved in making a TV programme. There's a real sense of everyone playing a unique part very skilfully. I haven't seen this kind of teamwork in any other profession.

The play begins with Frank and Alan having a fag in the bogs while assembly is droning on next door. This very long scene (remember, this was the first TV drama scene I'd written since I'd completed five theatre plays) establishes a number of things: Alan is into progressive rock, he's a rebel, he's bright, he's ambitious, he wants a risky life (he quotes Roger McGough '*Let me die a young man's death, not a clean and in between the sheets holy water death, not a famous-last-words peaceful out of breath death*'), he wants to get away from the life he's leading now. Frank is a conformist, not bright but future head boy. They are interrupted by Salter, the head of 6th form. He catches them smoking and sagging off from assembly. Salter is dismayed to catch Frank, one of his favourites but clearly has it in for Alan. When Salter demands Alan's fags and Alan refuses, he hits him across the head. Salter then tells Alan outright that he's never liked him. Alan responds angrily, 'You don't like me because you don't frighten me and you don't frighten me because I know what you're scared off.'

I spoke earlier of a generation of teachers who must have resented young people's freedom, their capacity to challenge authority, benefit from the NHS and the rapid expansion of higher education. This, I think, lies behind the remarks Alan makes to Salter. This scene is based on a real event, when the head of sixth form caught Chris Kenway and I having a fag in the bogs during assembly. Kenway and I were both rebels who were by now well beyond the strictures of an authoritarian organisation (Kenway had already been expelled from Manchester Grammar) and the head of sixth form really didn't like us. In reality he hit us both on the head which was a pretty extreme thing to do to two seventeen-year-olds. He must have been a very angry man. We were required to report to the head the following day. Fearing the inevitable caning I thought we faced the following day, I experimented with bathroom sponges and mats down the back of my trousers but they were all clearly visible as unnatural bulges. It was like something out of the Bash St Kids or Jimmy Edwards and Whack-O!

We faced the head the following day. As luck would have it, the head taught us General Studies and had recently covered the topic of penal reform. We both began to refute the key arguments which supported the notion of punishment. We demolished the argument from reform arguing that the cane wouldn't change our smoking habit. Nor would it deter us from smoking in the future. We were physically addicted. We added the affront to our dignity as adults and claimed the head would demean himself administering the punishment. The head bought it and quietly let us off. (Ironically, I was to revisit all this a decade later when I completed the dissertation for my Masters, 'Punishment and Penalties in Education'.) In the play, Alan takes the same route. However, my head is a character in crisis, a man questioning his own life and I was keen to give him humour and humanity in his time of suffering. Alan suggests a solution: 'Why don't you pretend to cane us? That way, everybody's happy.' The head agrees. He seeks assurance that they will respond to the whacks and afterwards tell people how much the cane hurt. The boys agree. The head whacks the desk. The boys cry in pain. Outside the head's study, Mr Salter is satisfied. 'Any more problems, send them straight to me,' the head tells him. I feel that, dramatically, this incident marks the head's breaking out of the professional behaviour expected of him and going his own way, something we will learn towards the end of the play he's never done in his life before.

The key scene of the play takes place at the prefects' dance. Alan and his girlfriend, Steph, are anxious to find somewhere to have sex. Their own homes are out of bounds because there are other family there (a very realistic problem at the time for us!) Alan has an idea – they'll go to the head, Mr Rush's office, where he was pretend-caned earlier. They open the door. There sits the head with a bottle of whisky. He thought he'd stick around to ensure the prefects' dance didn't get out of hand. The head invites them in. Steph disappears but Alan takes a seat, intrigued.

The head shares his whisky. For the head this is a confessional. He's disappointed in his children. What's more, he's disappointed in himself. He doesn't think much of the teaching profession. He thinks higher education is vastly overrated. Alan has got the impression of the head as posh, privileged and Cambridge educated. Rush puts him right. He left school at fourteen and only managed to get to Cambridge via evening classes and correspondence courses. Rush was, he says, head of English in Liverpool before coming to Manchester. And he cites one boy who was a difficult pupil, a rebellious unruly little horror. But only because even at school age, he had a 'talent for independence' and 'a single-mindedness' that Rush knew he would never have. 'His name was John Lennon.' Rush urges Alan not to make the same mistakes he made himself, to settle for second best, to 'end up'. Instead, he should follow Lennon's example. 'Make a mark,' he tells him, 'take risks, be outrageous, show your arse to the world but do it soon.' Alan refuses to acknowledge all this. 'You've nothing to teach me, sir.' 'Then, teach *me* something.' Rush replies. 'Like what?' 'Teach me what it's like to be seventeen again.' Alan returns to the dance. He has second thoughts. He grabs a Jimi Hendrix LP. Intending to play it to Rush, he runs back to the head's office. And opening the door, he sees Rush, hanging from the chandelier. I mentioned at the end of Chapter 1 that 'It was a tradition for departing 6th formers to enter the school the night before the last day and 'decorate' it. No vandalism this, just effigies of the headteacher on a scaffold, streamers in the staff room and such.' On watching the play again, I saw for the first time, as the prefects smuggled these effigies into school, where the seed for the ending might have been unconsciously sown.

I hadn't realised but TV dramas get two bites of the cherry: they get TV previews then, if they're lucky, reviews of the drama once transmitted. The previews for *Keep on Running* were universally good. For the Sunday Times it was 'a highly commendable play', for the Observer, 'a smashing play, witty and sensitive.' The Daily Mail thought it, 'startling…a sad and surprising play. Don't miss it.' Time Out had it as 'a charming hour's viewing' and for The Times it was 'a strong play'. The Evening Standard thought I'd made 'a successful TV writing debut with this lively drama.' The reviews, however, were more mixed. Hugh Hebert in the Guardian (whom I was later to take on) said 'If it had been done worse, it would have been very tedious. As it was, it passed the time.' The Telegraph was more generous, the Head's 'conflicts were absorbingly expressed and well-placed against those of the potentially similar Machin. Director Paul Seed gave them an entirely convincing background.'

Keep on Running was not about education primarily but was concerned with a theme I'd already set running in *Marking Time* and would run through the suite of BBC dramas. This theme was identity and about how you construct and express that identity in a way which is unique to you. This where my study of philosophy, my drama writing and teaching meld together. In philosophy, the exploration of personal identity concerns itself with how far we can say that a person is the same person over time and whether identity is naturally given or constructed. In my BBC dramas, Steve in *Brick is Beautiful*, is of the view that anyone can become an entrepreneur, espousing the shape-shifting of Thatcherite Liberal Conservatism or Neo-Liberalism precisely. In *Starlings* the redundant Consett steel workers spend their redundancy pay on retraining as butlers to join the burgeoning service economy. Michael, the biscuit factory engineer, reckons that in being recreated as a city banker, he's 'got behind the mask' and understood that social class is merely constructed performance. In education, I'd become a huge fan of Howard Gardner and had devoured his book *Frames of Mind: The Theory of Multiple Intelligences*, when it had been published in 1983.

'Gardner sees the traditional understanding of intelligence as limiting. He suggests that traditional understandings do not recognize the range of talents and abilities that many people have who do not excel in what he describes as 'logical-mathematical intelligence'. Gardner identifies and describes six other forms of intelligence as follows: linguistic intelligence, spatial intelligence, bodily kinaesthetic intelligence, musical intelligence, interpersonal intelligence and intrapersonal intelligence. For Gardner, these distinctive forms of intelligence are genetically based and influenced by culture, but can be enhanced through practice and learning.'

(Armitage, A., Cogger, C., Evershed, J., Hayes, D., Lawes, L., Renwick, M., *Teaching in Post-14 Education and Training* 5th edn)

This explained for me why so many young people were alienated from learning because the academic curriculum focussed entirely on logical-mathematic intelligence and education was not offering them opportunities to express and enhance their identities through their own special set of abilities. And I saw it as my job as a teacher to help learners do exactly this.

Although Maslow was discussing motivation, the pinnacle of his hierarchy of needs may be what Rush, the head in *Keep on Running*, had never managed to achieve:

'Maslow, whose work is closely related to humanistic psychology, saw 'self-actualization' as what drives people to learn; that is, the need to make full use of one's talents, become creative and achieve one's potential is what motivates us. Self-actualization is an ultimate human goal and need, but before that need can be fulfilled a set of other needs must be met. These needs are generally presented as a pyramid. At the bottom level are physiological needs such as hunger and thirst. Once these are satisfied the next level is the need for physical and psychological well-being which if met leads on to the need for love and a sense of belonging which involves having warm, friendly relationships. Next come self-esteem needs: to achieve, be successful, have the respect of others. Finally, at the top of the hierarchy is self-actualization, the desire to fulfil one's potential. This, according to Maslow may only be achieved by some people fleetingly throughout their lives, but the top of the pyramid is left open because human potential is not finite.'

(Armitage, A., Cogger, C., Evershed, J., Hayes, D., Lawes, L., Renwick, M., *Teaching in Post-14 Education and Training* 5th edn)

My interest in identity and role-playing had, earlier, spilled over into my teaching in FE and I had published a resource for vocational students called *What Do You Say? Guidance and Exercises in Oral Communications*. I was rather pleased with what I thought was the clever title at the time. It deals with self-presentation and body language, the technical elements of speech, expressing opinions, conversations, talk in formal contexts, phone calls, persuasion and negotiation. It has stood the test of time and I used a lot of its ideas in a book for apprenticeship mentors and coaches Alison and I published a couple of years ago.

What Do You Say turned me into a bit of an expert on oracy at the time and I started to get invited to in-service training sessions for teachers and to speak at conferences. One such was at the London Drama and Tape centre, a leading centre of training for London drama teachers. The session was on a Saturday morning. I made the mistake of eating a hot curry the night before. My good old digestive system was in paroxysms on the train into London, as I struggled to control the wind swirling round it. The utter fear of standing up and farting my way through the speech led to a shaking fit so that when I stood up to speak and grabbed the lectern for support, the shaking was transferred to the lectern and visible to the audience. The sight of this gibbering, shaking, arse-clenching 'expert' in oracy was too much for the audience who, as one, bowed their heads in embarrassment.

In writing this memoir, I have had a range of choices to make about the narrative. How much do I tell about intimate relationships? Do I use actual names or change names? How far am I critical of others' behaviour? When I wrote *Picture Friend*, a TV fiction portrait of my own family, I had no such questions. This was I think because I knew that I was going to fictionalise parts of the story and the audience would therefore not know which bits were fiction and which actually happened.

The story is told through the eyes of Sheila, who, drunk, falls off a bus and is taken to hospital. This is set in the then present, the 1980s but there are flashbacks to the family's life in the 1950s and then the 1960s, through her eyes. The key moment in the piece comes in a scene between the two girls, aged fifteen and sixteen. Sheila lies on the floor mooning over a photograph of Robert Wagner in her film magazine, *Picture Friend*. The more down to earth, realistic Christine says she still hasn't forgiven Robert Wagner for what he did to Joanne Woodward in *A Kiss Before Dying*. In fact, she reckons that film stars are, in truth, not very nice people and Shelia is starry eyed. Family members, and I'm sure this applies to all families, not just mine, often create fictions to protect them against uncomfortable realities. Ted, the father is a habitual practical joker. In the play, he comes home with his hand bandaged up. He was getting out of the car and someone slammed the door on his hand. The girls are horrified. 'They managed to sew two fingers back on but the third? They put it in a bottle for me in cases of advances in medicine. I brought it home. D'you want a look?' And he pulls a bottle out with a bloodied, severed finger. But it turns out to be rubber. My father did play the odd practical joke but I wanted to ramp this up in Ted's case to make clear that this was a distraction created by him. And we get an inkling that the uncomfortable reality might be partly to do with his war experiences when we hear him recounting patently fictional war anecdotes to David as the boy goes off to sleep. (Mind you, the tomatoes incident actually happened. Our next-door neighbour was continually looking over the wall and denigrating the pathetic plants in Dad's greenhouse. So, Dad bought large beef tomatoes and crept out to his greenhouse with them in the dead of night. He tied them to the actual tomato plants with twine. I'll never forget the neighbour's open mouth when he saw them. We stood as a family in the back yard and laughed.) But Ted must also rue his former wealthy status. Sheila shouts at the fur-coated, patronizing middle-class Mrs Gorrie who comes to use the la-va-tory on the way to the shops, 'My mum was rich once you know!' For her part, the mother, Mrs Goodwin, admits to Christine that she wanted to leave Ted many times but stayed for the two girls. That is her uncomfortable truth. (I invented this to make the story work. To this day I have no idea at all about my parents' relationship with each other. All I remember was that, as a tot, I was lying in bed with Mum when Dad shouted, angrily calling her a 'lion'. It was a long time later that I realised he was using the word 'liar'.) Sheila adores her father. And it looks as if she married someone exactly like her father when her (estranged) husband turns up at the hospital with a joke knife through his head. But the play ends with Sheila chasing him out of the hospital. Has she seen a truth at last? Is she no longer as starry-eyed as her fifteen-year-old self? The only character who does not seem to need fictions is Christine. She disapproves of her father's gulling of a work mate by telling him to bootblack his grey patches. The poor man ends up with bootblack all over his face. Christine sees through her father's antics. She intends to leave home and soon, after her father blocks her going to secretarial college.

Continuing its policy of developing regional drama programme making, *Picture Friend* was scheduled to be shot at BBC Broadcasting House, Bristol. Prior to this, myself, the director and designer took a trip up to Manchester. To get an idea of the part of the city where I lived, we went to Stretford and looked at the house I lived in at the time the play takes place. It happened that a neighbouring house was for sale. We got the key from the estate agents. An elderly couple had lived there and, inside, it was identical to my house a few doors down in the 1950s, even as far as the clothes horse on the kitchen ceiling (I remember, at the time, being most concerned about this bunch of posh BBC farts wandering round my childhood world at will and found it all quite invasive).

Cut to the day of filming. I walked into the studio and… there was my house, in detail. Suddenly, I was eight again. It was an extraordinary experience. I felt completely exposed. But I had no cause for complaint. I'd caused the exposure by writing the play in the first place. It got more bizarre. Unknown to me, the designer was a friend of my sister, Heather, who was also a TV/Film designer at the time. And Heather had given her family photographs. When Jim Broadbent arrived for his first scene, he wore a dog tooth check jacket identical to the one my dad had worn in the fifties.

The play was again well previewed and reviewed, with one exception: it was that Hugh Hebert in the Guardian again. ITV had chosen to transmit a similarly autobiographical play by John Osborne the same night and Hugh Hebert pronounced the Osborne superior to my piece. Although I was flattered to be compared with Osborne, albeit unfavourably, I was livid. Hugh Hebert had done for me previously. He'd done for me again. So, I wrote to Hugh Hebert pretending to be my mother and informing him that I had fallen into such a deep depression after reading his review that I'd had to be admitted to a psychiatric unit. He didn't take the bait. Which was a good thing. I believed and still do that it's the writer's decision to make their work public and they should be prepared to accept the consequences, including hostile criticism in the press. Hebert was to make up for this with a rather flattering feature about me in the Guardian a year or so later.

Later that year, another call from Brenda Reid at the BBC. 'Darling, we're sending writers all over the world for the next series – Zimbabwe, the USA, South America, chosen already. Come in and see me and, meanwhile, think about where you want to set your play.' Wow – the world at my finger-tips. In my head I travelled the world, wondering which country would have the best story for me. But, as per, I was on the Central Line to White City with no idea whatsoever.

When I went into Brenda's office, there was a tall, blond guy with her. 'Before you tell me where you want to go, Andy, well – you're going to Manchester.' 'But Brenda, of all places, c'mon, I grew up there.' 'Just hear David out.' She then introduced me to David Wheatley. David was a documentary director, a very good one (he directed the floating pink bottle for the opening credits of the Arena strand of arts programmes). He'd sold a film about the Belgian artist Renee Magritte to the BBC when he was still a film student at the Royal College of Art. David told me this extraordinary story and I knew immediately I had to do it. David had been working at Granada Studios in Manchester and had taken a cab to Piccadilly Station. However, the cabby took him on a very circuitous route round the Manchester back streets. David thought he was being taken for a ride by the cabby so confronted him. 'Street closures,' the cabby explained.

'There are warehouses collapsing in the street. People are knocking down the walls to get at the Victorian bricks that they can sell to builders.' Brenda was so intrigued with this (as was I) that she offered to fund David and I to do two weeks' research in Manchester. Full details about that odyssey in Chapter 5.

Meanwhile, back in Canterbury, I would often go into the city at lunch time for a bite and a wander. A former colleague from Orpington College lived outside the city in Ash. His partner had a knitwear shop in the city and I often popped in to say hello. The shop was staffed by volunteers. One day my jaw dropped when I saw the latest volunteer: this was Elaine, who was to be my partner for the next eighteen years.

At Canterbury Christ Church, I was running thirty-day courses, essentially for school-teachers, to equip them to teach technical and vocational programmes in schools in line with government reforms. At this time, I was still living in the flat in the College with the occasionally nude musician living next door. One of the students on my first programme, Phil Holden, lived in Eastbourne but taught in Tunbridge Wells. He decided, to avoid commuting, he'd bring his caravan over to Canterbury for the duration of the course and use the showers in the student union. As I lived in the flat close by, I'd work in my study until seven or eight at night. But Phil, who was incredibly enthusiastic, would also stay in our classroom next door. He'd pull me in to show diagrams of courses he was devising which I'd politely have to show the same enthusiasm for.

I'd mentioned Phil to trainees on subsequent courses and one day, after we'd advertised a lectureship in my area jointly with the local authority, there was a knock on my door. 'I've applied for this job,' said Phil as he came in the room. 'But first,' he said, 'I've got a bone to pick with you. I was on this course and was talking to someone who I discovered had been on one of your courses after me. He said you had talked about this mad PE teacher who lived in a caravan and stayed late designing courses. That was me!'

Phil's interview was hilarious. I was interviewing with my head of department, Paul Zec, the son of the cartoonist, Donald Zec, also an accomplished saxophonist, who had a very sharp but surreal sense of humour. Our principal, who was a rather vague and ...hesitant...hesitant...hesitant speaker was questioning Phil. 'This MA, he said, 'this MA... your MA...?' 'Sussex University,' Phil jumped in. 'Yes – I can see where you did it,' replied the principal, 'I wanted to know what you studied'. At this point, Paul Zec and I both had our hands under the table digging our fingernails in to stop us guffawing.

Phil aced the application and joined me teaching half the time at the College and half the time working as an inspector/adviser with the Kent Authority. We had great times both personally and professionally. Phil hailed from Stalybridge so it was two northerners together. We ran courses for teachers and eventually became in demand by local authorities across the region. We wrote two manuals together for teachers involved in the government's Technical and Vocational Education Initiative (TVEI). I remember an occasion in the College's senior common room when Paul Zec, Phil and I were discussing a series of management issues. What started as a serious professional conversation about management styles quickly deteriorated. We wondered whether people in each management role developed a walk specific to that role and so posited the ideas of 'role specific' walks. Myself or Phil, can't remember who, got up to demonstrate the walk of a particular senior manager at the College which was quite distinctive. As he or I began to walk the walk, the manager in question, as if on cue, emerged behind us and we crossed the SCR together. When I left, Phil had several roles at the College, including Director of the PGCE but, in the end, specialised in the training of head-teachers and finally became a director of a leading company doing this successfully nationally.

The deadline for completing the *Brick is Beautiful* script loomed but I had a two-week holiday booked with Liz in Crete. I was by then in the same position with Liz and Elaine that I had been a decade earlier with Mary and Monica, in love with two women simultaneously. This holiday was a sort of last-ditch attempt to save the relationship with Liz. I had to finish the script on the holiday in rather trying circumstances, both physically, in thirty-two degrees of heat, and emotionally with Liz. I take issue with Wordsworth's notion of literary creation as 'emotion recollected in tranquillity' because I seem to have done my best work at an emotionally fraught period in my life. It's almost as if an emotional crisis acts as the grit in the oyster. I would sit in the accommodation in the morning writing; the maid who cleaned the room would eye me with suspicion – why wasn't this guy like the other Brit lunatics, frying himself on the beach? But in the afternoon, I would join Liz on the beach.

The holiday hadn't worked. After some to-ing and fro-ing between Hampshire and Canterbury, I moved in with Elaine. Her flat I'd moved into had a balcony overlooking the Great Stour in the centre of the city. It was idyllic – birds in the tree overhanging the balcony, ducks and moorhens below on the river. Elaine had had a traumatic time the previous year. She had lived in London with a much older husband. He'd had a stroke which made him blind. They had moved to Canterbury to downsize and the husband had developed cancer and died.

A bond between us was our northern-ness: Elaine was originally from Sheffield. After O Levels, she had attended secretarial college but had then fled to London's bright lights: I think we were both caught between appreciating the positive aspects of living in the north and the constrictions and limitations of that life. So, one day, in the autumn of 1985, we both stepped out – I remember we had identical briefcases of different colours, naff but sweet, rather like matching anoraks – Elaine for her first day taking A Levels at the local FE college and me on my way to my newish job. This was the first day for Elaine of seven years of further and higher education as a mature student: A Levels, followed by a degree in history at The University of Kent and then an MA in Later Modern British History at The London School of Economics. She had impressed the historians at Kent and was offered a lectureship teaching both Sociology and History to preparatory students from overseas prior to their undergraduate studies.

Brick is Beautiful was shot later that year on location in Manchester and the North West. The film opens with Steve and his girlfriend, Maureen, at night, creeping past the security guard and entering the department store, where we subsequently learn Maureen is on a YTS retail programme. I liked this sequence, partly because I've always fantasised about a sort of supermarket sweep-type freedom in a department store myself – something the Royal Family apparently enjoy. But the opulence on display tees up one of the key themes of the film – the grasping materialistic 1980s. Maureen is content shovelling jelly babies into her mouth but Steve is on a serious search for designer label clothes, which establishes his acquisitive nature. The following morning, Maureen wakes in the bedding department. Steve's abandoned her. She's marched to personnel and sacked.

Meanwhile, Steve goes to collect Dez and Snapper to go out picking bricks. These are bricks from partially demolished buildings which legitimate demolition companies have the contract for. Our lads are therefore 'stealing' bricks. Both Dez and Snapper are on a YTS construction course and live in an abandoned warehouse because, we later learn, Snapper's mum's in rehab and Dez's father physically abuses him. Snapper's serious about training to become a brickie and chooses to go off to college whereas Dez isn't and goes picking bricks with Steve. They will run these bricks into Bennett's yard – he's the brick baron of Manchester. But it's at this point that Steve reckons they should set up their own brickyard in competition with Bennett. On the other hand, Dez, who has a strong artistic bent, wonders whether they should be helping demolish old buildings at all. I liked the crossed duologue on the demolition site which illustrates where Steve and Dez are coming from:

STEVE: *I don't see why we can't go off on our own.*
DEZ: *(HOLDING A BRICK) Mr Bainbridge says a brick is like this because it fits perfectly into a man's hand.*
STEVE: *All we'd need is a yard to clean them in.*
DEZ: *Just think – some bloke was holding this a hundred years ago. Only he was putting it on top of another. He was building something new.*

STEVE: *Get a yard – use our house as an office.*

DEZ: *I bet he didn't think, a hundred years ago, it'd look like this in a hundred years' time. He probably wouldn't have bothered, had he known.*

And later:

DEZ: *I don't think Mr Bainbridge was right you know.*

STEVE: *About what?*

DEZ: *Well – about a brick being this size and shape to fit perfectly into a man's hand. D'you know what a mandela is?*

STEVE: *Yeah – it's one of those boats in that ice cream advert.*

DEZ: *I read about it in this book. It's a load of shapes that stand for something. And they used them when they designed old buildings. And so, the buildings stood for something.*

STEVE: *Like what?*

DEZ: *That's why knocking them down's wrong.*

STEVE: *They're clapped out. They're old.*

DEZ: *But they stood for something. Take my block – what does that stand for? Nowt – because they didn't use these. They didn't use bricks. I think bricks might be mandelas themselves. That's why we shouldn't be doing this.*

We meet our final main character, Brad, Maureen's oppo, in the pub. Brad is very camp and larger than life and has an aspiration to sing and act. (The pub sequence was shot in a pub in Eccles. During the lunch break I would eschew location catering for a ham barm cake with my step-mum, Gladys, who lived around the corner. I also played the landlord who ejects the Anarchist Fortnightly vendor out of the pub.

A terrible performance. My step-children urged me to play it again and again when they first saw it and watched it with hoots of laughter.)

Steve meets the Tin Man on the way home. This is someone we found on a rubbish tip in Manchester. David filmed this tip and it appears early in the film, crowded with scavengers, making Manchester look like Mumbai. The Tin Man specialised in discarded tins. In the film he's got a basketful of tins but hadn't been able to get to them before the rain washed all the labels off. Steve asks how he knows what's in each tin. He shakes one – he thinks it's dog food but couldn't be a hundred percent sure. (This tin turns out to be mandarin oranges – much to the disgust of Steve's dog his mum tries to feed them to). David, decided to use the Tin Man as a kind of totem, protective figure for our main characters. He appears as a ghostly figure around Manchester, accompanied by strange music.

Steve, Dez, Snapper and Maureen set up a business which takes off dramatically. When Steve discovers Dez and Snapper have been selling bricks to Bennett because Steve hasn't paid them yet, he decides to go out on his own. Hearing about Steve's success, Bennett bulldozes Steve's van and stock of bricks. Steve confronts him. Bennett suggests Steve come and work for him:

STEVE: *I work for myself. No-one else. What's the matter –*
        can't you take a bit of healthy competition? Thought
        that's what being in business was all about.
BENNETT: *(Laughs) Who told you that? Being in business is*
        all about getting rid of competition.

Bennett tells Steve he needs to set up at least ten miles away from Bennett's patch. He does.

In one of my favourite scenes, Steve goes to meet the council's small firms' adviser, Mr Clark:

MR CLARK: *You see, Steven, our job is to advise, to counsel, people who want to set up small businesses and, quite frankly, your plan seems a bit half baked. It's a dog-eat-dog world out there. I don't wish to be rude but could you meet customers dressed as you are?*

STEVE: *I'm not selling insurance – I'm selling bricks to builders.*

MR CLARK: *Steven, ask yourself these questions. Are you tough? Do you refuse to allow your feelings to interfere with decision-making? Are you competitive?*

STEVE: *D'you mean can I be a bastard? Easy. No danger.*

MR CLARK: *As a matter of fact, I was describing the qualities of the successful entrepreneur. I mean – couldn't you think about something with a future? A car valet service, for example.*

STEVE: *Bricks have a future, Mr Clark – you can count on that. They're out there waiting to be taken.*

MR CLARK: *There is one small problem.*

STEVE: *What's that?*

MR CLARK: *Well – they're still attached to buildings, most of them, aren't they?*

STEVE: *Firms down south are crying out for these. They build new houses which look like they've been there for a hundred years. People want them. Firms like Bennett's are only selling bricks locally. They don't know there's*

> *an M6, never mind an M1. They think the world stops*
> *at Altrincham.*
> MR CLARK: *(Giving STEVE some leaflets) I hope I haven't*
> *been too discouraging. You might well be onto a*
> *winner. Those lads in Consett, those steelworkers – they*
> *set up a company to demolish their own steel works.*
> *Now that's what I call entrepreneurial flair.*

This scene encapsulates pretty much one of the key metaphors of the film. The brick trade sees the bones of the 19th century being picked clean for the wealthy in the 20th. The Thatcher governments oversaw the de-industrialisation of Britain, the evisceration of the manufacturing sector in favour of the service sector. It's a theme which will continue into my next film for the BBC, 'Starlings'.

Steve's business flourishes. At a dinner in Cheshire with Bennett and his wife and Maureen, it becomes clear that Steve is now more successful than Bennett himself. But Maureen doesn't like what Steve has become and she dumps him.

Steve has acquired the demolition rights to the warehouse Dez and Snapper live in. Dez and Snapper plead to remain but Steve's heavies remove them. The film ends with Steve and his new girlfriend/secretary going south to see the first house built with his bricks. He's taking a photo of his girlfriend on the bonnet of his car when the posh house owner emerges. 'What the hell do you think you're doing? I don't want to buy anything, so – piss off!' You don't get to join the middle classes that easily, Steve.

The romantic conception of creativity as the artist being seized by some powerful force in an almost passive way is a metaphor for a psychological truth that has been dramatically demonstrated for me on viewing my work some thirty years on, that is, the power of the sub-conscious over the artist. I can now see in *Brick is Beautiful*, continua I was simply not consciously aware of at the time of writing. Firstly, there is the continuum from anarchy/spontaneity to order and control. Anarchy litters the film. Maureen tells the personnel officer that she entered the store at night because she 'just fancied doing it'. The student tries to sell Anarchist Fortnightly to Steve, who rips it up. A man comes into the brick yard with a cart full of bricks. He's knocked down his front garden wall to sell the bricks. He'd brought his back garden-wall in the previous week. Alec, the drunken lorry driver who brings gravel into the brickyard instead of bricks, can't manage to complete the saying, 'God helps those – God helps those…well he does, doesn't he?' Mr Bainbridge tells Des that they'd still be in the stone age if everyone overslept like him. Maureen's mum drunkenly sings Edith Piaf songs, her dad's on the run from the police. Then there's the continuum from competition to collaboration. Steve and Bennett are competitors. The scavengers compete on the rubbish tip. 'It's a dog-eat-dog world out there,' Mr Clark tells Steve. Even the larger guppies in the aquarium in the pet shop where Teresa, Des's girlfriend, is on a retail YTS, are eating the smaller ones. On the other hand, the relationships between Maureen and Brad, Dez and Snapper are warm and supportive.

What the film illustrated dramatically was Brenda Reid's foresight in bringing David and I together. My writing was very much in the Social Realist tradition, a very strong thread in British TV drama. David's early interest in Magritte indicates how attracted he was to surrealism. In addition, he was interested in Magical Realism. He made a documentary about Gabriel Garcia Marquez and was to go on to make a feature film of Angela Carter's *The Magic Toyshop*. All this is evident in his direction in *Brick is Beautiful*. The shots of Manchester make it look like another planet. A brick glows gold. Dez legs it from the Arndale Centre where he's nicked a frozen chicken. As he exits, he literally disappears into thin air. Snapper wheels the wall Dez has built, back to the warehouse through the Manchester streets. Maureen's mum pushes 50p pieces made of ice into the gas meter, which then melt. 'Got very rusty in there hasn't it?' she says to the gas man when he comes to empty the meter. This was an apocryphal story we heard a number of times when carrying out our research.

Brick is Beautiful went out on 23rd July 1986, the same day as Andrew and Fergie's wedding. 'Someone at the BBC has guts,' wrote the Sunday Times previewer, 'scheduling on Royal Wedding Day Andy Armitage's marvellously sparky drama about another young couple, Steve and Maureen, YTS trainees in Manchester.' Indeed, the film began on BBC2 at the same time as *The Royal Wedding, A Day to Remember* on BBC1. The previews and reviews were raves. 'But the real gem of the week is in danger of being swamped by the pomp and ceremony. *Brick is Beautiful* – is a biting television film with cinematic depth,' wrote the Times. 'The BBC Drama Department occasionally turns out something that shows up most other work as dross' said The Observer. 'At last, a real play for today,' said The Guardian, 'the BBC's best play for ages'. The Telegraph thought it a 'clever film ', The Evening Standard a 'first rate play', The Mail thought it was 'a gem'.

The film attracted a lot of fan mail. The most impressive

was from the Director General of the Brick Development Association. 'We enjoyed the play immensely and we know that there is some talk of a sequel being produced and we felt it might be interesting to have a get together with you if you shared our view on this."

I will illustrate in the next chapter how good ideas for projects lie all around us and it's just a matter of nosing the truffle out of the ground. To use a contrasting metaphor, a good idea comes with a glimmering halo around it – it's unmistakable. The idea for *Starlings*, my next film for the BBC and with David Wheatley, came from a documentary about a butlers' school. A former butler in the Royal Household ran a butlers' school in a hotel in Crystal Palace. I tried to get access to the school but got the bum's rush. No matter – everything I needed was in the documentary: the silly exercises to improve posture, the lessons in etiquette, the mix of student butlers, redundant miners and steelworkers from the north east, ex public school boys. These were attracted by salaries of around £40K. This was a perfect metaphor for the UK in the late 1980s, the movement from a manufacturing to a service economy. It also introduced some of the key themes of the film: illusion, pretence and transformation.

The film begins with Gary, a biscuit factory engineer, getting his cards. His response is to throw his spanner onto the biscuit production line – after all, he's not going to need it any more. In a wonderfully surreal touch (David's idea, not mine) the spanner disappears into the machine on the production line which grinds to a halt – a real spanner in the works! It restarts and we see spanner shaped biscuits emerging from it.

Gary's parents are going to bed. Mum has been collecting cardboard cut outs of the royal family in a newspaper offer. They now fill the bedroom. She talks to them and ignores her husband, who has to lift the cardboard corgi to lay his trousers flat.

A number of times in the film, David will use a simple but very effective visual technique which has a surreal effect. So, Gary walks up his street and there is a dissolve to the job centre where he is introduced to an interesting opportunity. Later, he will walk up the streets with his suitcase, straight to the fountain in front of the Vernons' stately home where he will work. The opportunity is to retrain as a butler. We have a lot of fun at the butlers' school. The lads have to balance wine glasses on their heads in a deportment exercise; Scouse Dave has a hidden strip of elastic fastening his to his head. In a moment prefiguring Gary's later transition from butler to yuppie, the lads remark that the posh boys take to butlering – 'it's just another part they play'. Scouse Dave can't handle the job – 'all this bowing and scraping' and he leaves. But Gary will eventually graduate cum laude – indicating both a willingness to and ability to perform.

Mr Vernon is a northern self-made man, who, in Mrs Vernon, has married up into penniless class. On Gary's arrival, Vernon tells him, 'Don't bother with all that 'Sir' rubbish. Unless we have guests of course – then you do the whole act. But keep the bowing and scraping until then. As long as you do my fetching and carrying, I'm happy.' So, at the outset, Vernon is to deny Gary the dignity of carrying out the role he's been trained for.

Elizabeth, a friend of Mrs Vernon's son and daughter comes up to the house for a shooting weekend. She takes a shine to Gary and creeps up to his room that night to have sex with him. Afterwards, he thanks her.

GARY: *Thank you, miss*
ELIZABETH: *Thank you, Wilson.*
GARY: *That's one thing they didn't teach us.*
ELIZABETH: *Where?*
GARY: *At the butlers' school.*
ELIZABETH: *Can't learn everything in school, Wilson.*
GARY: *D'you get off on servants, then?*
ELIZABETH: *It's not so much that. These weekends are so*
              boring.
GARY: *Can't it get you into trouble?*
ELIZABETH: *One only screws other people's servants, never*
              one's own. That would lead to trouble.

The next morning, Gary is intrigued to see Elizabeth leaving the weekend early, looking vaguely disturbed.

By chance, Gary overhears the kitchen staff discussing where Vernon made his money. He discovers that it was Vernon who sold the biscuit factory where he worked, making him redundant. Gary is apoplectic.

Later, he is clearing the soup plates of the Vernons' weekend guests:

GARY: *How was the soup sir?*
VERNON: *See – he's got all the manners – they taught him to*
              do everything.
(GARY takes Mr Vernon's soup plate)
              Oh - very nice lad, yes.
GARY: *You didn't taste the urine, then?*
(Silence)
              I said – you didn't taste the piss? I pissed in the tureen.

144

(Giggles from the table. Gary now speaks with his real accent.) Remember Davidson's? I used to be there. You wouldn't let me work. And now you won't let me serve you properly.
(Gary drops the soup dishes onto the floor.)
VERNON: *'Ey – they're bloody Spode, them.*
GARY: *Sorry sir. Thank you, sir. Piss off sir!*
(Gary storms out)

Gary turns up at Elizabeth's house in London. He's invited to stay for a while, until he sorts himself out. But Elizabeth's got a proposal:

ELIZABETH: *I could get you some part-time at my place but I don't think you'd be very happy in a florist's in Covent Garden.*
GARY: *I could go to The States. Have to posh my accent up a bit, though. They go for that.*
ELIZABETH: *Listen – you're not going to get anything unless you lie, are you?*
GARY: *Doubt it.*
ELIZABETH: *Well – if you're going to lie – you might as well go the whole hog.*
GARY: *Eh?*
ELIZABETH: *Tell an enormous lie rather than a small one. I don't think you'll be ready for Ascot, nor Wimbledon – but you should be OK for Chatsworth.*
GARY: *What're you going to do – race me or play me?*
ELIZABETH: *We're going to pass you off as my new man. Mummy and Daddy are desperate for me to find*

someone. I'm on the shelf at twenty-seven, you see.
GARY: *I don't want to get married.*
ELIZABETH: *Oh – Christ – it won't go that far. But you may*
get an offer in the City or something. Come on – it's a
great wheeze. I mean, you've done most of the training
at your butlers' school, haven't you? You've learned to be
obsequious. It's only a short leap to the other side.

Elizabeth kits Gary out as a city gent and he works hard at a matching accent. She fills him in on his invented family, his education at Rugby and Oxford. And by the time of the Chatsworth International Event, he's ready to be presented to friends and family. It goes well. He's presented as Charlie Sayers and passes all the tests. Elizabeth's brother, Lance, lands Charlie a job at his stockbrokers and he's up and away.

Charlie's contacts enable him to swing two tickets for the Royal Garden Party for 'Councillor' and Mrs. Wilson. Gary picks them up from the Palace afterwards. Mum has been rendered catatonic by the experience. The scene actually plays:

74B. INT. TAXI. DAY
(MRS WILSON IS CATATONIC)
GARY: *What's wrong, Mum?*
MR WILSON: *Just get us to the station, son, I think it was a*
bit of a shock -seeing them.
GARY: *I thought she'd be pleased.*

The scene I actually wrote was:

74B. INT. TAXI. DAY

146

(MRS WILSON IS CATATONIC)
GARY: What's wrong, Mum?
MR WILSON: Just get us to the station, son, I think it was a
bit of a shock - seeing them. They're all so – small.
GARY: I thought she'd be pleased.

It was rumoured that there was someone at the BBC who looked after the Royal Family's image. Or maybe the production team or those higher up didn't want to field complaints from them. Either way, the reference to size wasn't meant to be a cheap jibe. It is known that certain Royal Family members have a diminutive stature. Meeting them in the flesh would have provided an understandable trigger for Mum's catatonia. In a scene afterwards, Dad is seen taking her cardboard cut-outs back into the house. He realizes she's better off with her delusions.

Elizabeth is rapidly coming to dislike what she's created: 'First Pygmalion, now Frankenstein!' There follows a series of scenes which provide the climax to the film. These take place at 'Workers' Playtime' – 'the one and only working men's club in the King's Road.' Charlie is there watching the cabaret with Elizabeth's brother, Lance and friends. The cabaret is presented by a troupe of dancing 'miners' (this was a decade before 'The Full Monty'). Elizabeth arrives and tries to out Gary, 'His name's not "Charlie", it's "Gary". He didn't go to Rugby, Lance, he went to some grotty comprehensive in Manchester. He's a fraud. A conman.' 'Hell hath no fury,' Charlie turns away. But Lance and friends believe him not her. She leaves. Lance says of her, 'It's not the first time,' he re-assures Charlie. 'She's always badly behaved like this when things don't work out.' Charlie follows her out of the club. Their final powerful scene is worth reproducing in full:

88. EXT. THE STREET OUTSIDE THE CLUB. NIGHT
GARY: You've got a bloody nerve. You dress me up like your doll and when you're tired of that game you want to play another. Well I still want to play this one.

ELIZABETH:You wouldn't have been acceptable to my family as you were. And you're not acceptable to me as you are.

GARY: Why?

ELIZABETH: You don't feel anything. For me. For anybody.

GARY: Feelings? You didn't give me any. You gave me vowels, you gave me clothes, you gave me confidence, you gave me contacts. You left feelings out. Anyway – I'm probably better off without them, aren't I? Your mob seems to manage without them.

ELIZABETH: What d'you mean?

GARY: Interfere with the bluff, wouldn't they – feelings? The sham, the scam. You've practised it for generations, centuries. Perfectly rehearsed, immaculately performed. Well – you've let me into the secret. I've crawled across the footlights and seen through the greasepaint. I've got behind the masks. And I'm grateful. I feel re-born. And I'm indebted to you.

ELIZABETH: 'Galatea never does quite like Pygmalion: his relation to her is too godlike to be altogether agreeable.'
(GARY RETURNS TO THE CLUB.)
(QUIETLY TO HERSELF)
*   You bastard.*
(SHE NOW SCREAMS)

You bastard!

Unfortunately for Gary, Duncan, Mrs Vernon's son, works at the same stockbrokers as Elizabeth's brother, Lance and Charlie/ Gary. Duncan makes the connection between the Vernons' butler and Charlie. The game's up. Charlie is sacked but not before turning the tables. He's taken a position which will lose the stockbrokers a large amount of money. Charlie will keep this and other indiscretions quiet for a sum: 'The fee is on the top, my account number along the bottom.'

In a postscript, Gary goes back up to Manchester. He has a bit of business to do. But he stops off at Mum and Dad's. Mum remains traumatised but Gary's brought her a corgi:

'WILSON: *We can't keep pets, son – they don't allow it.*
        Anyway, she doesn't like small dogs. They're like small
        people – you can't trust them.
GARY: *Dad – you know you said you wanted to buy this*
        place?
WILSON: *In time.*
GARY: *I'll be able to help you. Be sooner than you think.*
WILSON: *You've not been up to anything dishonest, have you,*
        son?
GARY: *Me, dad? Dishonest?'*

The film ends with Gary greeting a delegation of Japanese businessmen as they get off a coach. He's going to show them round a property he's acquired – the old Davidson's biscuit factory.

Starlings went out on Wednesday September 28th 1988 on

BBC2. It was preceded by a repeat of companion piece *Brick is Beautiful* the week before. The day after the *Brick* repeat, my nemesis, Hugh Hebert, wrote a lengthy piece in the Guardian. His mealy-mouthed appreciation of my previous work was replaced by a more positive approach. 'But the best reason for (*Brick is Beautiful's*) repeat last night is that it is a very funny and cutting piece about the entrepreneurial young and it makes a contrasting pair with *Starlings*, a new play from the same loft to be shown next Wednesday.' He cleverly picked up on the relationship between my teaching at the time and my writing:

'Armitage came south 17 years ago – he is 38 – and lectures in education studies at Canterbury. He specialises in the education of 14-18-year-olds, teaching people how to teach them, training some of the people who will work in YTS-type programmes: the kind of programmes that finally disillusioned the lads who believed they would become skilled men, layers of bricks and makers of walls and found themselves tearing them down.' (Guardian 22.9.1988)

As with *Brick is Beautiful*, the previews and reviews of *Starlings* were raves. The Independent thought it 'a film that is a perfect recreation of one of those sixties "new wave" North-South tragi-comedies starring Tom Courtney, Albert Finney or Alan Bates and a fine, entertaining film in its own right'. For the Daily Mail it was a 'hilarious satire'. Peter Patterson in The Daily Mail wrote 'There was an exuberance about last night's Screenplay, 'Starlings', plus a wonderfully ironic sense of the subversive that made it both compelling and highly entertaining. This was a play for our time, funny, tragic, cynical and ultimately manipulative - Not only did this play zing along. It also produced set pieces, like the butling school and a Chelsea nightclub called Workers' Playtime with a chorus of miners – which were hilarious in their own right. *Starlings* restored one's faith in the BBC's drama department.'

The following year, I was at Heathrow about to board a flight to Rome (see Chapter 5 about the German film producer and Arthur Miller's daughter) when I rang Elaine from a phone box - beep, beep, beep – no mobiles then although the car-phone made its debut that year. Exciting news – Brenda Reid had rung – *Starlings* had won a Gold Nymph at the Monte Carlo TV Festival for Best Film with Lynsey Baxter winning a Silver Nymph for best actress. After the Prix Italia, Monte Carlo is the most prestigious TV festival in the world. I have a letter in front of me:

'BBC

FROM THE CHAIRMAN MARMADUKE HUSSEY

20th February 1989

Dear Andy

I was delighted to learn that you have won the Grand Prix of the Gold Nymph at the 20th Monte Carlo International Television Festival, for your film, "Starlings".
Very many congratulations on this considerable achievement and thank you for all that you have done. These awards are a great encouragement to us all in the BBC.

All good wishes
Marmaduke Hussey'

Apparently, *Starlings* was apparently close to a BAFTA nomination for Best Single Drama that year. This from the BBC in-house newspaper, Ariel:

'One-eyed Wonders

The complicated process by which BAFTA picks the happy recipients of their one-eyed award has kept some good chaps down. Using suggestion and endorsement forms the 2000 enfranchised members cast the runes and come up with four candidates for each BAFTA category.

Alan Bennett does well in this year's nominations and so he should. His Brilliant *Talking Heads* appears in the Best Drama Series category. But when is a series not a series? At BAFTA time it would seem – as two of the *Talking Heads* series also make it to the best single drama category keeping others, notably *Starlings* (which picked up a couple of awards at Monte Carlo's Golden Nymph ceremony) out of the running.' (Ariel 9th March 1989)

David and I fell out over who would retain the Gold Nymph. As far as David was concerned, films were directors' films. I argued that without my authorship, there would be no opportunity for his directorial panache! We compromised on a time share: six months with David, six months with me. I remember bringing the nymph home in an Oddbins carrier bag for my six months' tenure. On the Victoria – Canterbury East train, I pulled the nymph's velveteen box out of the carrier, opened it and displayed the blingy nymph in all her glory, much to the amusement of the surrounding commuters. After my first six months, I handed it over to David and never saw it again. I mentioned this anecdote at the Celebration of David's Life and Work at the Electric Cinema in Notting Hill (compered by Alan Yentob) after his sad early death in 2009. I got the feeling the audience were on the bonny lad's side.

Following the success of *Starlings*, I felt it was now or never for a full-time writing career. So, I took the plunge and handed my notice in at Canterbury Christ Church. This was 1989 and it had been only five years since I had arrived. It was also the time to exit for a number of my contemporaries. So that we could keep in touch, with each other as well as with our comrades left behind, we formed The Sunshine Club, so called because all original members had been favourites of our beloved vice-principal Dr Graham Brown, who would use the soubriquet, 'Sunshine', when addressing his favourites, most of whom had enjoyed rapid promotion under his patronage. The Sunshine Club was in effect a gentleman's dining club, formed for the purposes of eating, drinking, reminiscing and bantering and we would invite our patron to join us whenever he could. We would meet thereafter every two or three years over the next thirty years. Meeting in Canterbury became more difficult as members were dispersed through the nations. New members would be co-opted at the suggestion of existing members but only after these had been consulted. Of course, during the pandemic, we have had the opportunity to meet on-line which has been a comfort for us all, during a period in which isolation has been a challenge for everyone and we have met every month. Only Robert Melville is still employed at the University. Phil Poole, Chris Bounds, Neil Morrison and Tony McCulloch remain in Canterbury, although Tony has moved on to teach at University College, London. Alan Norley and I are in the Faversham area, Peter Abbotts is in The Algarve, Fred Corbett in Norfolk, Carl Parsons in London, Phil Holden

The West Midlands, Grenville Hancox, Folkestone and France, Len Goad, The Highlands of Scotland and Geoff Howarth is in Margate. I was able to join the chaps this July from our summer retreat on the Greek island of Halki.

David Snodin had a producer's slot in the new Screen One series. What would I like to write? We started ever so simply with the notion of what would happen to someone, a paragon of civic virtue (like ourselves), who finds themselves on the wrong side of the law and ends up inside. We finally had *Home Run*, the third part of the trilogy of *Brick is Beautiful* and *Starlings*. If these two were about the rise of self-made men (although Gary/Charlie in *Starlings* is hardly self- made – he gets a leg up from his creator, Elizabeth), then *Home Run* was about the unmaking of the self-made man.

Bill English is a wealthy consultant who has recently returned to the UK from Brussels. His line is team building which he appears to be very good at. In fact, we get a strong sense from the group he is currently working with that his success is due to an ability to manipulate others. He has bought himself a swanky docklands loft apartment overlooking the river. He is joined by his French girlfriend, Anna. We quickly learn that Bill has returned to an East End he grew up in. The reason for this return is not clear. Anna thinks he wants to show locals how well he's done. We learn early on that all is not well between Bill and Anna. On the surface, this appears to be because Bill prioritises work over her. But it eventually appears that Bill has erected an emotional barrier around himself. 'I can't get into your life,' Anna finally acknowledges.

Bill begins to feel threatened by events in his surroundings. The doorbell goes in the middle of the night. There is no-one on the video phone. He leaves the office to find his car tyres are flat. He seems out of place, complaining about not knowing which suits to wear to functions, what social signals he ought to be sending out. He has a couple of disastrous meals with two local builders made good (who also have criminal involvement, it is suggested) and their wives whom he obviously despises. He loses his grip on his working practice and when his group of trainees turn against him, he walks out on them. One of his colleagues takes his work over. Terrified by youths whom he suspects are attempting to break into his block, he takes to standing guard by the front door. He goes out looking for an uncle. He's unsuccessful – he can't locate his past – it's been bulldozed. Anna has had enough. She leaves. His disintegration continues. One of the youths rings his bell – a young woman, Linda. She comes up to his flat. She is a wise waif. She tells him the truth about himself. He hasn't got the killer instinct East Enders are born with. He's soft. (It's clear to me now I used this character as the spirit of the old East End, the ghost of East End past.) His front door sentry duties continue. He pursues a group he thinks have been trying to damage the building and beats one of them up. He is rescued by one of the group, Linda, the wise waif and she takes him back to her squat and puts him to bed after this exchange:

BILL: *Miss Marshall*
LINDA: *Miss Marshall?*
BILL: *Our class teacher – form 4A. She always said I was a*
         good boy. And I thought 'yeah – I am'. I was always
         the kid who tried harder, who did his homework. The

one who kept things to himself. Always did what was
expected. It got to be a habit. Because there was going
to be a pay-off – one day. And I never did anything to
jeopardize that. Always turned the other cheek – gave
the other guy the benefit of the doubt.
LINDA: Sounds like looking after number one to me.
BILL: No – it's time I stood up for myself. Fought for what
I've got. What I've worked for.
(SHE CROSSES THE ROOM AND KISSES HIM GENTLY.
SHE PUTS HER ARMS ROUND HIM.
HERE ARE TEARS OF BEWILDERMENT IN HIS EYES)
LINDA: You're fighting for something, love. But I'm not sure you
know what it is.

Bill is surprised by three heavies waiting for him in his
flat. Unfortunately, the youth he beat up was the son of their
guvnor, local gangster, Guthrie. He watches as two other heavies destroy his BMW 316 with sledge hammers in the street
below. 'Everyone's got a 316 now, anyway, haven't they?' says
one of the heavies. 'Hairdresser's car.'

We see Guthrie's office building in flames with fire crews
attending. It becomes clear Bill set the fire. Bill is indeed fighting back. He is plucked from the street by Guthrie's men and
badly beaten.

GUTHRIE: Last time we did your car. Now we're going to
bruise you. Next time – well – I've run out of ideas.

In a spectacular shot, Bill climbs out of the Thames, his
entire body encased in mud. (The whole film was beautifully

shot by Philip Bonham-Carter and had a rich – a little bit over the top – sound track recorded by the Halle Orchestra.)

> (BILL HAS OBTAINED A SHOT GUN FROM
> A COLLEAGUE. WE SEE HIM SAWING IT
> OFF IN HIS CAR. BILL IS IN HIS PARENT'S
> GRAVEYARD -)

153. EXT. GRAVEYARD. DUSK

> (BILL FINDS HIS PARENTS' GRAVE.IT IS
> OVERGROWN. HE TEARS AWAY WEEDSHE
> KNEELS.HE TAKES OUT HIS WALLET)

BILL: *Wallet on the right.*
> (HE LAUGHS HE PULLS A STRING OF CREDIT
> CARDS FROM THE WALLET HE TAKES OUT
> ONE CARD AND TURNS IT)
> *Cash card. Looks nice, doesn't it?*
> (HE FLICKS IT AGAINST THE HEADSTONE)
> *Nice green that.*
> (HE TAKES ANOTHER CARD)
> *Credit card. It's HP really.*
> (BILL FLICKS THE CARD AGAINST THE
> HEADSTONE)

BILL: *(cont.) You used to give me hell when I took my flags-of-the-world cards to school and lost them all. I never -*
> (HE FLICKS ANOTHER CARD AGAINST
> AND ANOTHER
> AND ANOTHER)
> *there was some knack in aiming them – I never –
> cheque card – it's useless now – they've stopped my
> cheques. Now this – this is really special. You can do*

anything with this.
(HE FLICKS IT)
It's a gold card. I never felt happy with any of them,
though. You did a good job. But why...why did you
make me feel guilty about having things and then
drive me on to have more than you ever dreamed of?
Eh? Still confuses me that. Anyway – they're yours now.
Credit where credit's due.

Cut to Bill at night. He has the gun. He rings the bell. The door opens. No-one there. But the camera looks downwards. There stands a little girl. Bill goes inside. He points the gun at Guthrie who's having a family party. But Bill fires up into the chandelier and runs.

Bill is by the river with Linda. 'I'm not soft you know,' Bill tells her. 'You've got to defend what's rightfully yours. You feel strong if you do. You feel like someone then.' There is a sense that Bill feels he's proved himself fighting back against Guthrie. But the triumph is short-lived. 'You have to leave – now,' Linda tells him. 'There isn't anywhere. There never has been anywhere.' Bill has alienated himself from family, class, background and even standing up to the local bully has not enabled him to recover his lost identity.

Bill sits on the bench by the river all night. In the morning, Guthrie and his men come for him. A final irony – Guthrie recognises him as Billy English, a former classmate who passed the 11+ when he didn't. 'You've got the same smile. Superior.' Guthrie tells him. 'You're not though, are you? If only I'd known all those years ago – if only I'd known there'd be no difference between us, in the end.' For Guthrie, there's no difference between a successful businessman and a criminal in the new East End.

Previews and reviews of *Home Run* were mixed. The main complaint was around timing and that it trod familiar territory as other Yuppie drama (ITV's 'Capital City' had started the week before). This was summed up by Mark Lawson in the Guardian:

'Television was so quick to join the Yuppie backlash that there is now a real danger of Yuppie Backlash Drama Backlash, in which the viewer starts muttering about not being able to switch on the bloody set without seeing a broker being broken. That said, 'Home Run' was a strong competitor in the market, with a quirky eye.'

The Radio Times billed it as an 'enigmatic psychological thriller' with a 'spectacularly unhinged performance from [Michael Kitchen]'. The Sunday Mirror called it 'Another promising gem in what has been a shining series so far'. The Sunday Correspondent had it as a 'creditable psychological thriller'. The Sunday Telegraph thought 'Armitage is very sharp on class obsession. And the direction by Nicholas Renton is strongly evocative.' The Sun described it as a 'crisp drama'.

I said earlier that *Home Run* was the third in a trilogy. But, overall, the five BBC dramas over five years deal with common themes and could be described as a pentalogy. I said earlier that they were about identity and about how you construct and express that identity in a way which is unique to you. But there are also elements of tragedy in all of them. The leading characters in each are, if not *great* men or women, certainly every man or woman – Bill in *Home Run* even has the emblematic surname 'English' (Mark Lawson thought this was a bit too obvious!). Each main character has a fatal flaw (hamartia). Steve in *Brick is Beautiful* becomes a successful entrepreneur but at the cost of the loss of his girlfriend and friends. Gary in *Starlings* loses his identity as does Bill English. There is reversal (peripeteia): butler becomes businessman in *Starlings*. Bill English loses his partner, his wealth, his car, his job, his sanity and, probably at the end, his life. And there is learning/recognition (anagnorisis): Sheila in *Picture Friend* sees through the family fiction; Alan understands failure in *Keep On Running*.

Chapter 5 – You couldn't make it up

Research is the fun part of writing. Because, whatever the genre, writing is a lonely game, since writers themselves are entirely responsible for the quality of what they produce. However, those working in certain genres, screen and theatre writing, journalism in particular, get to meet other people for some of the time. This may be in a collaborative way with other writers, directors, producers, script editors, actors. Or it may be through conducting research. As I'm quite a sociable character, I found I was rather good at research and enjoyed it as much as the writing itself. Research can be inspirational and it can surprise you: the world is full of the bizarre things which you couldn't make up yourself!

I was born, grew up and lived in Manchester for the first eighteen years of my life, as described in Chapter 1. You can take the lad out of Manchester but not Manchester out of the lad and the city was to feature in a number of projects of mine – including *Coronation Street*, of course. It wasn't until I'd left and returned that I realised what a surreal city it was, particularly in its humour. When Gladys, my stepmother, died in 2002, I made the arrangements for her funeral and winding up of her estate. This involved several trips from where I live in Kent up to Manchester. The solicitor gave me permission to fly up and I would then hire the cheapest car at Manchester Airport to drive around the city, a city I'd lived in for twenty years but never ever driven in. I remember negotiating a five or six lane bit of motorway in Salford and I was weaving from lane to lane because I didn't know where I was going. I was conscious of a Golf trying unsuccessfully to get past me. He eventually pulled up next to me at the lights and did a wind-your-window-down gesture. I did so, fearing a road rage incident. But the driver was laughing. He shouted 'Eh – tell me where you learnt to drive so I can fucking steer clear of it in future!' before pulling away.

My dealings with the undertaker were macabre, starting with my first exchange with him. I told him I'd never arranged a funeral before and wondered whether we should start with him picking Gladys's body up from the hospital. 'I can't just go around Manchester picking bodies up, Mr Armitage, there are protocols.' We came to the interview at his offices. My step-mother was to be cremated at Eccles Crematorium where my father had been cremated nearly 30 years before and her ashes scattered in the grounds. 'Now,' he said, 'where do you want your step-mother strewn?' He explained that the crematorium rotated the strewing of ashes because they didn't have a very nice effect on the soil. 'Would you like the Wednesday plot or the Thursday plot? Your father was strewn on the Wednesday plot.' 'Right well, strew them together then please.'

Mancunians are great malapropists. I was in North Manchester with the producer of a proposed BBC series about a senior choir (never got made – see Chapter 8) when we stopped off at a back-street pub for lunch. The menu was a bit limited but the landlady pointed to three bins of curries. 'That one's very, very hot, that one's very, very mild and that one,' she said, pointing at the bin in the middle, 'well, that's mediocre'.

It was After David Wheatley had brought the idea for what became *Brick is Beautiful* in to Brenda Reid at the BBC that we were given two weeks in Manchester to research the brick story. We kept uncovering apocryphal stories: create 50p shaped ice cubes - push them in the gas meter and they'll melt by the time the gas man arrives. The film crew tried it. Impossible. We heard of a gang dressed as gas board employees who pretended they were digging the road up but were actually stripping pavements of their paving stones. Couldn't find them. We found the Tin Man. He specialised in scavenging tins from the tip. They were always thrown out when houses were cleared.

Then, as often in research, we got a lucky break – two in fact. Wandering up Deansgate, we came across two or three tents, young people in front of them. They were camping out, protesting about changes in social security laws. They were a feral, funny bunch. I always used a dictaphone on research trips. This was because it was easier to use and less intrusive than note-taking and I needed to be able to remember what people sounded like if I was to be basing a character on them. We ended up visiting them on several occasions. We had our five main characters – in one tent. One lad revered Margaret Thatcher – 'she's made this country great' 'I'm one of Thatcher's boys' 'My mam hates her but I love her'. All this in spite of being impoverished and unemployed. He became Steve – our brick entrepreneur. We even gave his mam a cameo. She blamed Thatcher for everything. Dropping a tea tray, she exclaims 'Look what the bloody woman's made me do now!' She brandishes a rubber brick at Thatcher on a TV news report. Maureen was based on a very beautiful young woman. She was disarmingly straight and honest about everything and Maureen became the moral heart of the film. One of the lads professed an interest in the arts and mysticism and we thought he'd be a terrific foil for the other characters as Dez. The lad we based Snapper on wanted to go to college to be a skilled construction worker but we intended to put Snapper on a YTS scheme which he would later realize would not give him the higher-level construction skills he was expecting to acquire. Finally, there was an outrageous, camp cross-dresser with heavy make-up. Every time you spoke to him, he'd respond by performing a Tina Turner number. He became the basis of our character, Brad.

Our second break came when I was having a pint with an old school friend. He asked me what I was doing up in Manchester again. When I told him, he said I should contact Colin and Mike, two other school friends of ours. 'Yes,' he said. 'They've got a second-hand brick company.' David and I went to see them the following day. These two turned out to be the brick barons of Manchester. As we stood in their yard, we watched our film being made. Lorry loads of bricks were coming in. Bricks were being vacuum packaged ready for delivery. One man walked in with a handcart full of bricks. 'He brought his backyard wall in last week. That must be his front wall,' said Colin. Colin and Mike were happy to collaborate with us as long as we didn't give away their price range. Both Colin and Mike were larger than life figures. Both had left in the 5th form and originally went into blue collar jobs. The second-hand brick trade had made them a lot of money. Most of their bricks were going to builders in the South of England who were building houses in middle class enclaves which were new on the inside and over a hundred years old on the outside. We had the central metaphor for the film. The bones of the 19th century were being picked clean to provide housing for the wealthy bourgeois in the 20th. Mike urged Colin to tell us what his next project was. Colin was excited. He planned to import sand from the Sahara to the Canary Islands so that their black volcanic beaches looked like proper beaches.

Mike invited David and I to his beautifully appointed house in Cheshire footballers' territory. He clearly needed to show us how well he'd done. And he had. Only, he hadn't really made the cultural transition. Picking up a very expensive solid silver cocktail shaker, he said, 'Nice that, isn't it? Fucked if I know what it is.' Colin became the model for Bennett, an existing brick entrepreneur Steve eventually outdoes. In the film, Bennett and his wife invite Steve and Maureen to a Cheshire restaurant where they try to impress them with their culinary sophistication.

In the early 90s, Granada Films commissioned a feature film from me, to be directed by David Wheatley, called *Femme Fatale*. Granada Films had already had recent Oscar nominated success with *My Left Foot*. *Femme Fatale* was what Screen International called a 'Gothic comedy', when Granada announced its 'big league film slate' for 1992. The film follows the fortunes of a Manchester hairdresser who becomes a vampire when bitten by a 700-year-old shape-shifting Manchester vampire, Sherratt who morphs into club owner, Tony Chicane. Sherratt/Chicane was based on Mr Manchester, Tony Wilson, whom I'd first seen in an 80s documentary (this was a decade before Frank Cottrell-Boyce and Michael Winterbottom's excellent *Twenty-Four Hour Party People*, and I completely understood the fascination which must have underpinned the drive to create that film). I was intrigued by Tony Wilson's relationship with New Order in the documentary. On the one hand, they were treating him as their Svengali and in the next moment he was a hectoring head-teacher. On the one hand, they seemed heavily dependent on him, then he appeared dependent on them.

I was very interested when I recently dug out my notes and realised the very different types of research I had carried out in writing the film (BTW It went through three years of development but never made it to the silver screen). The film opens with a flashback to a Northern Soul night at the Tower Ballroom, Blackpool in the late 1970s. Jo's parents, the Pendleburys, are Northern Soul fanatics. I needed to know about Northern Soul – it post-dated my departure from Manchester - and I am now looking at my notes of two interviews, one with an NME journalist and one with the then journalist (later to be Head of Programmes at Channel 4) Stuart Cosgrove, both of whom I discovered knew more about Northern Soul than anyone. I have details of typical dance routines, key venues, clothes worn, the music and the culture.

I also needed to meet with Tony Wilson himself. This proved easy to arrange. Tony continued his journalism at Granada and his hosting of *So It Goes*, his regional Manchester arts programme, in parallel with his recording and club-owning career. Steve Morrison, the producer of the film (and Managing Director of Granada), was a colleague. I had a number of happy, informative meetings with Tony. At the first one, he insisted on taking me round Manchester's cultural institutions, starting with Affleck's Palace, as it was then called, the famous indoor market. After about an hour of this, I stopped him and said, 'Look Tony, thanks for this but I know all this – I'm a Mancunian'. 'Oh shit, sorry, I didn't realise.' It turned out we had a lot in common. We were born in the same year, both to mothers then in their mid 40s. We were very appreciative of Manchester humour. Most of all, I think, we were aware

166

of the huge cultural potential of Manchester and the North West. I was very interested in the Situationist International and I saw in Tony's work, as a programme host, music promoter and club owner, someone in a direct line from the Dadaists and Situationists. Malcolm Maclaren owed a debt to the Situationists; Tony gave the Sex Pistols their first TV gig on *So It Goes*. I went to the Hacienda on a number of occasions but, having just turned 40, stuck out a bit in the crowd, making research which was best carried out anonymously, problematic. On one occasion, I went to the Hacienda with Steve Morrison himself. I remember Steve was sporting a sheepskin coat, not the usual attire for the club. This freaked some of the clubbers who thought the drug squad had arrived.

TV documentaries have been a reliable source of stories for me. *Starlings*, *Frankie's House* and *Femme Fatale* were all prompted by TV docs. Newspapers, obviously, but newspaper magazines and Sunday supplements in particular, are a potential source of great stories. Journalists might have found an idea for you but, as there's no copyright on ideas, you can use the idea as a beginning of your own story.

One cracking idea came from a story in a Sunday magazine about the Herald of Free Enterprise, which sadly sank in Zeebrugge harbour in 1987. Only one of the dead from the disaster couldn't be identified. He had a passport on him which was false. So, the authorities published his photograph in newspapers across Europe. Did anyone know this man? As a result, some four or five women across Europe, including a woman from Sheffield, claimed the guy as their husband. It turned out this man had four lives in four different countries with four different families. Wow – you can understand why I thought this a wonderful premise for a great drama. In the end, I never wrote the piece but it remains a classic starting point.

Murder Weekend (never made) was inspired by a remark by the detective, John Stalker, whom the Sunday Times sent to sample murder weekend events at several hotels. 'It occurred to me,' he observed, 'that a real murder committed at a murder weekend would probably go unnoticed until everyone had gone home.' So, I set about writing a one-off film about a real murder taking place at a murder weekend event. This involved desk research scrutinising a range of brochures from hotels across the country but I needed to experience the real thing and squeezed as many murder weekend events in as I could. I was surprised by the range of organisational structures/models, the professionalism or complete lack of it and the wide variety of guests who attended. Each weekend had incident rooms, where relevant evidential items were kept: one contained autopsy reports for each of the murder victims. Undoubtedly the best weekend was the Joy Swift weekend at the Talbot Hotel, Oundle (I note that Joy Swift received an MBE for services to tourism and celebrated the 38th anniversary of her weekends in 2019). A scenario explaining the context of the murders was sent in advance, as was a series of tips on how to play the murder game, a set of ground rules really. (In contrast, at another weekend, we were simply put into different sleuth groups with whom we would work on arrival and urged to cross question other guests. The groups contained planted actors who played the characters. However, these were anonymous so that it was a matter of chance whether you came across them or not.) At the Joy Swift weekend, a number of very skilled actors were identified whom guests could interrogate at any point. At another weekend, one event was surreal. In a lecture delivered by a Hitchcockian ex forensic pathologist, a series of slides were produced. Two or three had been shown before the audience realised that these were photographs of real murder victims the pathologist had dealt with in his career. It was a kind of snuff lecture. Several audience members fled. 'If you feel ill, sit at the end of the row,' the pathologist advised. The guy was brimming with medical in jokes: doctors know everything and do nothing; surgeons know nothing and do everything; psychiatrists know nothing and do nothing; pathologists know everything but one hour too late. A very useful by product of the murder weekends, and an important point about project research, was that I had seventy character sketches of guests I'd made at the weekends which was a rich resource when I came to plan the characters in my film.

My favourite research activity was travelling. After *Starlings*, the BBC commissioned *Car Wars*, with David Wheatley once more as director (never made). This film followed three sets of people travelling from Sheffield to Wolfsburg. One of these was the VW Franchise owner and his wife who were on their way to VW HQ to collect his golden tie pin for being the best-selling UK franchise that year (they would also watch the friendly between Sheffield United and Wolfsburg Vfl with the VW CEO in the directors' box). The second group are young executive car salesmen who 'borrow' franchise cars for the trip to see the match. And the third group are a bunch of Sheffield United supporters who, after discovering they have forged tickets, watch the match in a bar near the ground.

Car Wars was about national identity, racism and prejudice, manifest from the 1970s in football hooliganism. We based our film in Sheffield because we learned that a franchise there had been one of the first to import VWs in the 1950s. This necessitated a trip to Sheffield, where we visited the franchise and other Sheffield landmarks we felt our characters would have visited, including pubs and clubs, as well as local characters such as Rony Robinson, writer and broadcaster, who would go on to complete forty years with BBC Radio Sheffield. However, only the first part of the film was set in the city and the rest of it was part road movie and part matchday drama. As for acquainting ourselves with football violence, we thought the best way was to go and find us some. It would be a couple of years before Bill Buford's seminal book about football violence, *Among The Thugs* would be published, detailing his eight years of attending football matches. We only had a couple of days. This was 1988 and the Euros were being played in Germany. We contacted John Williams at Leicester University, an expert on football violence, to get his view on which of England's matches would go up. He reckoned the most likely would be v The Netherlands in Dusseldorf.

So, David and I flew out to Dusseldorf the morning of the match. We managed to buy tickets from some lads at the hotel. When we arrived at the ground it soon became clear that we were in the centre of the trouble makers, which was what we wanted. I believe sociologists call this 'participant observation'. There was an extraordinary bond between the fans. I've observed this at league matches I've attended but this was my first England match and this was entirely different. We got hammered by the Dutch 3-1, a Marco Van Basten hattrick, and knocked out of the competition. Again, for us this was a great result because the English would be more likely to want to exact their revenge. And they did. After the match, we were swept along with the English on to the tram, which would terminate at the main station. Being something of a wuss, I was beginning to get nervous but I looked over at David who was anything but and appeared to be revelling in the shouting and chanting. Interestingly, Bill Buford was to enjoy the same experience:

'I was surprised by what I found; moreover, because I came away with a knowledge that I had not possessed before, I was also grateful, and surprised by that as well. I had not expected the violence to be so pleasurable....This is, if you like, the answer to the hundred-dollar question: why do young males riot every Saturday? They do it for the same reason that another generation drank too much, or smoked dope, or took hallu-cinogenic drugs, or behaved badly or rebelliously. Violence is their antisocial kick, their mind-altering experience, an adren-aline-induced euphoria that might be all the more powerful because it is generated by the body itself, with, I was convinced, many of the same addictive qualities that characterize synthet-ically-produced drugs.'

(Buford, B, *Among the Thugs: The Experience, and the Seduction, of Crowd Violence*)

The battle outside the Hauptbahnhof was not what I had expected. Apart from a few scuffles at the edges of the crowds, there was very little actual violence. There was posturing, taunt-ing, gesticulating, a kind of mock violence. Eventually, David and I repaired to the hotel for a meal. From the hotel, we were able to watch further conflict unfold. How this happened was fascinating. The English seemed to have formed into what I can only describe as platoons of 8-10 men. Each platoon had a leader, an officer, as well as an NCO who communicated with the platoon. It was almost as if WW2 was being re-enacted on the streets of Dusseldorf.

Later, in a bar, we witnessed a funny and revealing series of events. The English were singing anti Dutch songs and eventually, the Dutch left. So, the English began singing anti German songs at the neutrals in the bar. These also left, leaving only the English. A hiatus. The Arsenal supporters then began to sing anti Spurs songs. The lads needed enemies. It didn't matter where they were from!

We took the decision to follow the fans home on land to the Hook of Holland and back with them on the ferry to Harwich. What this trip illustrated for me was the importance of experiencing what your characters were going to experience, enabling you to write them from the inside.

My most ambitious research travel was for a series about a group of young women Interrailing, *Off The Rails* (never made). Again, the most effective way of getting inside your characters' heads is by experiencing what they would in the drama. I therefore organised an Interrailing trip. I foresaw some problems, however. What kind of response was a forty-two-year-old man, claiming to be a TV writer, get from young women he approached randomly on a European train? The solution was to be accompanied by my partner, Elaine. Elaine approached the interviewees and made the interview notes which she then transcribed into a journal recording the trip. Elaine was well equipped for this, having worked in TV previously. It's amazing how funding sources open up when TV programmes are mentioned. We got free, unlimited European travel via British Rail, free passage and accommodation on a Brindisi to Patras ferry. Most of the interviewing took place on trains but at each of our stops we would go to local youth hostels where we thought Interrailers might be staying. First stop was Paris. We then took the overnight Rome Train from the Gare de Lyon (free 1st class sleeper). In Rome we went out to the youth hostel near the site of the 1960 Olympic Games I'd stayed in as a student twenty years before. We then took the train from Rome to Brindisi. A very funny, very Italian event took place at Roma Termini before we left. We boarded the train, managed to get seats but the train quickly became very packed. So packed that people were sitting in the corridors and still more people wanted to get on. And the train being a hundred per cent full of Interrailers, each passenger was accompanied by a rucksack, which took up as much room as its owner. After a bit of head scratching by officials and a great deal of shouting, several empty coaches were added to the train – an initiative you wouldn't see in the UK! At Brindisi, we boarded the ferry, were separated from our new friends from the train and led to a beautiful cabin with white-sheeted bed and flowers and fruit on the table. We peered outside at our now very pissed-off new friends who were going to have to sleep on the deck! Having reached Athens, we had a problem about our next stage. The Balkan Wars were raging at the time and there was no rail connection from Athens up to Eastern Europe. The solution was to fly from Athens to Budapest. We then made our way from Budapest to Vienna and from Vienna to Prague. Our most enjoyable trip was a Sunday morning Prague to Dresden journey which took us through the heart of Bohemia. This was enjoyable not only because of the spectacular scenery but because of the breakfast we were served. The food was prepared in a kitchen carriage and then served in our compartment by uniformed waiters. The Full Czechoslovakian! From Dresden, we made our way to Berlin. Having stayed in hostels and one- and two-star hotels round Europe, we decided to blow our budget for a couple of days at the five-star Kempinski. And, now somewhat rail-weary, we flew back to London.

Off The Rails had been commissioned by Channel 4 from the producer, John Goldschmidt, at Viva Films. It would be made using a European Fund for projects that were pan European but only if all the European partners (of which Channel 4 was one) gave it the green light. John decided to take me to pitch the project to another partner, ZDF, a leading German TV network which was based in Frankfurt. And as we were in Germany, we could then go on to Berlin to do further research. The advantage here was John's native German (he is half Austrian, half Mancunian). We could also afford to hire a minder based in Berlin. This made sense because she would be able to arrange interviews so that the research could be completed more quickly and therefore the trip would be more economic in the end. I've pitched to some difficult drama controllers in my time but ZDF was a nightmare. This wasn't helped by John having to translate – my A Level German not being up to it. So, the conversation was rather like you imagine dignitaries meeting each other accompanied by interpreters might be. I tried to explain that *Off The Rails* was a comedy drama and told the story of what happens in Episode 1. Not a titter. 'So, what happens in Episode 2?' they asked. I explained. Grimaces from the Germans. Episodes 3 and 4 got the same response and John and I left with our tails between our legs. We took the commuter flight from Frankfurt to Berlin, in a plane full of returning Berlin business people. In the departure lounge, before boarding, they each picked up a tray of cellophane-wrapped food with integrated cup and walked out to the plane – so organised, so German!

We had better luck with the Berlin research – doing a whole range of things to get a feel for a country and city which had begun re-unification only three years before. Berlin, always a louche, lively city, had become something of a Wild West, frontier town. The minder was brilliant – I wished I could have brought her home as my resident researcher. We interviewed refugees flowing out of Eastern Europe, went out on patrol with the Guardian Angels, ubiquitous at the time. We went into the former East. These were still two cities – everything dramatically changing as you went from one to the other and back. We found a squat in the former East – a squat with a difference. The German Government had allowed Western German young people to live rent free in apartment buildings in the East, as long as they renovated them. A whole room in the squat was devoted to tools, neatly lined up in rows on the walls. These weren't hippies – they were very together, organised, ambitious young people. They made fun of John and I, calling us the 'acht-und-sechsigers' (the sixty-eighters), alluding to our revolutionary generation. We interviewed students in a Burschenschaft, one of the influential student fraternities. We even went on a shopping trip to KaDeWe (Kaufhaus Des Westens), the exclusive department store on the Kufurstendamm that is more opulent than Fortnum and Mason or Bloomingdales.

I had continued full time at Canterbury Christ Church from my appointment in 1984 until 1989, when I'd had a series of successes and felt I was able to support a full-time

175

writing career (which I did for the next decade). I was in my study one day when the phone rang. It was my agent. She had a German producer with her who was interested in discussing a movie idea with me. She put him on. 'I'd like to meet this Friday night,' he said. 'OK – what time?' '9pm', he said. I hurriedly consulted my Victoria – Canterbury East train timetable. 'Well – that doesn't give us a lot of time – my last train leaves London at around midnight'. 'No – not in London,' he replied. 'In Roma'. So that Friday, I picked up a Business Class BA ticket at Heathrow, paid for by the producer and took a 7pm flight to Rome. I sat alone in Business Class, quietly sipping champagne, thinking that this was the kind of research I really liked to do.

I took a cab from the airport to what turned out to be a very plush block of flats in central Rome. Over the intercom came my producer. Sorry – he was in the middle of having a 'discussion' with someone else in the apartment. Could I come back for breakfast? He gave me the address of a hotel he'd booked me into and off I went. I returned the following morning. The flats were indeed plush, luxurious even. The other person there turned out to be Rebecca Miller, the daughter of playwright Arthur Miller and the Magnum photographer Inge Morath. Rebecca would go on to have a distinguished acting, writing and film making career of her own, as well as marrying Daniel Day-Lewis and becoming Lady Day-Lewis. We were served breakfast by the producer's staff and then had coffee on the rather extensive terrace overlooking Rome. The producer's idea for a film was about an art heist. The three of us then discussed the idea before the producer decided he needed to get out of the city to think clearly.

So, we all leapt into his Merc and off we went. We left Rome in a westerly direction. I asked the producer why we were going that way. He replied that it was the only way he knew out of the city by road. We ended up in Ostia, an important archaeological site and resort on the Tyrrhenian Sea. There we paced the beach intensely discussing the movie plot with Rebecca contributing as she jogged along beside us. Eventually, we returned to central Rome and I was dropped off near the Colosseum. Could I get a cab to the airport? I gave the cabby my very last lira note, holding my finger over the tear, in case he declined it. I never heard from the producer again. But it was a hugely enjoyable and exciting twenty-four hours.

An independent company came to me with an idea for a series set on a cruise liner, POSH (Port Out, Starboard Home – some believe this where the adjective 'posh' comes from. On voyages to Africa, India and Australasia it was considered desirable to have a cabin on the port side to avoid the sun's glare and a starboard cabin on the way back for the same reason). I thought it'd make a cracking series but I really needed to go on a cruise myself to research it. Which I did.

We managed to blag a free cabin with a major cruise company on a world cruise. The cabin was only free on the Southampton-Barcelona leg of the cruise. Dinner on the first night was a scream. Passengers sat round large circular tables – about ten to fifteen of them round each one. As dinner progressed and the passengers chatted to each other, it soon became clear that they all had Black Country accents. 'Where you from, then, Dudley?' 'No – we're West Bromwich.' The cruise company had grouped the passengers by geography, obviously thinking they'd appreciate sitting with folks like themselves. The pleasure at being seated next to locals was, however, short lived. Soon they were discussing where they'd bought their cruise and how much they'd paid. Which were, of course wildly different amounts. The meal was completed in a grumpy silence.

I needed to interview the ship's crew from the captain downwards and I had permission to interview a range of passengers. The cruise company had given me a PR minder, so I was sure they had stuff they didn't want me to find out. More than one crew member told me about the pugnacious first officer, a man for whom no cruise was complete without his sackings reaching double figures, dismissing each victim with the query 'Chicken or Beef?' relating to their dining preferences for the flight home from the next port of call. I learned that emergencies were frequent occurrences. Embarkation on Day 1 of a cruise could be overshadowed by the frantic search for a passenger who had left a suicide note behind him at home. Cruise holidays are often chosen as an appropriate setting for intended suicides. Since helicopters only have a range of a hundred miles and cruise ships will only divert in life or death cases, most medical emergencies will be dealt with on board. And with two thousand five hundred people, anything can happen. The doctor on our ship on a previous cruise had allowed engineers to cool a piston cylinder in his one-berth mortuary freezer and was then overwhelmed with a higher than average number of deaths and was forced to plead with the head chef to stow the bodies in the galley's ice cream fridge, along with that evening's raspberry surprises.

An important aspect of any cruise is the next meal, with passengers photographing the sumptuous buffet before devouring it. The crew told me that veteran cruisers brought clothes several sizes larger because they were aware of how much weight they would put on during the voyage. I identified a single serial eater whom I followed. He consumed two breakfasts and two lunches, all in different restaurants, continuing through afternoon tea to dinner and then the midnight buffet.

Some of the most interesting and useful research has been spending time in other people's working worlds. I have had many outings with the police. I was doing research for the Rik Mayall police comedy, *Constable, Constable*. This involved Rick as a philosophy don who, bored with the contemplative life, decides to lead a life of action and joins the police. (You will read an extract of the prose version of this in Chapter 8.) My local force was very obliging and I joined both uniform and CID officers on their shifts. This had a cost – I had to go through various rites of passage. One of these involved shutting me out into the police station back yard and setting a K9 on me. Even though it did nothing but bark savagely, I was utterly terrified, while the other shift members watched through the windows and giggled.

'Doing a comedy then, son?' said one of the two officers at the start of one shift. 'Nothing funny about the police,' he went on. Later, we arrested a man who'd done a runner from a city centre restaurant. But a call suddenly came through about a burglary in progress and, not wanting to miss a much better collar, the two officers jumped into the area car and roared off leaving me holding the runner by the arm. When the car was out of sight, he said, rather plaintively, 'Let me go, mate'. So, I did. Later still, we were out in the countryside and a 999 call came in. As the two tried to accelerate away, the car instead shuddered to a halt. 'We can't be out of fucking petrol,' exclaimed one. 'We fucking are', the other responded. They blamed each other for this and had to decline attendance at the call, pleading technical difficulties. The three of us had to push the car to the nearest garage. One motorist after another slowed down and laughed out loud, some doing dickhead gestures. The officers were incensed: 'I know who you are, mate. I'll have you for this'. The garage manager was delighted to see me, dressed in my white mac. 'So, you're taking it seriously, then?' 'What's that?' I replied. 'Last week's robbery. Glad they've got the CID on it now.'

On one shift I went out with a woman PC. She'd had more collars that year by far than any other officer. I recall she was checking the boot of a suspect's car when a suspect for a different crime drove by. She radioed in for this second suspect to be stopped. Two for the price of one. On a different shift I went out with the same woman PC. This time she was in plain clothes because we had the job of following a prominent local criminal through the city. As we closed in on him she linked my arm: if we pretended to be a couple we'd be less likely to attract attention from him. I was rather unnerved because our route took us past my block of flats and I wondered what Elaine might have made of my strolling past our home arm in arm with another woman.

The beauty of established series and serials is that a lot of basic research has already been done for you. So, I have in front of me, character notes for *The Bill*, each a side of A4, which help enormously when writing – you have a 3D picture of every character at all times. There are sample premises for stories, sample storylines and scripts, all of which help different writers keep to the same house style. As a regular *Bill* writer, you were required to go out with the Met every few weeks: this was very important, enabling writers to live the job on the inside. It was also exciting and I saw clearly what the attraction of the job was.

I have my notes for a 2-10 shift at a major South London police station. The first shout is to a dispute between two bedsit tenants, the younger man has accused an older man of threatening him with a knife. The police team go in with shields and batons. The dispute turns out to be six of one and half a dozen of the other. I describe the team I'm with: a big blond man, always picked on by the others; a thin, lizard-like character, an expert on anatomy; a squat scouser; well-spoken CAD (Computer Aided Dispatch) Room operator; 3 older women (40s) together in one car; cheeky 25-year-old woman who prides herself on getting away with things – very ambitious; bright, quiet Welshman; bald man who seeks affirmation all the time. At parade, there is a summary of yesterday's exploits – a lot of black humour. The station working/shift pattern: 2-10 for 3 days, 3 days off, nights for 3 days, 6-2 for 3 days. Vehicles – each shift, 3 response cars, 2 area cars with advanced drivers, 1 inspector, 1 van. Separate crime squad, burglary squad, robbery squad. We are sitting in the CAD Room. The inspector on duty spots on CCTV a robbery in progress in the street outside the station – he legs it along with others he grabs on the way. False alarm. Later, two boys arrested on the premises burgling a house. This is a five-star collar. Arresting officers very proud. Both boys 15, one at a special school, the other of Portuguese extraction. His parents have no English. Communication fraught. Police note how crimes peak after school and during holidays.

The Bill encouraged its writers to engage with a range of activities with the Met. One memorable event was the National Investigative Interviewing Course at Hendon. We writers acted as interviewees but that event appealed to the dramatist as well as the drama teacher in me because the course consisted of a series of role plays. It was an important lesson in police procedurals.

At the time I was on the writing team, you came up with your idea for an episode in the form of a premise. This then went to a weekly meeting and a storyline might then be commissioned. If that found favour, a script would be greenlit. Each episode then was a self-contained story. And the writer had the responsibility for researching the material for that episode. You had immediate access to three ex senior Met officers permanently employed by the programme. They would then put you in touch with relevant professionals. My episode about domestic abuse, *No Victim*, involved a number of key courtroom scenes and I spent a lot of time talking to criminal barristers and the CPS. For *Beasts*, my episode about a police officer who goes undercover with a group of animal rights activists and experiences the Stockholm Syndrome (very topical), I met on several occasions with animal rights activists at secret locations. More detail about these episodes in Chapter 6.

I can't recall any group of people, workplace, profession, who didn't welcome me into their lives and help me in my research. People are often flattered by your interest in their world. For me, theatre and TV drama were centrally concerned about telling the truth about human experience. And without research which explores this experience, your work will lack the veracity and authenticity it needs to convince its audience.

Chapter 6 – Around the millennium

The early 1990s was a time of major change in UK TV and in TV drama in particular. The single drama, a jewel in the BBC's crown for 20 years, suddenly became a rarity (although Screen 1 continued until 1994). This was partly because of the increasing importance of ratings: series and serials could build audiences week on week. And single dramas, particularly on BBC2, had been seen as culturally important, state-of-the-nation events rather than mainstream entertainment. The BBC quickly moved to develop projects for cinema release with the establishment of BBC Films in 1990, among the first being Anthony Minghella's *Truly, Madly, Deeply*. We were told that *Starlings* would have been a certainty for cinematic release had it been transmitted a year to eighteen months later. At the same time, the era of the autonomous BBC producer-auteur was at an end, commissioning being subject to central control. And control of ITV programming was also centralised. In house producers at both the BBC and in ITV companies now competed with independent producers, one result of the Broadcasting Act of 1990, which required them to be commissioned to make 20% of programming. During the 90s, satellite and cable television was breathing down the necks of terrestrial broadcasters. (A similar, although much greater, challenge is of course currently being launched by large international streaming companies against both terrestrial and satellite broadcasters!) These changes were not in my favour:

I had always seen my strength as that of a single drama writer (and still do). However, needs must.

Frankie's House

Tim Page first came on to my radar in 1977, when he was introduced in Michael Herr's *Dispatches*, his memoir about the press in the Vietnam War:

'He was twenty-three when I first met him, and I remember wishing that I'd known him when he was still young. He was bent, beaten, scarred, he was everything by way of being crazy that everyone had said he was…'

Then, in 1979, The National Theatre did a stage version of *Dispatches*, with John Salthouse playing Page/Green. That year, the BBC produced a documentary about Page in the Arena strand. Page was an Orpington boy who hitched across Asia in the 1960s and ended up in Laos, then Vietnam, where he became one of the most celebrated photo-journalists of the Vietnam war. He is allegedly the model for the mad photographer played by Dennis Hopper in *Apocalypse Now*. I was fascinated by his emphasis on the excitement of war rather than taking against it. While recuperating from his fifth injury, he got a letter from a publisher asking him to write a book taking the glamour out of war. 'Page remembers his bewilderment. "Jesus! Take the glamour out of war. How the hell can you do that? You can't take the glamour out of a tank burning or a helicopter blowing up. It's like trying to take the glamour out of sex. War is good for you."'

He teamed up with the good-looking Sean Flynn, Errol's son, on assignment for Paris-Match ('A Playboy Goes to War'), as well as John Steinbeck IV, the author's son. It was cool to be in Vietnam. One day in the mid-eighties, I was fetching sandwiches and doughnuts for my staff crew in college at the bakers in the Walnuts Shopping Centre in Orpington, when who should limp across the shop window but Tim Page himself. He had to be visiting his parents who lived in Orpington. I took this as a sign that I had to write his biopic. A couple of years later, I contacted him and secured his co-operation. Initial Film and TV, then run by Working Title's Eric Fellner, commissioned a four-part series, established a co-production with Anglia Television in the UK and Roadshow, Coote and Caroll and ABC in Australia and Arts and Entertainment in the US. It was block buster time.

The first task before embarking on the script was to scope out exactly what this series would focus on. The nineteen-seventies/eighties had seen a plethora of Vietnam movies: from *The Deer Hunter* and *Apocalypse Now* to *Platoon* and *Full Metal Jacket*, these had focussed largely on combat or combat-related stories (apart from *Good Morning Vietnam*). What interested me chiefly was the character of Page himself. Our Australian colleagues called him a 'larrikin', an Aussie word for a boisterous, rebellious, maverick youth. He was one of a cadre of what Michael Herr called 'young, apolitically radical, wigged-out crazies running around Vietnam.' He was this but he was also incredibly English: 'What do you mean, of course I love the Queen. The Queen's a very lovable bird.' At the same time, he was very American influenced: he both loved and derided the USA in equal measure. I watched a recent interview with Page in Australia and you would have sworn he was a Californian.

Above all, and this is what interested me most, he was a

committed professional who would do anything to get his shot. He had the reputation of putting himself in harm's way to do this, 'Hey Page, there's an airstrike looking for you.' However, his propensity to get hit arose from his tenacity, his willingness to stay with his subjects for days on end while his press colleagues peeled away. No more so than with the ambush of Charlie Company of the 173rd Airborne in the Iron Triangle:

'The press gang faded too, leaving me alone with B Company of the 2nd 503rd…The sign at the side of the road had read, according to the hastily summoned interpreter, 'ALL AMERICANS READ THIS DIE!' The VC had artfully rigged a dud-fused, American 105-mm howitzer shell behind the placard. As the troops bunched up on the derelict Michelin rubber road, machine guns opened up from the concealed positions simultaneously with the detonation of a recycled claymore mine. The results were devastating. Six dead and nineteen wounded in the time it takes to blink three times…My mind went blank. Memory serves up a jumble of crouching, dodging, snapping and dragging back wounded…Four of us grabbed a GI with legs and arms virtually amputated, and as we ran out of the firing zone towards the rear, a leg detached in my hand. The camera was at my eye in the right hand as the dust-off bird clattered in towards the centre of the red marker smoke farther along the reddened road.'

(Tim Page *Page After Page*)

This photograph made a two-page spread in Life Magazine. I have the copy in front of me, October 22nd 1965. It's a bizarre publication. The cover photo is of Mary Martin performing

'Hello Dolly' for the troops. There are articles about American football, Italian fashion, adverts for perma-lift bras, the latest Dodges and Cadillacs and two-reel tape recorders. Then – wham – Page's double page spread, 'And then the trap was sprung,' the aftermath of the ambush – foreground, dead and wounded soldiers, blood-soaked bandages, their colleagues tending to them, a medivac descending through the pink haze. Quite what the good American public made of this, I can't imagine.

Many argue that it was this kind of press exposure and, later, TV coverage which turned the American people against the war in Vietnam. Press accreditation was certainly straightforward and, at one point, there were around 600 western journalists in Vietnam. The West learnt its lesson, however and, by the time of the Gulf War, less than 20 years later, there was a strict pool system whereby a small group of press exchanged information and footage with each other and with organisations outside the pool. And because of the limitations of this material, media organisations were often happy to accept military footage.

Because of their freedom, Page and his colleagues were able to access a whole range of events in the war theatre. This introduces another key theme of the series – the moral and professional dilemmas of journalists, particularly photo-journalists, covering combat. Page doesn't have a problem with the situation described above: he managed to help the wounded while still taking shots. (He told me that he was staggered after this event that he'd got all his horizons level – a difficult enough task for a photographer at the best of times.) But there were other, more nuanced situations when he and other photographers wondered what side they were on, if any and most experienced moral dilemmas about their craft. This was clearly expressed by the British photographer, Larry Burrows:

'I was trying to take a shot of this guy who was dying in the helicopter. I never took his face. I don't like making it too real. I've wondered about that point quite a lot. I think if the pictures are too terrible, people quickly turn over the page to avoid looking. So, I try to shoot them so that people will look and feel, not revulsion but an understanding of war...I was torn between being a photographer and the normal human feelings. It is not easy to photograph a pilot dying in a friend's arms and later to photograph the breakdown of the friend. I didn't know what to do. Was I simply capitalising on someone else's grief?'

(Phillip Knightley *The First Casualty*)

A lot had been written about Vietnam through the 70s and 80s, much of it by combatants, some of it by journalists, so there was ample reference for me to use. There were the two great histories: Stanley Karnow's 1983 *Vietnam – A History* and Neil Sheehan's 1988 *A Bright Shining Lie*, the war as seen through the life of John Paul Vann. Also influential was Rik Atkinson's *The Long Gray Line*, about a West Point class's journey to Vietnam and back, Erik Durschmied's *Don't Shoot the Yanqui*, the war of a TV cameraman-reporter, Bao Ninh's *The Sorrow of War*, an account from the point of view of a North Vietnamese soldier. Tim Page's *Nam* had been published in 1983. Tim O'Brien's story about his platoon in Vietnam, *The Things They Carried*, left a lasting impression. Best of all, in two volumes, and 38 parts, lovingly collected by Tim Page himself, was Orbis's brilliant *Nam – The Vietnam Experience 1965-75*. This had a whole range of features about life in the Vietnam War: American military and political strategy; battles; operations and campaigns; the role of helicopters; life in base camp; R&R (Rest and Recuperation); even details of Vietnam's 131 poisonous snakes. There was a very useful chronology at the end of each part.

My most important resource in writing the scripts, however, was Tim Page himself. By the late eighties, Tim had moved down to a small hamlet near Lenham in Kent with his new partner, Lindsey, some forty-five minutes from my place by car. At one point, I travelled over daily. Tim was still all the things Michael Herr had noted in him over 20 years before:

'His talk was endlessly referential, he mixed images from the war, rock, Eastern religion, his travels, literature (he was very widely read and proud of it), but you came to see that he was really only talking about one thing, Page.'

However, with age, he seemed to have become less open-minded, less tolerant, easily irritated, impatient and this made him tricky to interview. In his accounts of his experiences, he often drifted from one event to another and back, which was no good for me because I was writing a drama which was basically chronological. However, I could usually sequence/order his accounts using his memoir supplemented by the Orbis history.

I was writing the scripts with the support of Initial's Eileen Quinn and it wasn't long before tensions began to arise with our colleagues in Australia. Thus far, I had worked as a signature writer for the BBC, writing my own original dramas with little or no interference from producers, script editors or directors. But international mega dramas were another game entirely.

International TV had its own grammar. I had, for example, knowing Page so well, attempted to include in his dialogue the creative epithets, conundrums, jokes, verbal ticks that I heard in his everyday speech. (His dedications to me in two of his books illustrate this clearly: in *Page After Page* he writes 'No such thing as emulsion only reality. Or is this just fantasy?' In *Nam* it's 'R&R forever now' and in *Derailed in Uncle Ho's Victory Garden* it's 'Methinks that M.Frankie would possibly turn over in his proverbials.') The Australian attitude was that an international audience needed to find the dialogue accessible, they needed to know what was going on. I suspect the British broadcasters were of the same mind.

David Wheatley had been on board since the beginning as the director and I think, on the basis of the highly individual dramas he and I had produced, as well as others he had directed, the broadcasters were rather fearful of what we might produce together. David went. (Ironically, David then went straight on to direct Bernard McLaverty's *Hostages* for Granada/HBO about the incarceration of John McCarthy, Brian Keenan and Terry Waite in The Lebanon which was released at the same time as *Frankie's House* and also garnered international acclaim, each reviewed on the same page of Variety!) There was also a sense that some of the more excessive behaviour of our characters was out of bounds. I was told, for example, that one Frankie's House resident had been getting dressed one morning when single false teeth began falling out of the underpants he'd worn the night before. There was apparently a Saigon bar you could sit at, underneath which women would give you a blow job while you drank. Er – no thank you – not on international TV thank you very much. Either way, two

Australian writers were brought on board, Matt Ford and Sue Masters. This was the dawning of the age of the fax so Matt, Sue and I had a faxual relationship – each sending one another drafts, amending and sending them back. Not so much writing by committee but by continent.

Frankie's House in Saigon was, in Page's words, 'the frat-rat dwelling for a hard core of residents, all bao chi (journalists).' Although it was essentially residential, it became in the series a night club and brothel as well. I think this was an example of the features of Page's life which he felt were invented in the series. But, and I can't remember whether this was my decision, the Aussies' or both, this enhancement of its role, opened it out dramatically as a meeting place for bao chi, the military and locals. It also tapped into the glamour and rather sordid hedonism which was everywhere in Saigon (Page actually complained there was too little drug-taking shown in the production!).

The USA has a long history of press freedom, which is at the heart of its constitution and its democracy. In times of war, this freedom had always been curtailed. However, war had never been declared in Vietnam and there were therefore none of the constrictions which might have been applied had it so been. As a result, it became the most widely covered conflict in history. In the early days there was real tension between bureau chiefs on the one hand (represented by Meadows in the series) and their much younger staffers and freelancers who brought them their copy. The former were likely to have been veteran journos who cut their teeth in WW2, when there was absolutely no moral ambiguity about the allies' attack on fascism. However, as the rhetoric of Vietnam became detached from the reality, the copy, photos and footage produced by unfettered journalists, became increasingly credible. I remember in my late teenage seeing nightly on TV news, sets of statistics produced by the US Government about US and enemy casualties in a desperate attempt to claim victory, which was then completely undermined by TV footage which suggested the opposite.

I commented earlier in this memoir that, on re-viewing or re-reading my work from earlier in my life, I suddenly saw the significance of something I might have understood subconsciously at the time, but only now, consciously. This happened again with *Frankie's House*. I suddenly realised how important still photos were in telling the story of the reality of the war. In one scene, exiled in the South of France between tours, Page and Flynn watch TV footage of the Tet Offensive. Page derides TV footage as wall paper while extolling still shots which 'draw you in'. This is the photo-journalist's professional competitiveness but he's right. The photographer captures a significant moment and has to be close to the action to do that, closer than the TV cameraman and closer still than the print journalist.

We decided to make the relationship between Page and Sean Flynn the heart of the drama, which did reflect the reality between them (Granada made a very moving documentary in 1991, *Danger on The Edge of Town* showing Page's search for Flynn and Dana Stone in Cambodia. It shows Page planting a Bo tree on the 117th parallel in their memory, a moment which ends our series). Part of the dynamic between them is their difference: the ordinary Orpington lad and the playboy from Tinseltown. But they have startling similarities and a strong bond: the need for each to establish their own unique agency and achievement. Page seems clearer about this than Flynn. Flynn is a failed film star – well, if not failed, never achieving the starry heights of his father. But being in front of the cameras isn't enough. He wants to be on the other side of the camera, with Page. This proves to be enough for Page but not for Flynn. He begins to go out in the field but leaving his camera behind. Page challenges him. Of the shots, 'They're up here,' he says, pointing to his head. In the end, Flynn seems to be more interested in being alongside combatants, rather than accompanying them, as a journalist. 'Real bullets,' he says in the series, 'real fear'.

Frankie's House went out on four consecutive Saturday nights in May 1992 in ITV prime time. The P/reviews were good. It was called: 'Action packed' 'A good yarn' 'A cracker of blood, sweat and tears', had 'A pacey treatment', was 'Poignant'. John Naughton in The Observer, summed up the series thus:

'Journalists who covered the Vietnam war experienced the conflict between moral and professional values in its most acute form. For that reason alone, *Frankie's House* would have made timely viewing, based as it is on Tim Page's true story of a gang of war correspondents sharing a house in Saigon. But in fact, this four-part series, adapted by Andy Armitage from Page's book, held its own in straight dramatic terms. This was partly due to fine performances by Iain Glenn as Page and Kevin Dillon (of *Platoon* fame) as his charismatic mate Sean (son of Errol) Flynn; but it was mainly attributable to the way the script avoided sentimentalising a set of alliances made under grisly circumstances.'

It is common for the subjects of biopics to react unfavourably to adaptations of their life stories and Tim was no exception.

He dissociated himself from the series, which he clearly hated. This was widely reported and did, I think, damage the programme's reception. 'I want nothing more to do with it,' he said. 'I won't watch it when it's on – in fact. I hope I'm out of the country.' And he was. In Cambodia. He had a number of complaints: 'It's the worst of pop television. The combat scenes will be laughed off the screen.' He complained that he wasn't used as an on-set adviser during filming (as he was for *Apocalypse Now*). He complained that we invented scenes and used dramatic licence and we didn't film in Vietnam. The Australian co-producer, Matt Carroll, defended the series. It would have been impossible to film the whole of Page's account in *Page After Page* he claimed. 'Tim is obsessed with the detail of the thing and you can never re-create someone's life in that way, no matter how many hours you have. You have to look for the emotional heart of each person, deal with the central core of what Tim was searching for. We have tried very hard to get that right. And hope that when Tim sees the finished version, he'll agree.'

There was a lot of interest in Australia in the programme, partly because Roadshow was one of their premier drama production companies but partly because of the prominent military role Australia had in Vietnam. It was widely reviewed, from the Sydney Herald to the Illawarra Mercury, Wollongong to the Western Australian, Perth. And the reviews were as good as, if rather better than, the UK ones. *Frankie's House* was 'gripping', 'one of the best things on television', 'stunning drama', 'impressive,' 'not to be missed', 'damned good TV', 'The acting is sensational and the atmosphere brilliantly re-created. I loved it.'

But the best reception of all came from the US press. They

raved from coast to coast. This surprised me because, as a country so powerfully affected by the war, you would expect much greater criticality, particularly for a depiction of it by an Anglo-Australian production. For the New York Times, the programme stood out against the entire Vietnam canon:

'But *Frankie's House*, by playing it straight, is somehow more persuasive (than the other Vietnam movies), with music by Jeff Beck and Jed Lieber instead of The Doors and with a director, Peter Fisk, who doesn't think he's more important than Vietnam.'

'Better still,' claims USA Today, 'is *Frankie's House*, the first significant Vietnam TV drama since "China Beach" went off the air. It is randy, more and more provocative than US network TV generally is allowed to be.'

For Life, it was a 'strong movie' and for the New York Post 'lots of surprises, tense scenes and good acting enliven this drama.'

The Philadelphia Enquirer admired 'top flight drama' while the Orlando Sentinel hailed 'Apocalypse Again!'.

But it was Newsday's veteran TV critic, Marvin Kitman, who encapsulated the American response (his review was personally delivered to me via A&E in New York. Never happened to me before or since):

'The gripping script by Andy Armitage also manages to examine the ethics of being a war cameraman, how he steels himself against atrocities. It's in the camera, Page learns, not him. As long as you get the pictures, or dispatches, that's all that matters … *Frankie's House* is the *Born on the Fourth of July* and *Apocalypse Now* of TV shows about Vietnam. It captures the horror, passion and recklessness of the war, the friendships, the sex, drugs and rock and roll. I am not a 'Nam head, but it's hit me like a claymore mine, leaving shrapnel of scenes and words and pictures that I haven't been able to get out of my mind. You will never forget visiting *Frankie's House*. Don't take my word for it. Go there on A&E.'

Coronation Street

The first episode of *Coronation Street* was transmitted on December 9th 1960; the genesis of the programme beautifully told in Daran Little's 2010 film, *The Road to Coronation Street*. (This marked the Street's 50th anniversary in 2011. I have this very morning received a £150 royalty payment relating to the programme ITV put out for the 60th anniversary, *Coronation Street: 60 Unforgettable Years*. They must have used material from my episodes in the programme.) I was a ten-year-old in 1960 and nightly family viewing of TV was already a tradition. And my family gawped. We'd never seen anything like it. Here were people like those in our street. They spoke like those my mum would hail for a natter across King Street nearby with an 'Oo-oo'. The alleged model for Coronation Street, Archie Street, was in Salford, less than three miles from our door. The programme was, of course, shot and transmitted in black and white. Which was entirely appropriate: the first twenty years of my life spent in Manchester were entirely monochromatic. Colour? Luxury - you should be so lucky. I remember one summer, looking at the sun glinting off the grey slates on the roof of the house opposite after a rain shower and thinking how unnatural it was. Sunlight wasn't meant for us. Initially, 'Coronation Street' was raw, in your face, social realism

– a genre I felt I cleaved to as a writer some twenty years on. However, within a decade, I was seeing it as a vacuous parody of Northern life. In fact, my mate Ian and I would make up dialogue caricaturing the programme on our way to the pub, when swotting for our A Levels:

A: Aye when you're young you're not old....
I: Nay, lad, when you're old, you're not young...

Mind you, at the time, we were rather snobbish eighteen-year-olds, anxious to get to university away from what we saw as a suffocating, illiberal, reactionary world. (Ian still sees it that way at seventy-two!) This latter view of The Street coloured my view of it well into adulthood and it was a programme I never watched – doing so was like re-entering a world I'd managed successfully to get away from. It was probably this that was behind my passing a number of times on invitations from Street producers and executive producers to join the writing team. (With four out of my five BBC dramas in the nineteen-eighties set in Manchester, I think they felt I was a natural.) What also put me off was that, having been a signature author with almost total freedom about what I created, I felt writing alongside fifteen others for a programme with established characters and format would leave little room for innovation. (My instinct was correct and this was one of the reasons I left the programme after a year.) Mind you, I was behaving rather grandly at the time. I had a meeting with *Emmerdale* producers who asked if I'd join the programme. Only if I could wipe out all the characters and start again, said I. I didn't get invited back (however, that's exactly what they did themselves with the plane crash in 1993!).

By 1997, with the run of *Annie's Bar* finished (See Chapter 7), I approached Granada myself to join the Street team. I'd already returned to Canterbury Christ Church, as a part-time sessional tutor. This was partly because I'd missed the interaction with students but also to guarantee a regular income – Elaine and I were buying a rather grand three-storey town house in the centre of Canterbury and had a mortgage for the first time in a decade. The producer invited me up to Manchester to sit in on one of the fortnightly story conferences which I would then be attending regularly for the next year. The company paid first class rail fare but, since flying was cheaper, myself and a few other southern based writers, including the indomitable Adele Rose – then the Street's longest serving writer – would fly up and back together in the day. (This led to some very funny, desperate moments at story conferences. With the last London flights leaving Manchester around 8pm, the southern brigade would start looking at their watches and twitching as 6pm arrived. The writing team would have been locked in at 1pm and not allowed out until the story editor and his team had material for eight episodes.) Arriving in Manchester by plane was weird. The cab would go all the way along Princess Parkway into town, passing Uncle Sam and Aunty Jenny's house at 599 Princess Road. I'd only known this because of the old red phone box ten yards from their door, since each house for miles along Princess Road was identical. I'd sat as a boy in their front room in the fifties and early sixties watching the distinctive light and dark blue airport buses passing back and forth and thinking that this was the way to the rest of the world. And here was the man, forty years on, coming back from the rest of the world.

On my first day, a posh floor manager walked me round the

set at Granada. She had to because some writers were writing impossible shots, 'You can't see the Kabin from Number 7'. As I stood in the yard of The Rovers Return, I waxed all post-modern, 'D'you know, it's weird standing in a real back yard in a fictional soap, three miles from the real back yard I used to play in.' 'Oh, you're from round here are you?' she said, surprised. And, indeed, by the time I joined, Corrie was no longer the Mancunian social realist drama I'd grown up with but was a huge international phenomenon.

Coronation Street stories began their lives at long term story conferences. These were held a couple of times a year. Each writer was mandated to arrive at these with an agreed number of possible stories and the conference was spent evaluating the potential of these, as well as discussing long-term programme strategies. For obvious reasons, these conferences were subject to maximum secrecy with the venue only disclosed to everyone days before. It was as if you were in the security services. When the waiting staff trollied in the tea and biscuits, the producer would pause meaningfully and we would all follow. The poor waiting staff would complete their task in silence and then depart, looking like they'd been suspected of a major crime. At one conference, the producer began sternly: one of our team had been selling stories to the papers and he was determined to discover who. It was indeed rumoured that the tabloids would pay £10-20K for a story. However, the writers eyed each other with incredulity: every one of them was there out of love for and commitment to the programme and it was hard to believe any of us would betray it in this way. And for what they would be paid anyway for 3 or 4 episodes? The miscreant was never caught or, if they were, we never found out.

Story conferences took place every other week. Most of the writing team would meet up in the bar ahead of the 1pm kick off. Word was that when the Bernsteins had built Granada in Quay Street, they forbad alcohol in the building and the staff bar had had to be located in the decommissioned Methodist chapel across the street. The old hands needed several glasses of white wine – it had to be Chardonnay – to fortify themselves for the task ahead, to oil the cogs of their creative machines. The writers were a terrific bunch – many believe the consistent writing talent available to the Street over the years has been the secret of its success. They were mixed: some were northerners, some had been on the team for twenty or thirty years. There were newbies like me who had already had a writing career, newbies who were just starting out. There were experienced writers who would go on to have stellar careers as signature writers/producers/directors – Sally Wainwright springs to mind. What they all had in common was a total commitment to the programme and a clear, shared understanding of its identity.

Story conferences would begin with the producer or story editor reminding us of the three or four storylines carried over from the previous batch of eight episodes as a starting point for that afternoon's eight. We would then begin to describe how these storylines would develop, or indeed how they might be resolved/concluded and others begun. It was usually the producer who called the big ones – a departing character, a new character, a new story. I remember writers' jaws dropping when the producer introduced Julie Hesmondhaigh's character, Hayley Cropper, soaps', nay the world's, first transgender soap character.

The way this creative process worked out was something of a

free-for-all. 'So Deirdre at this point won't have anything to do with John…' 'Of course she would, she trusts him completely.' 'Come on, our Deirdre's got more nous than that…' 'No - no, we know what our character would do…'. This kind of Darwinian survival of the fittest contest would go on and on, with producer, story editor and story liners as referees. I found it very difficult, a kind of competitive creativity and I don't think I was alone. All the creative endeavour in my life thus far had been a private affair and I hadn't been used to sharing it (although *Annie's Bar* had involved some small team brainstorming). I did try to use my twenty-five years' teaching experience, involving extensive group management, to suggest more fruitful ways of working but I came to realise that only by managing one group process was the producer able to keep a firm handle on the creation of the story.

Sometimes – particularly when the situation had the potential for melodrama - we would go off on silly, impossible narrative rants. One such concerned the reign of terror of Don Brennan, Ivy Tilsley's mad, taxi driver husband. We knew he would die at the end of a particular episode, but weren't sure how or what events would occur leading up to this. Our favourite ending involved Don shaving his prosthetic lower leg down to a vicious point (the character had acquired this after an earlier car crash had meant amputation at the knee). He would then proceed to threaten those pursuing him with the weapon, a hopping fugitive, before finally turning the weapon on himself. However, we couldn't agree whether it was physically possible to stab yourself to death with your own prosthesis, so Don met his end more mundanely by crashing his car into The Railway Viaduct.

A week or two after the story conference, eight writers would be commissioned to write the eight episodes concerned. It was rare for any writer to be commissioned for more than one episode per block, probably because the producers wanted to make maximum use of the pool of talent available to them. And, of course, it would be hard for any one writer to pen more than one episode in the fortnight available. Each commissioned writer would then receive a story outline for their episode. This told you which characters were available and gave you a suggested scene by scene plot summary – usually around nineteen or twenty scenes for a half hour episode. Once you digested this and had planned your episode in some detail, you attended a commissioning conference at which the sequence of eight was firmed up. This was the opportunity for some bargaining – could you have an extra external scene, could the plot sequencing be slightly adjusted? You were then sent off to write the episode and given a deadline of around a fortnight.

I can only describe this period as a kind of relay race which changed day by day. In the course of writing the episodes, the writers often had brainwaves, creative moments when they wanted to change something in their episodes. But, of course, this might have implications for episodes up the series of eight or indeed backwards down the series, so the negotiations went on between the eight writers. And because writers are as bad as actors, if not worse, at stealing one another's thunder, you would often get a request such as: 'You know the [incredibly dramatic, life-changing] moment at the end of your episode? Well, wouldn't it be better to move it to the beginning of my episode with a cliff hanger at the end of yours?'

I was extremely lucky that, during my year at The Street, I

penned episodes around Deirdre Rachid's (false) accusation of fraud which led to the 'Free the Weatherfield One' campaign supported by none other than Tony Blair in the House of Commons – one of the most explosive stories of the last twenty years on the Street. This appears as one of four stories in the story outline in front of me, with John, the supposed airline pilot, attempting to convince the police that, Deirdre, not he, set the whole thing up. The other three stories concern the fall-out from the end of Fiona's long-term relationship, Curly Watts' attempt to exact justice for the pouring of anti-freeze on the frozen prawns at Firman's and the budding relationship of Chris and Samantha.

Once the draft was complete, it went through three further drafts (pink, yellow and blue as I remember – the final shooting script was white). Each of these was subject to a phone conversation with the producer and story editor before you moved on to the next draft. It was possible, and indeed likely, that a writer was doing a first draft, editing a first or second, attending rehearsal for another in production and seeing another they'd done earlier at home on screen. It was like playing three-dimensional chess, although in a time scheme that was a reversal of the natural time scheme: you had to adjust to seeing the past on the screen now, in relation to the future you were currently creating! It would be enough to make Einstein have to redesign the theory of relativity.

Writers didn't often attend the recording of their scripts. This was because they weren't a lot of use at this stage: directors pretty much shot the script as written. Also, as I was to find, they were quickly taken hostage by a number of parties. I didn't attend many shoots but I was always assailed by actors who were desperate to know what the future held for their characters: chopping and changing characters was a popular pastime among soap producers. Of course, you could never tell 'em owt. Also, some directors unscrupulously used writers as a tool in their directorial armoury with actors, openly asking writers if the actor's interpretation of lines was what the writer intended. However, there were some glorious incidents to enjoy which gave insight into behind-the-scenes life. On one occasion, during the recording of an episode of mine, Alec Gilroy (Roy Barraclough), Jack and Vera Duckworth (Bill Tarmey and Liz Dawn) had a scene in the Rovers' parlour. As the scene progressed, Alec and Jack's dialogue made perfect sense, while Vera's interjections didn't. Roy and Bill giggled away because they knew exactly what was going on. Roy and Bill were off the script, whereas Liz still held hers. After a couple of runs-through the director said, 'Liz, love, er - what script have you got because we're on Wednesday's.' Liz looked at the front of her script, 'Oh – I've got Friday's.' She gave me a sweet, apologetic smile, 'Sorry love.'

A year into my time with The Street, I was still not contributing at story conferences for reasons I explained earlier. Without that, my only creative contribution was turning the prescribed scenes with established characters into scripts and this began to feel like a bit of a treadmill, writing by numbers. I began to wonder whether I was cut out for soap writing and the producer agreed. My departure from The Street was by mutual agreement. I was flattered by the response of my colleague writers: I fielded at least ten phone calls from them who felt my eight episodes had been among the strongest of the year.

An amusing postscript. I used to meet regularly with a

journalist on my local paper, the Kentish Gazette, to give her career updates. After I'd left The Street, but round about the time of the transmission of the John/Deirdre story, I casually mentioned that it had been based on what had actually happened to a friend of the executive producer. I thought no more of this until, one afternoon, the phone went. 'Hello Mr Armitage, it's the Daily Mirror, could we have a word?' 'Yes, of course,' I said. 'No – you see – we're outside your flats.' And they were. The reporter and his cameraman. Not only did I find myself giving an interview but I was then manoeuvred behind the railings of the Poor Priests' Hospital, a museum next to my flats in Canterbury. There was a photo next day in the Mirror of me holding the railings with the caption, 'The Man Who Jailed Deirdre'. I was very lucky I didn't become a national hate figure. The poor actor who played John was exiled to Spain in the end. When I got back in the flat the phone rang off the hook and a similar story graced all the tabloids the following day. Radio stations were trying to get hold of me as well as TV news programmes but I managed to dodge them. What really scared me about all this was how quickly and powerfully the media can turn individuals over in their search for a story. It arrived like a whirlwind and just as quickly became yesterday's news.

However, the builders finishing off the town house Elaine and I were shortly to move into, decided it would be funny if they wrote 'Free Deirdre' slogans in the whitewashed windows. And some months later, one sunny summer's day, I was working in the third floor study which overlooked the street when I heard, 'Coronation Street – blah, blah, blah – Deirdre Rashid – blah, blah, blah…' I looked out and there, in the street below, looking up, was a couple in a tourist rickshaw, the rickshaw driver giving a running commentary. I'd arrived - I had made it onto the tourist map of Canterbury!

The Bill

Shortly after leaving The Street, I took a call from Richard Hanford, who had produced *Annie's Bar*. He was now Executive Producer of *The Bill* and wanted me to write for the programme. Although, like The Street, *The Bill* had an established format and regular characters, unlike The Street it was then a drama series rather than a drama serial. Each episode was a self-contained story, originated, story-lined and written by the individual writers. In terms of autonomy and creativity, then, writing for The Bill was a very attractive prospect.

My first episode was *Good Relations*. Following the election of the Blair Government in 1997, there was a dramatic increase in public-private partnerships with particular growth in the health and security sectors. At the same time, street crime, particularly in London, had been rocketing through the nineties and there was a perception that the police were overwhelmed by crime and that private security might be one way of helping them stem this tide. I therefore wanted to place public policing and private security operation side by side and, of course, to sharpen the drama, bring them into conflict. Of the regular characters in The Bill, I was most interested in PC Reg Hollis as the central focus for my story. I hadn't really taken in the character notes on Reg but on reflection, the description equips him admirably for the central role of practitioner of community policing:

'Undeniably odd and offbeat, Reg is the maverick copper who can be found in every nick. A hypochondriac, a gossip and a model train enthusiast with a passionate interest in abstruse pieces of information, he is above all a good copper with a genuine belief in the value of routine police work. He will occasionally madden his mates with his dogged insistence on investigating something that appears perfectly straightforward, but his instincts are surprisingly accurate and he has had some spectacular successes. And Reg definitely has his uses – it is he who resuscitates the station garden, and he who has the idea of setting up the mobile police office (in an elderly caravan). He has a real rapport with the vulnerable, the young and the elderly which his colleagues secretly respect, although would never admit it.' (Thames Television *Character Notes*)

Superintendent Brownlow has two issues. His bosses are keen to make the partnership with the local private security company work. The latter are keen to show they can produce results while plodding police work doesn't. Secondly, he is keen to test Reg Hollis' community policing initiative: Reg has refurbished an old caravan as a Community Liaison Centre and Polly tows it onto the local estate. The press are watching both initiatives carefully.

A burglary on the estate is investigated. It is one many that have blighted the area. The security staff have already interviewed the victim who has named two local gang members, Tyler and Mills as responsible. The 'honey monsters' (as the locals call the security staff) are keen to go and arrest the perpetrators. Our PCs tell them to hold on – there isn't any evidence yet. And it's difficult to get this: the victim won't give a statement because she feels intimidated. Meanwhile, Reg's van is proving popular with the relief: it's an ideal spot to have a break instead of having to go back to the nick!

A serious incident on the estate: a large group of youths has surrounded and attacked a private security van. Most of the relief attend. It turns out that the security guards were easily provoked when the lads were taking the mickey out of their uniforms. One of them admits they don't know how to handle most of the situations they find themselves in. 'Didn't you get any training?' enquires one officer. 'If there was, I must have missed it,' responds the guard. The security guard recruitment consisted of 'finding bodies to fit in the uniforms.' The relief twig that the van attack might have been a distraction and so it appears when Reg returns to his caravan to find one of the gang members in the process of torching it, Zippo lighter in hand.

The following exchange between Reg and Tony, the gang member, proves the value of best practice in community policing: Reg recognises where Tony's coming from, empathises with him and makes him an offer – he'll put McDonald, the gang leader, away if Tony informs on him. Tony accepts. McDonald is brought in in connection with the burglaries but he can't be touched. It's known he instructs gang members what and where to burgle and then tells them where to fence the stolen goods. All he does is collect the money at the end of the process. Reg takes a statement from Tony implicating MacDonald in the whole process. Meanwhile, Macdonald offers police officers a deal: he'll shop his gang members if he can walk. CI Conway consults Brownlow: Brownlow says they need the collars to demonstrate their effectiveness in contrast with the private security company. 'It's not what we do, it's what we're seen to do that matters,' he tells Conway. As Macdonald exits Sun Hill,

Tony watches. Reg has let him down! Community policing doesn't stand a chance against politics and PR.

Looking at this episode after twenty years, I was impressed with the plotting of it: plotting has never been my strongest suit. However, when I looked at the commissioning process, I was not surprised and this contains an important lesson for TV drama writers. *Bill* writers initially submitted a premise to the weekly story conference. This was one side of A4 and stated what the episode was about – an abbreviated storyline and who was involved. If this was greenlit, the next stage would be a storyline. At nine or ten pages, this most closely represented a proposal or treatment that might be written for other films or TV dramas. This was very detailed, with scene by scene action specifying who does what to whom and when. Only when this was approved could the writer consider themselves commissioned and go ahead to write the episode. So, at this point, the writer had done a lot of the thinking about the action, the characters, the shape and the pace of the piece. It's forethought and discipline that a writer, working outside the structure of an established programme, might find it difficult to adhere to but might be recommended to follow.

As outlined in the chapters above, a key theme of my writing has been the creation and re-creation of identity. With regard to policing, I was most interested in how an officer's identity might be tested by undercover work. One *Bill* episode, *Beasts*, explored this. The episode was transmitted 20 years ago but has gained topicality by recent actions against undercover officers whom activists married and, in some cases, had children with. In *Beasts*, PC Sam Harker is requested by Special Branch to go undercover as an animal rights activist: he went to school in the North West with Steve, an associate of Ged Melling, a leading activist whom Special Branch would like to see convicted. Harker is 'managed' by a Special Branch officer and Sun Hill's DC Duncan Lennox. Harker is initially arrested with other protestors and is convicted of assault on a police officer to maintain his credibility. Green, who owns the abattoir which the protestors were targeting, accuses them of breaking in and causing damage. (It turns out later that this was faked damage enabling Green to make an illegitimate insurance claim.) Steve introduces Sam to Anna and Star, fellow travellers with Ged Melling. Anna, although passionate about protesting, is more ambiguous in her support for direct action. To prove his credentials with Melling, Sam proposes he and Steve break into Green's abattoir and spray paint the offices. This takes Sam into dangerous territory: if the law-breaking is seen as incitement, Sam could be regarded as an agent provocateur which might compromise Special Branch's pursuit of Melling. But the operation is successful, Sam videoing the proceedings to up his cred with Melling. He and Steve take refuge from the security guards in the pig enclosure, the pigs repaying the activists' support for them in not giving them away. In turn, Sam and Steve free the pigs, causing traffic mayhem that night and the following day in the Sun Hill area.

Sam's becoming increasingly confused. He begins to admire the activists' idealism: for the first time, he has come into contact with people who are motivated by their beliefs. But he wonders where he should draw the line in terms of his activities with the group. His minders urge him on: he has to stay close to the group to get the evidence they need. He has begun to feel like a traitor to the group. A kind of Stockholm syndrome is coming into play.

Finally, Melling comes up with a plan: they will hit the fur trade by planting incendiary devices in clothing in the local department store. The operation goes ahead, the relief and Special Branch staking the store out. Success! The activists are nicked – and there is evidence on the store CCTV. 'You must be over the moon,' Harker's fellow officers congratulate him. 'Yeah – I must be, mustn't I?' says Harker, unconvincingly. Ged Melling, however, has something up his sleeve: he has a tape (which he's obviously edited – wouldn't get away with that now – forensics would be able to show it was tampered with!) showing clearly Harker's incitement and provocation, which undermines any attempt the police might have to convict Melling and the others. Harker's only hope is to appeal to Anna's law-abiding nature to support his story v Melling. But Anna's having none of it. Why should she support a traitor who has no ideals, against someone who has – albeit someone who breaks the law in order to fulfil them? Harker just does what he's told. It is clear the episode leaves Harker questioning his professional identity as a police officer.

I'd been struck, on my outings with the Met, how problematic it was to prosecute domestic abuse perpetrators. And, without being able to establish that a crime had taken place, there couldn't be a victim of that crime. So, *No Victim* became my final episode of *The Bill*. Sarah is threatening to jump off a bridge into the river. A man emerges from the crowd who Dave Quinnan recognises as DS Terry Collins from Stafford Row nick. Why is CID interested in a jumper? She's his wife, he says.

Casting a colleague officer as a potential abuser quite neatly draws on the conflict of interests of the relief: possible crimes are on their patch while they have professional and personal links with Terry Collins. Some remember Sarah as something of a man eater while others recall a difficult, unstable woman. Police are called to an alleged mugging. It is Sarah again. Terry Collins attempts to prevent the police doctor from examining Sarah but Di Worrall, who has taken up Sarah's case, insists and it appears that Sarah has extensive bruising, some of it older than that allegedly caused by the mugging. Di, who has been looking at CCTV footage of the 'mugging', sees that there doesn't appear to an attack but rather Sarah falling over in the street, apparently being chased. She admits she was being pursued by Terry who had attacked her for involving the police in their domestic.

Threaded through the episode is the unrelated story of colleagues Dave Quinnan and Polly Page, who have been having an affair. Dave has promised to tell his wife, Jenny, about the affair but so far hasn't. Polly wonders how serious Dave is if he hasn't told Jenny. Tony Stamp, a mate of both of them, implores Dave to stop the affair which he claims is bad for everyone. Dave, however, thinks Tony is motivated by his own feelings for Polly. I think this story was a continuation from previous episodes – a serial story, the purpose of which was to build the audience. (Not long after I left, The Bill moved to be a drama serial rather than a series, with all stories ongoing, a development which was obviously ratings driven.) Nevertheless, in my episode, the Dave-Polly-Jenny story reflects the main plot: here, in the sub-plot, is a man emotionally damaging women as opposed to the physical damage allegedly being meted out by Terry Collins.

Inspector Monroe warns Di Worrall of the serious nature of the accusations for Terry Collins: they will result in automatic disciplinary procedures whether he's found guilty or not. Terry Collins comes in for a voluntary interview. Initially, he claims Sarah's injuries are drink related, falling down stairs, crashing into furniture. But when Di claims some injuries don't fit this pattern, he says he thinks Sarah is self-harming. But he then accuses her of attacking him and claims that her injuries were caused by Terry defending himself. But Di Worrall puts it to him that this is the abuser's oldest trick and that these are her defence injuries incurred while Sarah defended herself from him.

After Di Worrall discloses her own abuse at the hands of her partner, Sarah agrees to give a statement. She then withdraws this, arguing that Di has forced her to make it, Terry having apparently got to Sarah. The CPS will not prosecute without a statement from Sarah, which she finally agrees to give.

The trial goes badly for Di and Sarah. Without any proof of the cause of injuries, it is essentially Sarah's word against Terry's and Terry Collins gets off.

The episode ends with a shout to the Collins residence. There has been a fatal stabbing. And down the stairs comes…Sarah, cuffed.

Chapter 7 – Annie's Bar

Easter 1995. A producer friend of mine called me and asked if I'd be interested in writing a series set in Parliament that Channel 4 had expressed an interest in. I was happy to meet the production company, Ardent Productions, which sounded vaguely familiar but my friend had deliberately omitted to give me a contact name – I think because he feared I might have been frightened off. I went to their offices in Charlotte Street and was buzzed up. When the lift doors opened, there stood Prince Edward. Apparently, some people have bowed when he met them at the lift, one person even sinking to their knees. We chatted about the PM's Question Time he'd just been to. I'd always thought Edward would turn out to be a bit naïve. Not a bit of it. John Major was then in the driving seat (just) and Edward gave a very trenchant analysis of current parliamentary politics.

As I write, the media are awash with details of the David Cameron/Greensill lobbying affair, as well as Boris Johnson's interior decoration, with many talking about the return of the Tory sleaze of the late nineties. And it is easy to see what attracted both Ardent and Channel 4 to a Parliament-set satire at that time. Sleaze dominated the political world in the nineties: David Mellor's resignation after the alleged affair with Antonia de Sancha; Michael Mates's support for Asil Nadir; 'cash for questions' and Neil Hamilton which led to the establishment of the Nolan Committee to review the issue of standards in public life; the government's 'back to basics' policy, hoping to restore the virtues of neighbourliness, decency and courtesy to British life (eventually rather undermined by revelations of John Major's affair with Edwina Currie); Jonathan Aitkin's 'Paris Ritz' allegations. Of course, the sleaze didn't end with the disappearance of Major's government but continued under Labour: Bernie Ecclestone's donation to the Labour Party; Peter Mandleson's loan from Geoffrey Robinson; Ron Davies and the Clapham Common case.

Ardent had interested Channel 4 in a political soap. I seem to remember a short pitch document: the key elements C4 had bought were a) that it would be a soap involving those who worked in Parliament, principally MPs b) that it would be satirical c) that it would be shot close to transmission so that the issues in each episode would be bang up to date, political events changing with such rapidity.

I hesitated about getting involved. Even though the fiasco of 'It's a Royal Knockout' was nearly a decade old, I was aware of the hostility shown to Edward at the time by the media. It was an ongoing hostility that was not just connected with that particular programme but seemed to be related to outrage that Edward would dare to try to carve out a media career and use his privilege to help himself (a view which seemed to ignore what I'd already seen in a media career of then fifteen years – how dependent many in the media were on the patronage of family, friends and other connections for their success!). And, as Andy Beckett points out in a Guardian article, 'From the start, there were many people in television keen to see him fail. "There was a lot of envy," says Vernon Lawrence, a senior executive at ITV at the time. "Only a few lucky production companies have a big backer."' Added to this was a vague republicanism: was it really appropriate for a member of the monarchy to take the piss out of the executive and legislature?

At the same time – the prospect of creating a ten-part, high profile series which my chum would produce was very attractive. Ardent was obviously well resourced: a human dynamo called Eben Foggitt ran the business side and Graeme McDonald, producer of ground-breaking Plays for Today, BBC drama head and then controller of BBC2 was their Head of Drama. I also needed the money: TV drama writing tends to be feast or famine and I'd got nothing off the ground for two or three years. I took the gig.

The initial commission was three-fold: a broad treatment for a ten-episode series; main character sketches; a written first episode. The research for this was relatively limited: the deadline was tight. I already had quite extensive contacts in Parliament and I was given a number of advisers and researchers. Among the former were Michael Brown, who I believe was the first MP to out himself and Derek Draper, Peter Mandelson's former researcher, who shortly after was to be involved in Lobbygate: we determined that the programme would only work if it satirized political parties equally, so we needed advisers from each. My assistant was a former researcher for a Lib-Dem MP and was able to arrange meetings with her contacts. I decided that by far the best way in to the series for the audience would be to follow a newly elected MP from his election. This would provide us with a narrative focus for the entire series: the birth and journey of an MP, from innocence to experience, with idealism pitted against realism, the early episodes inducting the audience into the culture and procedures of Parliament, a potential barrier for viewers, at the same time as the series' protagonist is. I also thought it would be nicely ironic for the new MP to be a Toryboy in the dying days of the Major government.

I completed the treatment, character sketches and first episode, submitted them and promptly forgot about them: most projects don't get off the ground so it's hardly worth worrying about them. Then, in the middle of a sunny weekday morning my producer friend was on the phone. His voice was quivering with excitement and the words tumbled out of his mouth: Channel 4 had commissioned a series of ten episodes and committed to transmission the following February. Excited company executives rang me one after the other. But my exhilaration quickly turned to panic. Shit - this was June. I didn't know a great deal about the production process but I reckoned that developing ten scripts, producing, shooting and editing them in little more than six months was probably impossible. Nevertheless, no-one is going to say no to an offer of a ten-part series which might be recommissioned, even if it was impossible to make. Ardent was a new company with great ambitions. And – I didn't know it at the time – C4 were in the market for a long runner. After the read-through of the first episode months later, Peter Ansorge, commissioning editor for drama, turned to me and told me he thought he'd found another *Brookside*.

The characters were created for their potential to be involved in interesting stories. Some were based on existing MPs or an amalgam of several (the Guardian ran a Guess Who? article before transmission) whom I'd observed in the media or interviewed as part of my research. Most were to be back benchers, the Rozencrantzes and Guildensterns of parliamentary politics.

The squeaky-clean David Dashwood, the new member, is the tabula rasa arriving at Parliament in Episode 1. There are a number of key characters eager to take the new boy under their wings. On the Tory side there is David's neighbour, the oleaginous Stiggy-Bedford Bounds, with his creepy interest in passing young women. Stiggy turns out to be class sneak, a useful plot device in future episodes, given an oily patina by Geoff McGivern. I was struck how, for many MPs, the public-school common room had simply been replaced by their university junior common rooms and then the Commons Tea Room. Paul Brooke's Vernon Du Chine is a sad front bench has-been in search of a seat at the next election, on the 'chicken run', his rail timetable constantly in his hands. Larry Lamb's Terry Dunning is a magnificently terrorising chief whip: 'avoid the 3 A's – arrogance, alcohol and adultery,' and 'Never get caught in bed with a live man or a dead woman', - advice apparently given by actual whips. Elizabeth Bennett's vamp, Antonia Courtney, who has 'provided many an opening for upright young members,' (oo-er-missus) quickly takes Dashwood in hand (oo-er-missus) and asks if he'd like a quickie (in Annie's Bar) before lunch (oo-er-missus). Gwyneth, Dashwood's secretary, is an expert on Commons procedures. Finally, there is Jonathan Coy's clubbable Philip Salisbury, who, teetering on the edge of bankruptcy which would disqualify him as an MP, is used ruthlessly by Terry Dunning.

On the labour side we have Blairite Graham Keegan, earnestly played by Eamonn Boland, with his snake of a researcher, Darren Watling. Gavin Richard's Nick Buckley is Labour left (although he quietly confesses to colleague Jilly Jones that his daughter is at Cheltenham Ladies College). I noticed (and this was confirmed to me by a number of members) that there was a disproportionate number of very pretty American female researchers in the House so I gave Candy Aloha, played by Sarah Lee-Jones as a not so ditzy air-head, to Nick Buckley. Sarah Neville's Gilly Jones is an early Blair Babe, a forerunner of the record 120 women MPs who were to be elected to the House in the following year's general election. In contrast, Joan Fairlie, made very credible in Marjorie Yates' performance, is old labour, as is Jimmy Mackenzie, ex-Communist and Clydeside ship worker, who sits at the bar, unwilling to accept a drink from anyone to avoid accusations of corruption (I was told about the Three Jimmies, three Scottish Labour MPs, who propped up one of the Commons bars). I was very drawn to the only Lib-Dem, Brian Lightfoot, who dithers at the bar about which soft drink he should have.

The opening episodes included vignettes of the kind which would feature throughout the series. So, Candy gets her own back on Nick Buckley's condescending attitude towards her speechwriting by filling an envelope with blank sheets which he only opens just before his after-dinner speech to business-men. Jimmy Mackenzie has been convinced by Graham Keegan to remodel himself as New Labour, in the hope of getting a place in Blair's future cabinet and employs an image consultant, 'Image Shapers', to re-brand him. He is persuaded to wear a suit the shade of 'subtle, steely midnight blue'. Further fun would be had later when Jimmy takes the 'Spoken Module' of image shapers. The consultant tries to remodel what she calls his aggressive Glaswegian style in favour of a more person-able style but, in the end, Jimmy prefers the passion of his old communist party rhetoric. Antonia Courtney's researcher,

Bruce, is in a gay relationship with Graham Keegan's ex. Bruce, believing gay public figures should out themselves, let's the tabloids know about Keegan's historical conviction relating to public decency. How will Keegan respond? He accepts an invitation to go onto *A Day in Politics* and, admitting his sexuality, gives a stirring speech about New Labour and equality. The watching Labour whips are pissed off: they wanted him to deny the claim and then they could accuse the Tories of smearing a New Labour leading light.

One feature which didn't survive much beyond the first episode was planting real MPs among the fictional ones. This came from Ardent and I thought it worth trying. So, we have Austin Mitchell welcoming Dashwood to the Labour end of the Tea Room: 'Must be the quickest defection in history!' And Edwina Currie is selling *A Woman's Place*, her second novel, out that year. She gifts a copy to Philip Salisbury whom she knows has had problems with Lloyds. In the end, this turned out to be a gimmick which didn't work, a collision of real and fictional worlds which just seemed weird.

We also began a number of longer stories which would run over several episodes. Dashwood's endearing, but somewhat naïve, idealism is illustrated following a TV appearance on *A Day in Politics*, ironically set up by Dashwood himself. He intercepts a phone call meant for Philip Salisbury and offers to step in for Salisbury on the programme. What he doesn't realise is that Labour's Graham Keegan has got hold of a list of maxi-mental hospitals the Government plans to build in an effort to roll back Thatcher's Care in The Community initiative of the 1980s and has tipped off the TV programme. The list includes Dashwood's constituency of Westling-On-Sea: the

Government plan is to site the hospitals in the constituencies of compliant Tory MPs to attempt to minimize the NIMBY response. However, the Government has managed to conceal the existence of the list, in particular from Dashwood himself who, on national TV, appears to have lied to his constituents about its existence during the by-election, or been lied to by his own senior ministers.

The whips attempt to thwart Dashwood's attempts to challenge the Health Minister but in vain. Dashwood chooses his maiden speech, supposed to be non-controversial, to threaten to resign if the hospitals are built and Care in the Community is abolished. This would normally be political suicide for a new MP but with a razor thin majority, the Government need him to vote in favour of their upcoming health bill. On the day of the vote, Dashwood is courted by tea with John and Norma Major at Number 10. Finally, in his first act of pragmatism, he votes with the Government.

Later, Dashwood's constituency wife Laura will become something of an embarrassment to him when she engages in radical social action and chains herself to the girders of the White Knuckle Sky Ride at Westling-On-Sea Funfair. 'Red Laura' (so named by the blue rinses in Westling) is arrested after allegedly kicking four police officers in the groin during a protest and makes the front pages of the dailies. Dashwood thinks Terry Dunning has framed Laura to keep him on track voting with the Government but it appears to be the handiwork of Vernon Du Chine. If Dashwood is forced to resign the Whip as a result of his wife's anti-social behaviour, he won't be able to stand as a Conservative at the next election, making room for Du Chine to grab his seat.

The first division in the series is a vote on the Government's proposal to tax caravans. Graham Keegan thinks this will anger the C1 and C2 voters and that Labour will repeal it immediately after they are elected, although Jilly Jones reckons it's a law that might appeal to the 52 million people who get stuck behind caravans each summer! Vernon du Chine, thinking this will be the last straw for any remaining Tory voters, agrees with Keegan although Reg the barman considers the caravan a national symbol. The hack at the bar tried to break into the national press via Caravan Fortnightly but failed because any scoop had to involve caravans and not many of those came along. The Gypsy Forum think a caravan tax is a threat to their culture and lobby Jimmy Mackenzie to table an appropriate amendment. Those with caravan parks on their land offer to grease Stiggy's palm if he manages to make static caravans exempt. Brian Lightfoot, for the Lib Dems, is sensitive to the environmental impact of caravans and, instead of a tax, proposes a series of measures which will minimise this impact. Among them is a daytime curfew in high summer, obliging caravans to travel at night only. In addition, he proposes that any time five caravans are travelling behind each other on the highway, they have to come to a compulsory halt. This would be signalled by any driver going in the opposite direction to the caravan at the front, raising the hand and stretching the fingers in the 'Caravan 5'.

I'd heard of parliamentary workers who'd been disciplined for running paid tours of the House and I decided Candy Aloha would be ideal for this. She specialises in wealthy American tourists and enlists Stiggy to pose as the 'Vice Prime Minister' giving an after-lunch speech for them. Candy's boss, Nick

Buckley, finds out but Candy claims the tourists are his constituents. Nick wonders how many American ex-patriots live in his Humberside constituency! Candy augments the income from the tours by reselling items from the Houses of Parliament Shop at more than the retail price to her guests.

Vernon du Chine bribes a court official to give him information about a fellow MP prosecuted for kerb crawling in an early morning sitting arranged by Terry Dunning to avoid any press coverage – Vernon's after the miscreant's seat. Vernon du Chine threatens to expose Terry Dunning's protection of the kerb crawler unless Dunning finds him a safe seat at the next election. Dunning, pushing Du Chine into a toilet cubicle, reminds him that Dunning himself has enough dirt on Du Chine to expose him and reminds him that Dunning does the blackmailing of MPs, not the other way around – pushing him down onto the only seat he'll have – the toilet seat!

Darren Watling takes Brian Lightfoot's researcher, Jane Browning, out to dinner and manages to wheedle out of her proposed future Lib Dem policies. He's particularly taken with the plan to take all waterways back into public ownership: angling is the most popular participation sport in the country. Nick Buckley seizes on Darren's stolen policy. He discovers that the Ramblers' Association is to organise a right to walk protest across an aristocrat's estate. This will conclude in a mass fish-in on the banks of the estate's salmon-packed river in protest at the private ownership of river banks. Come the day, there is huge media interest but the protest misfires badly: there is a counter protest by Biteback, an anti-angling group, who disrupt the fish-in.

Originally, there were supposed to be two or three writers

but they didn't emerge at first. Richard Stoneman and Farrukh Dhondy were to come on board further down the line. John Fortune turned up to one script meeting but I never saw him after that! Interestingly, he's billed on the programme's credits as an adviser but I'm not sure what or whom he advised. I also remember a programme day trip to meet the 'Yes, Minister' creator Anthony Jay in his beautifully appointed Cotswold home. I don't remember much about the day except that it was very convivial! Anthony Jay was also credited as an adviser: I think the programme makers in giving both he and John Fortune credits were hoping for some stardust to attach itself to the programme. Meanwhile I cracked on to write the first six episodes. Time was short and, if I'm honest, by this point, I was regarding the series as my baby. There was little time to develop scripts and what was done was largely by myself and the producer and Peter Ansorge and his assistant Beth at Channel 4. Edward wasn't involved in the development of the scripts: he would attend the odd script meeting but took no active part. The script meetings were slightly inhibited as a result of our knowing there was an armed Royal Protection Officer sitting ten feet down the corridor.

My chum jumped ship as producer. I think he sensed that the task ahead was impossible and Richard Hanford came on board. Richard was a very experienced long series producer. One coup of his was finding a decommissioned Victorian asylum in Berkshire which was to double for the House of Commons (no irony intended there).

The series was shot at Teddington Studios and the read-through and rehearsals took place in the Twickenham Sea Scouts hut. The first episode read-through was quite an occasion with

Peter Ansorge and the Earl of Wessex in attendance. It went very well and all concerned were convinced they had a sure fire hit on their hands. However, as we neared transmission, we only had four or five episodes in the can.

Two royal asides as part of the production process. There was a rumour at the time that Princess Diana was considering standing as a Labour MP. Quite apart from the tradition that royalty didn't enter the Commons (although, as an earl, Edward himself had the right to sit in the Lords) this did raise the question about what relationship a New Labour Government would have with the monarchy and this was discussed animatedly in one of the episodes. I loved the idea that supporting Diana stand for New Labour was just the completely barmy sort of thing they might have done as part of a sovereign-public partnership: the princess of the people as a representative of the people. I asked Edward to enquire of Diana whether she'd be up for a cameo: I just wanted her to cross the end of a corridor or be seen entering the Labour whips' office. I guess we could have used a lookalike but I was after a water cooler discussion about whether it was her, given we'd used real MPs in the show already. I never heard back from Edward.

The producers were keen to use the crowned portcullis, the symbol of Parliament, as the central image of the programme credits and approached the parliamentary authorities for permission to use it. They demurred, politely informing them that licensed use of the symbol was the gift of the Queen. It was agreed that to ask Edward to request from his mum permission to use the symbol might be a request too far with any agreement looking too much like a licence by the monarch of the programme. 'By Appointment to HM the Queen, makers of satirical comedy programmes…!' In the end, as you can see from the programme currently running on All 4, a rather fetching version of the symbol was used, minus the crown on top of the portcullis.

Publicity for the series was wall-to-wall as transmission approached. A fortnight before, Michael Brown MP hosted a launch event at the Commons for the press. By invitation only, people were still turned away at the door. Although TV cameras were banned, radio journalists were able to do recorded interviews. Driving home down the M2, I switched from station to station, listening to myself saying pretty much the same thing. An old mate actually rang my mobile and exclaimed, 'Andy – you're on the radio!', as if I might not have known about it. Preview copies were unavailable to the press because the final version of each episode was subject to a final cut the week before transmission to accommodate last minute topical events. Previews were therefore descriptive and anticipatory, rather than evaluative. On the day of transmission, I spent the day racing round London doing more radio interviews before sitting down to watch a preview of the opening episode with Edward and the others at Charlotte Street. I then legged it to catch the Victoria train and ran into the flat in Canterbury as the credits went up to watch it live with Elaine.

Critical response to the opening episode was largely positive with a couple of fence sitters reserving judgement until later in the series. Max Davidson in the Mail thought it was a 'stylish debut' with a 'sharp script' and '[deft] performances'. Thomas Sutcliffe in the Independent thought, 'as a maiden speech it wasn't bad at all'. Matthew Bond in the Times thought it 'looked terrific' with 'top flight, middle-aged character actors' and Sean Day-Lewis in The Observer thought it made 'an accessible, sharp pacey start'. Banksy, in The People, liked the 'cracking one-liners'. And Christopher Dunkley in The Financial Times thought, 'The opening episode was quick, funny and – pleasingly naughty'.

In the end, the decision to re-edit each episode the week of transmission to make it topical didn't work. And I do think someone in the team with a modicum of technical knowledge should have known this. The routine was that I'd go into Channel 4 the Monday morning before each episode on the Thursday. I'd confer with Peter Ansorge, Beth and Richard Hanford before catching a train back to Canterbury. I'd spend the afternoon and evening either re-writing existing scenes or adding new ones. These would go back to C4 and Teddington overnight and the director would rehearse and record the new material on the Tuesday. This would be edited on the Wednesday, ready for transmission on the Thursday. There were a number of problems with this. Firstly, the sheer technical challenge of integrating the new (sometimes filmed on outside broadcast) material into an already locked off episode was underestimated. The aspiration was to have a *Drop The Dead Donkey* kind of topicality. But when you look closely at DTDD, the new material is added, as voice over, at the end of the first half and over the final credits only. This was technically quite straightforward. Secondly, it was quite possible that nothing remarkable happened that week at all. Or that the story would break on Tuesday to Thursday so that we'd miss it completely. Either way, given the speed at which political developments occur, events which happened only a week before would look unremarkable by the next Thursday and be lost in the episode overall. After five or six weeks of this, I convinced everyone it wasn't working and the practice was dropped.

Although *Annie's Bar* began with an audience of 1.9M, very respectable for a C4 programme, it didn't hold on to that figure. We did try a number of ruses to boost viewers during the run but the audience numbers didn't improve on the first episode. Peter Ansorge implored me to write an all-night sitting episode but I couldn't work out how that might sit with the narratives we already had running.

I believe we sustained a high standard of writing throughout the series: in fact, I'm particularly proud of the final episode, which I recently watched for the first time in twenty-five years. It's the night of the crucial vote, following the health debate. In the chamber, members are discussing the new Government policy, Care on the High Seas. The plan is to use decommissioned warships as psychiatric hospitals to house patients, or 'customers' as the Minister calls them. Customers can purchase basic accommodation or 5-star accommodation on the refitted Royal Yacht Britannia.

Vernon Du Chine is afforded a helicopter to take him to two potential constituencies, on the understanding that he returns to London in time for the vote.

Terry Dunning's desperate not to lose the knife-edge vote. He makes the walking wounded attend the House. He discovers intending abstainers hiding in the bogs, their feet up on the toilet seats and kicks them out. On the phone to the very poorly Greville Beacham's wife, he enquires about Beacham's current condition, 'His doctors reckon he'll die if he's moved? Well, I'll take the risk if you will, Mrs Beacham……No, no, it's not a problem that he's not conscious – many in the lobby

228

aren't as it is.' In New Palace Yard, Dunning and the Labour whip, Graham Keegan go in to the ambulance in order to nod through Greville Beacham, on a stretcher, with an oxygen mask on. Keegan asks how can be sure this is Greville Beacham. Does Keegan think Mrs Beacham is a con artist? Dunning asks.

Meanwhile, a Labour member, Bunter Hargreaves, has expired having sex with his secretary. The vote gets tighter.

Vernon du Chine's helicopter abandons him at a constituency selection because of a fog warning and he doesn't make it back for the vote.

Finally – the vote. Dashwood goes into the Opposition lobby. The Government lose…by one vote. Dashwood's. He apologises to the Minister of Health who is forced to resign. Apologising to him, Dashwood is told by the Minister: 'You can only afford principles when you've nothing to lose. You'll learn that.' A touching ending as Jimmy Mackenzie and Dashwood pass in the corridor. Jimmy thanks him for his vote. 'Virtue is its own reward – I think that was Aristotle.' 'I certainly can't think of any other advantages,' Dashwood replies. Admiringly, Jimmy tells Dashwood he reminds him of himself thirty years ago. 'Passionate…I still am…sometimes.' The direction was also of a consistently high standard, as was the acting, with only a couple of ham performances from minor characters.

I believe there were a number of factors contributing to the programme's failure to attract an audience. One was the short lead time between commission and transmission. Ardent's Malcolm Cockren makes this clear, 'It could have been a huge success for Ardent. Channel 4 found a spot but then they decided to bring the whole thing forward by something like three to six months.' Peter Ansorge, who commissioned the programme, confirmed this. '…we lunged into it. Our problem was not with the company but that we had bitten off more than we could chew. Edward had surrounded himself with good people.' This meant that we didn't have the time to think through the structure and tone of the series as a whole. Nor did we have the time to develop all the scripts before the series was then shot, edited and transmitted. We were still producing first drafts of later episodes as the first episode went out! On other programmes I've written for, each script would go through at least three or four drafts over a lengthy period before being handed to actors.

A senior BBC executive commented to one of our directors six or seven episodes in that *Annie's Bar* still hadn't worked out what it was and I feel this was very perceptive. We had a whole range of comedy genres represented: some Carry On here, some farce there, elements of comedy drama, sitcom and even Grand Guignol. Furthermore, our narrative structure fell between two stools. If we'd followed soap rules, we would have had three or four strong story lines continuing through the series, maybe dropping one or two and picking up one or two on the way. This would hopefully have kept and built an audience. On the other hand, we could have taken an anthology approach. So, each episode would have one or maybe two stories which were resolved at the end of the episode. As it was, we had stories which lasted two episodes and could then disappear and pop up several episodes later. Or stories which lasted one or two episodes and finished.

All this aside, I have a strong sense that, however long we'd had to develop the programme, the media wouldn't have allowed it to succeed for reasons I outlined earlier. This narrative of flop and failure preceded the programme, ran alongside it and interestingly, hardened up after it. So, we have Stuart Miller, in his article above, casually describing it as 'a horrific flop...it wasn't even funny'. And journalist John Naughton includes it in his 50 worst UK TV shows. I was miffed that we only made Number Five behind 'Naked Jungle', 'Minipops', 'Triangle' and 'Quickfire Balls'. And, if *Annie's Bar* was so dire, why are Channel 4 running the whole series on All 4, a quarter of a century after transmission?

Chapter 8 – The ones that got away

The pitch of a proposal to a broadcaster might then result in a commission for a script. Further scripts could then be commissioned for a serial or series. You might then be asked for redrafts of scripts. If you were very lucky, something would eventually get made but usually it didn't. Don't be a screenwriter. My life's work is in a four-drawer filing cabinet. Three of the drawers are full of stuff which didn't get made and only one drawer is full of produced scripts. This chapter will focus on the former.

Sometimes, pitches just don't get anywhere. I remember going to a broadcaster with a great idea for a cruise ship project which I mentioned above. I'd meticulously researched it and had a really hot pitch document. The drama controller didn't even look at it. He simply invoked an earlier seaborne series that had been unsuccessful. 'Got anything else?' he asked, eyes glazed over. At some point, British TV drama stopped being original. Broadcasters were only interested in ideas that were like something else which had already been successful. So, it's now the turn of my projects in the three lower drawers. I said in Chapter 4 above that good ideas for projects lie all around us and it's just a matter of nosing the truffle out of the ground. And, to use a contrasting metaphor, a good idea comes with a glittering halo around it – it's unmistakable. All the projects below share these qualities.

The BBC single dramas I wrote but which didn't get made were all pitched as ideas directly to producers in the days when producer-auteurs had slots in BBC single drama series such as Screen 1 and Screen 2. Producer Fiona Finlay was interested in an idea I came up with for *Moonlight and Roses*. My dad had died in the early 1970s and I'd seen my step-mother, Gladys, regularly thereafter. She'd had a tough life. Born in 1920, she lived in the house she was born in, in Eccles, until the day she died in 2002. She had worked in a munitions factory the other side of Manchester in WW2 ('I had to get three buses there and three buses back'). There was some sense that she'd been unlucky in love, even lost someone in the war but no-one ever went there! Although they'd been close partners for five years, they married in 1971 but Dad had died two years later and she spent the last thirty years of her life widowed. I was then forty and was beginning to get my first intimations of mortality. I looked at Gladys and wondered about life seventy plus. Was it depressing reaching the end of your life, knowing there was little left to achieve, you'd thrown life's dices and won or lost? Or was it, as I suspected, being forty and feeling eighteen, nothing like that: that love, success and achievement were still all there for the taking?

So *Moonlight and Roses* (it was Gladys' favourite song) follows Ellen into an adult education centre. There she bonds with members of the drama group. Mid way through the course, the centre decides to chop drama and other non-vocational courses which don't hit 'performance indicators' like progression or employment. Ellen is livid and rails at the Principal:

*ELLEN: Listen – you can tell those masters of yours – the ones
you're really accountable to – that it's places like this
keep the geriatric wards from overflowing in this city.
I know you can't measure it but it's true. You can tell
them that turning off brains is as bad as turning off
gas, turning off electricity. No – it's worse – far worse.
And you can tell them we'll go out and do something
for people, not because it generates income but because
it gives them pleasure and us pleasure. And you can tell
them – we shan't be measuring that either!'*

I had been struck, doing research for this project, what
a melting pot Adult Education was (I'd already known this
having taught in Adult Education myself for some years). I
also knew that it was a favourite political football of both local
and national politicians. I visited a wonderful adult education
centre on the corner of Oxford Road in Manchester and, six
months later, decided I'd like to make a return visit. When
I rang to arrange this, a painter and decorator answered the
phone. His voice echoing in the empty building, he said the
council had sold the building and moved the centre to Moss
Side. I chuckled at the thought of left-wing Labour politicians thinking that if the blue rinse ladies of Altrincham really
wanted to crochet, they could travel to Moss Side to do it. In
fairness to those politicians, this relocation was probably about
serving the greatest need and when I visited the Moss Side
Centre, I saw it was just that.

The film follows Ellen as she becomes the driving force of
a senior choir which tours care homes in the area and enter-
tains the residents. There is great debate over the repertoire:

they begin with music from the 30s and 40s, thinking that's what the residents want to hear but, in the end, consider this music over-sentimental and whimsical and they include more contemporary, gutsy numbers such as *Hey, Big Spender*. Ellen has a love affair with fellow chorister Vic but Vic, feeling he's second fiddle to the choir, walks away. Ellen lets him. I didn't know that 'Young at Heart', a chorus of elderly folk, had been formed in the US in the early 80s but didn't hit our shores until the 90s. Life (pre) imitates art!

I've just finished reading *Turkish Delight* for the first time in thirty years. It was commissioned by Ruth Caleb as a BBC Screen 2. I'm not surprised it was never made. It reads like an episode of a comedy drama. In fact, I was reminded of *Benidorm*, which I'm an enormous fan of. Derren Litten's writing and the acting of a very talented cast were sublime. I've always been tempted to write about package holidays and tried before with *Too Much in The Sun*, a theatre play inspired by a package holiday to Tenerife in the late 70s. There was a power station a short way along the coast, which you couldn't really ignore. Five lads who had already been expelled from one hotel were in residence in the chalet next to us. They dive bombed everyone in the pool and, when we complained, all five urinated against our chalet door when they returned from the bar. They were from Luton, as I remember. Package holidays offer endless comic possibilities, as *Benidorm* demonstrates. People think they can leave their troubles behind them but their troubles always follow them. Holidays offer folk the opportunity to start afresh, meet new people who might be impressed with them, particularly when they lie about themselves. They can demonstrate British superiority over other cultures, particularly that of their host country. They can indulge in all manner of delusions. Linda has come away with husband Barry – they have been trying for a baby and this will be the magical trip. But it goes badly. She has a sunset conversation on the beach with Steven, a laid-back guy who's there on his own:

LINDA: Nice at this time, isn't it?

STEVEN: I can't understand why nobody comes down to watch the sunset. Sunrise and sunset. They travel all this way and miss the best bits. Not surprising, I s'pose. People seem to spend half their holiday thinking about the past – how the food was better last year, the hotel the year before – and the rest of the time obsessed with the future – getting a tan they can swank about, taking snaps they can show around when they get home.

LINDA: The tan fades and no-one's interested in the photos.

STEVEN: Yeah…why can't people just live for the moment… in the moment?

LINDA: Because they get off the plane with dreams that… (She starts to sob) …turn into nightmares'

Steven will oblige Linda with the task allotted to husband Barry on the last night of the holiday.

An independent producer contacted me. She'd received a story idea from someone who'd spent time in a spinal injuries unit. Would I be interested? We went up to meet with the originator of the story, Alan Snell on The Wirral. Alan was a paraplegic who had been admitted to the Merseyside Area Spinal Injuries Unit in the Promenade Hospital, Southport, following an accident. Most of those in the unit were young and, because of the nature of their injuries, had previously led highly active lives and therefore their adjustment to lives with such severe disabilities was particularly difficult. What gave the film such potential was the camaraderie in adversity that the lads developed. A key draw for me was that Alan described their meetings in the unit's bogs, like naughty school boys. A running theme of these meetings was the lads plotting the perfect fantasy crime. They reckoned they could hoodwink the police who wouldn't be able to believe that people in wheelchairs were capable of committing such crimes!

I produced a treatment for a single drama, *Walkie Talkie*. This was the phrase used by the lads to describe able-bodied people and the successful completion of the 'crime' was a way of getting one over on them and the closest the lads would get to being like them again. My main character was Gary, a British Transport Police Officer, admitted to the unit following a fall while chasing a fugitive and the early stages of the film shows him adjusting to his injury. Gary's neck is broken and his spine is severed at T8. He will be paraplegic for the rest of his life - paralysed from the waist down. In the unit, he meets his fellow patients. There is Alan, ex-marine, ex-forester, who fell thirty feet from a tree and like Gary, is a paraplegic: he's reached an angry uncomfortable stalemate with his injury. Dave is a quadriplegic (paralysed from the neck down) a witty, chain-smoking biker who dived into six feet of water in Blackpool and hit a girder. Rick is a posh graduate drop-out who was injured in a dangerous sports accident and, although a paraplegic, is the least injured of them all and, as a result, the most embittered because, physically, he's closest to the able-bodied existence they've all lost.

The film follows the struggles of each of these characters as they come to terms with their new lives. The relationship between them strengthens because they share a predicament and become alienated from those outside, particularly their families. And the fantasy crime becomes an actual crime, the 2nd Great Train Robbery. Alan's had it in for the railways ever since, on a recent trip home, he was made to sit in the guard's van (this was the 1990s – there were still guards' vans where the mail was stored. But the railways can still be appalling in their treatment of disabled people in other ways today). Alan drew the line when mailbags and parcels were thrown in on top of him. Passengers in wheelchairs are themselves treated like cargo – as if railway staff can't see them. Gary confesses that before he became a BTP officer he worked, like many of his colleagues, on the railways. In fact, he worked as a guard! He confirms what Alan said. Wheelchairs were always a nuisance to guards: he never thought he'd end up as the nuisance himself. But Alan may have something – as a guard and transport police officer, he knows vans are insecure. The guard is constantly up and down the train collecting tickets and can't possibly guarantee the security of the contents of the guard's van. And, of course, no-one'd suspect the poor guy in the wheelchair, locked in the cage with all of it!

Gary learns from a mate of his in BTP CID of a Liverpool drugs gang who they think are sending regular consignments by Red Star and receiving the cash payment by return the same way. So, the police are staking out the train in question. And the sort of money being talked about would save the spinal injuries unit from its threatened closure (it was important to keep the audience on the side of our lads as per an Ealing Comedy).

It is Gary who is pushed up the ramp into the guard's van of the Liverpool train. The plan is that Gary will locate the suspect parcel. Meanwhile, Alan will pretend to get his wheelchair stuck on a level crossing after the barriers go down to let Gary's train through. The train would come to a halt, leaving the guard's van, as they have carefully calculated, on the bridge above Dave and others below. Gary will push the parcel of drugs cash out of the window to be retrieved by Dave below. However, once on the level crossing, a helpful Samaritan responds to Alan's plight and, in spite of his desperate protests, pushes him to safety. So, Gary is stuck with the cash parcel but, at Lime Street, he is able to pass safely by his monitoring colleague BTP CID colleagues who wave him cheerily through, the cash hidden under the blanket of his wheelchair.

In the 1990s, trade wars began between EU countries. In particular, French farmers started to wage warfare in order to block British lamb imports. They blockaded ports, hijacked trucks, set up roadblocks, destroyed carcasses and dumped them in front of town halls and police stations in what became known as 'The Lamb Wars'. The heart of the problem was that French sheep raised on small family-owned farms couldn't compete against imports from large British farms that had close links with big meat-exporting companies. (There is no primogeniture in French inheritance law. Unlike in Britain, where the oldest sibling wins all, on a French farmer's death, his property is divided between all the siblings. So French farms become smaller from generation to generation.) French lamb production had risen sharply to meet growing domestic consumption, but so did British imports. French farmers blamed the jump in these imports, up thirty per cent in the first four months of

1990, for the collapse in prices. The idea to base a film on this was brought to me by David Stacey, then a fledgling producer (destined to be the High Sheriff of Shropshire in 2015-16) and Josh Golding, whom I'd met when he was Kennith Trodd's script editor at the BBC.

To research this project, David persuaded a Welsh meat exporter (he lived on the Welsh borders) to allow us to accompany a lorry loaded with lamb from Wales down to Poitiers in the hope that it might be attacked. We chose a re-frigerated wagon rather than get involved in the dubious ethics of accompanying live exported animals. I sat in the cab with the driver and David followed in his car at a discreet distance behind. We caught the overnight Poole – Cherbourg commercial ferry. In the morning, having heard that French vets were making only cursory examinations to check on exported animals' welfare, I decided to follow a vet on his rounds at Cherbourg port. This was 1991 and my primary evidence gathering tool was a (rather cumbersome) camcorder. This I secreted under my coat as I stalked the vet from wagon to wagon. I was curious that, every time I switched the camcorder to Record, the vet swung round and stared at me. I abandoned my pursuit and wondered what had drawn the vet's attention. On inspection, I discovered the camcorder had a large red light attached to the lens which glowed when the device was switched to Record and it was this the vet was seeing. Investigation foiled!

The six-hour journey to Poitiers was uneventful but we had a good look around the town for a day or so; it was to become Pondriers in our film. On the way, David used his (extensive) French contacts to get us introduced to members of the French farming community. His French was impressively fluent which helped enormously with these meetings.

Fleeced was therefore to be essentially a road movie, starting in a Welsh border country town. Livestock trader and lorry fleet owner John Verne, landed farmer Beaumont and two young farmers as well as a Beaumont's tenant farmer, Geraint, decide unanimously that they will take a convoy of live sheep down to Pondriers, in an attempt to take their goods to market, by force if necessary. Their departure is widely covered by the media…which doesn't go unnoticed by the British Transport Secretary who is also scheduled to go to Pondriers but on the TGV from Bordeaux. He is to celebrate Anglo-French co-operation with his French counterpart M. Lafayette and Pierre Vivier, the mayor of Pondriers. Vivier's son, Jean, is a leader of the regional activist farmers. Mackay, the Transport Secretary, fears that the British farmer's convoy will keep him off the front pages so arranges for a couple of MI6 'mischief merchants' to stop them getting there. French Securite are also sending a couple of operatives who are going to pretend to be English as a form of disguise and attempt to stop the convoy.

Meanwhile, Brigitte, Pierre Vivier's daughter, is returning from the UK where she is a student and hitches a ride with Alan, one of the convoy drivers at Portsmouth Harbour. On the same ferry will be Janet Saville, Inspector with the People's Society for the Prevention of Cruelty to Animals and Bob Fleming with his two children Kirsty and Luke, who are pretending to be the model, France-bound, caravanning family. Saville is following the convoy in order to monitor the welfare of the livestock.

French farmers try to turn the convoy round at Port St Quentin but the Brits call their bluff and drive the wagons at the very expensive French tractors forming the blockade which reverse out of the way at the last minute.

After overcoming all the hazards put in their way, the convoy finally approaches Pondriers. But the French, posing as garage hands, have managed to fill the diesel-engined wagons with petrol. Their valves are burnt out and the injectors have melted. There's nothing for it but to drive the sheep into town by foot. As the sheep approach the town centre ceremony, the French farmers, led by Jean Vivier, let off bird scarers and klaxons, as part of their demonstration. The sheep scatter ending the ceremony. As the French approach the Brits, who ready themselves for the battle, Alan, the lorry driver, gives a stirring speech, translated by Brigitte at his side:

ALAN: *British farmers have their problems. French farmers have theirs. But neither side has caused the others'…. We only fight when we feel we've lost control over our lives, when others are taking decisions we feel we can't do anything about. But, in the end, the people can't be made to do what they don't want. Any of us. So, we've got far more in common than anything which divides us. We shouldn't be fighting each other but the real enemy…*

Both French and Brits applaud loudly, cheer and whistle.

The producers who commissioned *Fleeced* hated it. They thought it read like a sitcom. Thirty years on, I'm ready to take issue with them. It reads like a comedy drama verging on farce in the Ealing Comedy tradition. Like *Car Wars*, it is about nationalism, prejudice and internationalism. Although set very firmly in the early, pre-Channel Tunnel, 1990s, its issues are directly relevant to post Brexit Britain and Europe. Of the ones that got away, it is one of the most deserving of production.

In 1997, Richard Hanford and I developed a proposal for a single drama, *Twitchers*. Twitchers are fanatics who will travel hundreds of miles for a 'twitch', a sighting of a rare bird, earning them a 'tick' to add to their lifetime's list. For them, the rare bird is everything and they should be distinguished from ornithologists and birdwatchers whose interests are of a more general nature. Twitchers are usually men, generally from their 30s to their 50s, from all social backgrounds. Any women tend to be hangers-on, or twitching widows who refuse to be left at home again. With an R.S.P.B. membership of over 1/2 million and a hard core of 20,000 keen birders, there were reckoned to be around 3-4000 regular twitchers. Although an interest in birds may simply arise from disillusionment with urban, hi-tech living and a consequent turning to the natural world, twitching seems to offer its devotees everything they are desperate to recapture - the playground seems to permeate their activities. Male friends, in intense competition with others, often travel together, collecting ticks compiled compulsively into lists and, if they're very successful, national league tables. Like kids camping out in the garden, they brave freezing nights waiting for the dawn chorus. They have their own magazines, their 'comics'. Their language is partly Famous Five/Biggles ('Duff Gen' is misleading information about a rare bird's presence, possibly obtained from the twitcher's coded enquiry, 'Anything about?') partly macho laddish (A 'mega-crippler' is a near miss - a 'cosmic mindfucker' a particularly rare sighting).

Apart from exploring this refusal to grow up, an unwillingness, perhaps, to accept the pain and responsibilities of adult life, the peculiarly obsessive nature of twitching had, for us, enormous dramatic and comic potential. What makes a 30/50-year-old go to the lengths of driving long hours, even chartering planes and hiring boats just to see a bird through his scope? One prominent twitcher, Roger Johnson, crept out of his wedding reception and drove two hundred miles in morning suit and carnation to see an Isabelline Shrike on Portland Bill. Unsurprisingly, wife Susan left him eighteen months later citing mental cruelty. He'd abandoned his sister-in-law's birthday to see a Harlequin Duck on Shetland but when he got back there were reports of a Brunwich's Guillemot so he was off again before Susan could tell him she was leaving him. Why are the Roger Johnsons driven by this feverish urge of the collector? Collecting, list-making, compilation certainly seem to be obsessions among middle aged males if not our culture as a whole: hardly a week goes by without a list of some kind dominating the media: Best Britons, Rich List, All Time Sporting Moments. Is our culture so impoverished, our lives so sterile that we are left to catalogue the achievements of other times? Or is classification an attempt to impose some order on a world which we, and in particular the contemporary male, feel we have lost control of? Or, is there something else linking the migrating birds and the flocks of middle-aged men who follow them? One twitcher pointed out that rare birds were often where they shouldn't be as a result of freak weather conditions or the mechanism in their heads which gave them a sense of direction going badly wrong. And, more often than not, they die. Aren't disorientation and a sense of doom major features of the crises of middle age?

Our tragi-comic drama would have focussed on a twenty-four hour race which the central character, Frank Gillot, enters, the object of which is to spot as many birds in that period as possible. He enlists the support of lifelong best friend, Barry Alcroft, who, although a keen birder, is less obsessive than Frank. However, Frank's wife, Pat, refusing any longer to be a twitching widow, decides on coming along. Not to be left out, Barry's Jean insists on joining the party too. So, the foursome, much to Frank's irritation - this is a race to be won, not a day out - set off in two cars. The Gillots and the Alcrofts have a lot in common: now in their 50s, they went to school together, grew up and stayed in their part of the North of England, bringing up two children each. But they differ in important respects: Frank has been seen to have done so much better than Barry in spite of the reverse being expected. While Frank took an apprenticeship as a draughtsman after leaving school at sixteen, Barry stayed on, took A Levels, went to university and became a school teacher. Frank eventually started his own building firm which he developed into a major concern, selling it recently for reputed millions and retiring at fifty. Barry refused to climb the management ladder in education, preferring to stay in the classroom where he remains. Pat Gillot could afford, and indeed was ordered by Frank, to stay at home after the children came along, whereas Jean Alcroft continued with her nursing job. It is, however, recent changes that bring events to a dramatic climax in the course of the race. Pat - now following a return-to-learn access course at her local college and having undergone in one term a transformation from pale housewife to assertive intellectual - begins to question the quality of their life and Frank's boastfulness about their wealth. Frank's dominance and control begins to fragment for the first time. Jean, bitterly resentful of Frank's patronizing treatment of both Barry and herself over the years, summed up in his sneer that the Alcrofts have devoted their lives to others instead of looking after themselves, needs no encouragement to be open with Frank now. And she foments rebellion in Barry, encouraging him to confront his lifelong friend (hesitantly, as it turns out) with his feeling that their friendship exists simply to allow Frank to enjoy his assumed superiority.

We would have followed our characters, for what would effectively have been a twitching road movie, pursuing birds from North Norfolk to the South Coast, Dorset to Morecambe Bay, from Flamborough Head to the Western Isles. They would have become involved in some bizarre incidents at unusual venues (Tesco shoppers were trapped in the Maidstone store in 1992 when 3500 twitchers converged on the car park after learning that a Golden-winged Warbler had landed there. A Rose-Coloured Starling took a liking to a lady in the remote Surrey village of Christmas Pie but refused to budge from her garden. Twitchers formed an orderly queue to climb a ladder to see the bird - their sleeves were tugged if they stayed too long - and were obliged to make a cash donation to the R.S.P.B.).

As a result of Frank's confrontations with the other three characters in the course of the twenty-four hours, each deserts him. The film does, however, end hopefully. Filthy and exhausted from spending a night in a ditch, a lone Frank is rewarded with a dawn sighting of the lesser short-toed lark - its first appearance in Britain for thirty years. After reporting his sighting to Birdline and anticipating kudos and celebrity in the birding world, Frank has second thoughts. He calls again and apologises for his false report: he's mistakenly identified the creature. The man obsessed with winning, with success, has deliberately thrown it away. In the lost lark, he has suddenly seen a reflection of his own life blown off course. As he watches the bird, he realizes he is looking at something perfect which needs nothing more to complete it. And Frank finally accepts himself the way he is - with no need for achievements, particularly rare bird sightings, to make him feel he is somebody.

Both Richard and I thought James Bolam would be perfect as Frank (I wonder if the Manchester Library Theatre script report - Chapter 3 - comparing the relationship of Alan and Frank in *Marking Time* with *The Likely Lads* had stayed with me over 20 years?). We went down to see James at his home in Billingshurst, West Sussex and had a very enjoyable lunch of smoked salmon and strawberries with him and his wife, the actor Susan Jameson. I'd fallen in love with Susan Jameson when she appeared in *When the Boat Comes In* and was delighted to finally meet her.

White Lies was a single drama proposal created in 1989. Leo Benedictus writes in The Irish Times: '...Rahila Khan's... stories about British Asian teenagers were broadcast on the BBC, leading to a book called *Down The Road, Worlds Away* being published by Virago in 1987. Khan was in fact a man teaching religious education at a girls' boarding school. Her real name was the Rev Toby Forward.

Forward had wanted modern writing with a Muslim background to use in his lessons, but found little, so he wrote his own. He wondered if BBC Radio 4 might be interested but was terrified of rejection, so he sent a story under a nom de plume.

…Listeners loved (Khan's) work. She was encouraged to publish. The only imprints taking this type of short story were the Women's Press and Virago. Forward hoped that Virago would back out when he refused to meet them. When they didn't, Khan signed a contract. She was supposed to promote the book, give a radio talk, write a newspaper article. There is no good time to admit you've been deceiving people, but later is worse. Forward confessed to his agent, who told Virago, which removed the books from sale and pulped them, furious.

Critics said that Forward had stolen an opportunity from a real Asian woman. He insists this never occurred to him, nor would it, because he doesn't see fiction that way. He was writing about being an outsider, a feeling he knew well from his own poor background. The alter egos, as he wrote at the time, "released me from the obligation of being what I seem to be so that I can write as I really am. When it comes to an author's life…It shouldn't matter to the reader who this person is.'"

I was interested in key questions about Forward's experience, questions which seem even more relevant today than they did thirty years ago. Was the selection for a nom de plume that of a minority ethnic woman an immoral deception as Virago believed? Or was it understandable that Forward realized that authors were often published because of who they were, rather than the quality of their prose? Witness the contemporary plethora of celebrity memoirs of varying quality. Didn't Forward's alter egos free him to say what he really wanted, rather than being conscious of his identity as a priest and teacher? In my piece, the character based on Forward says to his wife at the end of the film: 'I didn't know who I was once. Then I thought I'd found out. Now – I don't know again.' There is a long literary history of first-person narratives by fictional characters, from *Moll Flanders*, arguably the first novel, onwards. Interestingly, though we know Defoe as the author of *Moll Flanders*, the original printing did not have an author, as it was an apparent autobiography. The attribution of *Moll Flanders* to Defoe was made by bookseller Francis Noble in 1770, after Defoe's death in 1731. The novel is based partially on the life of Moll King, a London criminal whom Defoe met while visiting Newgate Prison.

Granada TV approached me. They were making a series of films each of which Rik Mayall would star in, called *Rik Mayall Presents*. I had been amused by the recently established graduate entry route into policing. I thought the comic potential of intellectually over-developed graduates entering what was essentially a practical, down-to-earth pragmatic plod culture were endless. So, my main character, which Rik was to play, was John Constable. A philosophy don at a nearby university, he wanted to swap a life of quiet contemplation for its opposite, a life of action. But of course, John wouldn't be able to leave his enquiring mind behind and it would lead to some rather eccentric policing on his part. As luck would have it, one of the students on an Open University philosophy module he was teaching was Superintendent Sproate, who ran Bramdon police station and this became Constable Constable's first posting. I met with Rik several times as I was writing the piece and he loved it. On one occasion, he stood up in the Shepherd's Bush coffee shop we were in and acted out the scenes below, which were then in dialogue form. During his first shift, John is on foot patrol.

'It wasn't long before the question of gait began to exercise him. John's natural walk was, he observed for the first time, rapid, consisting of very short steps with a high degree of shuffle. It was not far removed from a mince. This wouldn't do. Although much had been made of self-presentation during initial training, the question of walking style had never been addressed. It possibly would in a future in-service module, but his problem was immediate. Apart from provoking inappropriate responses from the public he served, John calculated that he would cover the beat in a little less than ten minutes unless he adapted his natural walk. He experimented. At first, he dramatically lengthened each step but was quickly aware that he was executing a bizarre lope. He shortened his stride and decelerated until he found himself at a very pleasant stroll. He smiled. But there was still a problem: what to do with his hands. At first, he meshed his fingers together in front and pressed them down which, although comfortable, made him appear as if he was about to go into a song and dance number. He eventually felt at ease with them clasped behind his back. The routine was completed by stops during which he would jab his hands together and then blow on them, stamping his feet simultaneously, actions he'd often observed foot patrol officers carry out.

P.C. Constable couldn't believe his luck. The lights had failed at one of the busiest junctions on the high street and it fell to him to control the traffic. As a child, the policeman on point duty, together with the conductor, represented the apexes of his ambition. He had done well in this module at the staff college. Everyone could manage the stop signal and the differing go and keep moving signals but only the better co-ordinated mastered first time the multiple signals such as stopping one queue with the left hand while waving on a second queue at a ninety-degree angle with the right. And John had been among the high fliers. After an hour at the junction, however, his arms were aching and the novelty had worn off. He was by now interested in the unquestioning obedience the drivers showed. Had the traffic decided to ignore him, he would have been powerless to do anything. He decided to test this willingness to follow rules further. Instead of waving on the High Street queue after stopping the crossing traffic, he paused, with all vehicles at a standstill. He then pointed to the driver of a leading car and mimed - film, two words. The driver climbed out and approached. John began the mime. A furious trucker opposite bellowed 'Oi mate!' The driver turned on him.

'Leave it out. I've gone and bloody missed it now!' He turned back to John. 'Hellboy 3?' he asked.

John arrogantly shook his head, sighed and held two fingers up. 'Two words, yeah – I got that,' said the driver. 'First word, second syllable. Go on…'

The switchboard had been jammed. John had been hauled off duty and now stood head hanging low in front of Superintendent Sproate.

'I think it was boredom, sir,' John confessed.

Sproate sighed, 'I know, John, I know. It's a pointless waste of resources but everyone has to do their two years on the beat, even graduate entrants. I wish it were otherwise - that you could assist with operational decision-making at the highest level but, as things stand, those are the rules. I want you back in the car, though. Straightaway. A talent like yours should be mobile.'

In spite of Rik's enthusiasm, Granada turned *Constable, Constable* down. I knew at the time that the philosophy jokes, of which there were many, would not exactly be mainstream ITV fare. I took it to David Liddiment (whom I'd first known at Granada) who was now Head of Entertainment at the BBC. Unfortunately, David had just greenlit *The Thin Blue Line*, a sitcom set in a police station starring someone called Rowan Atkinson and written by a bloke called Ben Elton. Luck – good or bad – is an important element of a writer's success – or failure. I had first discovered this when I was a member of the script panel at the Croydon Warehouse Theatre. This would meet periodically and invite writers to pitch ideas for plays. One particular writer had a stream of bad luck. On one occasion, he sat down and began to gush: 'So it's about this disabled bloke John Merrick who was treated at the London Hospital…' We had to stop him and inform him that *The Elephant Man* by Bernard Pomerance about John Merrick had had runs at the National Theatre, on Broadway and was being made into a film with John Hurt…'

He was undeterred and returned to the next script panel. 'So – there was this guy who entered the round-the-world yacht race…' We had to stop him. A play about Donald Crowhurst, the lone yachtsman, was shortly to open at the Warehouse and the panel pointed to the boat itself, currently being constructed on the stage. We never saw him again.

I learned something else about writing from the *Constable, Constable* affair. I thought it was such a good idea that perhaps I'd try it in another genre. So, I wrote two sample chapters and the outlines for a further seven chapters. I asked my agent to give it anonymously to her colleague who handled prose fiction, thinking it might make a decent comic novel. Her colleague responded once she'd looked at the material. Not a comic novel, she thought. But it'd be a wonderful TV sitcom, she went on! And the moral is: find out what you do well and stick with it. I once made an input to a Creative Writing Class at the University I taught at (there are now undergraduate and post-graduate degrees in Creative Writing there – in fact, apparently everywhere!). I repeated to the students my observation above. The lecturer took me aside afterwards. 'I wish you hadn't said that, Andy,' he said, 'you see, for their final assessment this year, they have to do one piece in a genre they feel they're strong at and another in a genre they feel weaker at'. Which is why from that day I kept well clear of Creative Writing courses as well as theatre, film and TV courses at the University.

The final series David Wheatley and I devised was *Anything Goes*. As the title implies, we thought this series had endless story potential, centering as it does on a disparate group of people who create a company offering the ultimate in service industries: they will be or do . . . well, anything legal. They are: Michael (30) a redundant hedge fund manager; Charlotte (25) beautiful, with a cut-glass accent, lives on her looks but her sophisticated veneer belies her rootless life in an army family constantly on the move - a girl educated to sound wealthy who isn't; Vin (45) is a Yorkshireman who commuted weekly in a double decker bus to building work in London until being made redundant - he continues to commute but those at home don't yet know he's unemployed; Jane (19) is a cheeky Mancunian regularly seen in Michael's supermarket eating food as she wanders around - selling the fruit of the earth is an abuse of nature and, anyway, she's skint; Ian (20) a funny, sharp Liverpudlian - he managed to get a place at a London drama school but, because of the difficulty of getting a grant for acting courses, was unable to take it up. He thought he'd come down to the capital anyway.

We envisaged this as a long-running, popular series which could play pre- or post- watershed, with selfcontained episodes offering a main storyline and one or two subplots, provided by *Anything Goes* operations. These may require role-play: our characters dress as a policeman- and woman-o-gram but get mistaken for real police on the way to the gig; they are paid to attend a dinner party in character so as to surprise and entertain other guests - obnoxious, rock star, man-eating vamp; one is a svelte male escort accompanying an upmarket female to a business dinner; another pretends to be a client's new wife to irritate his divorcing partner. Further jobs may take our characters into the world of security: guarding prize pedigree show dogs after attempts have been made on their lives; getting back the father of a young woman who asked her best friend to flirt with him in order to test her mother's suspicion about his philandering, only to see father and friend run off together.

Requests could be bizarre, made by clients unable to find the service they require in Yellow Pages: a lifer rehabilitated through sculpture, has been invited to show his large master-piece at an exhibition. Forbidden to take it himself, 'Anything Goes' are commissioned to transport it - but when it tumbles from the back of the transit and shatters, the artist is discovered inside his oeuvre; our team, summoned to a house where a ghost climbs the stairs every night, rapidly solve the mystery when they find the staircase on the other side of the wall in the neighbouring house to be constructed from the same wooden planks as their client's - the phantom comes back down the stairs when next door's bell is rung; our characters are asked to find a use urgently for three tons of bananas before they turn to liquid; there is a request to provide lookalike celebrities as decoys. Problems arise when both decoys and celebrities claim to be the real thing. There are the standard caretaking tasks such as a flatsitting job which goes wrong when team members are taken for the real owners. There are forays into the leisure sector: Wimbledon tickets secured by *Anything Goes* are unfortunately discovered to be fakes only when the clients present them at Centre Court; our team is asked to organise entertainment ranging from children's parties to cossack dancers, from majorettes to sword swallowers. And then there are the routine tasks which everyone is keen to avoid but provide the bread and butter: the contract to replace a missing packet of rawl-plugs in four thousand flat packs, or the apples omitted from the lunch-boxes of a large international conference. And *Anything Goes* find themselves fielding challenges that others have passed on: how, in the end, is the desperately unattractive man going to find a partner if the dating agencies insist on a photograph?

Each episode was to be centered on the company's base office space in central London which they occupied rent free in return for looking after it, a setting which pulsated with life as the jobs came in, the phone promising to ring at any moment with a request *Anything Goes* would always say 'yes' to and desperately wonder what they've taken on once the receiver goes down.

As the business grows and customer requests become more varied, there is room for a range of minor characters to be co-opted temporarily. Although *Anything Goes* is London-based, there is potential for stories which have a national setting, involving say car or boat delivery, as well as with international settings when, for example, team members act as air couriers.

As important as the self-contained narratives, however, are serial elements which may run through several episodes or the entire series. And it is these recurring aspects which would have acted as a central focus of both dramatic and comic interest. Our five characters share one important feature apart from their versatility - each has either lost, discarded or is yet to find their identity: Michael is now left with nothing apart from his financial acumen; nowhere has ever been home for Charlotte and possibly never will be; Vin travels to work which doesn't exist; Jane turns out to have been a runaway who still feels she can't contact her parents; Ian seems most at home pretending to be other people. How will these characters develop as individuals through their involvement with *Anything Goes*? Will they locate their real selves by constantly playing others? How will they be changed by the demands of customers, some of which may be impossible, unethical, or dangerous? Will they baulk at being treated as commodities? Where do they find the resources to complete difficult tasks? Will allegiances, affairs threaten the group? Will success and expansion lead to conflict and disillusion?

We are told that young people face an era of unprecedented geographical and social mobility, of structural change in the economy. Identity will no longer be easily found in the family, the home or the traditional workplace. *Anything Goes* follows the fortunes of a predominantly young group of people who come from all over the country to London where you can be who you want to be. We watch them find out who they are... and who they pretend to be along the way.

Miracle Girls was my only attempt at adaptation. It was

based on Ed Jones' novel '*Come Again – The Second Greatest Story Ever Told*'. Late at night, a sixteen-year old girl is the victim of a hit and run driver on the bleak Sunnymeadow Estate, Bolton, Greater Manchester. In the morning, Theresa miraculously recovers, picks herself up and makes her way to her best friend Betty's house. Theresa discovers she is capable of amazing things like disappearing and reappearing and psycho-kinesis. When a small group of her mates from the youth club run by local priest, Father Vernon, come around, they enjoy her ability to levitate all of them at the same time.

A strange UFO disgorges two figures on the Sunnymeadow Estate, an event witnessed by a crowd of youths. One of the figures is Canon Drinkwater, Father Vernon's mentor, who died some time before; the other is God. The apparently resurrected cleric makes contact with Father Vernon and explains how God, angry because humanity has turned away from Him, has been persuaded by the Canon, now an Archangel, to give it one last chance. But, after what happened last time, He isn't prepared to risk another member of the family, so has chosen to bring the lowly Theresa back to life as the new Saviour. The two of them have come down to Earth in human form to monitor her progress. They will need Father Vernon's help.

After a shopping trip in Manchester during which the girls buy what they want without having to pay, courtesy of Theresa, and Sunnymeadow heart-throb, Pete, cleans out Johnny Roadhouse, Manchester's top musical equipment store, acquiring the gear his band have always dreamed about, Betty accuses Theresa of just buying friends. When Theresa asks her what she's supposed to do, Betty suggests doing something with her powers for people who really need it.

Theresa announces to the girls that they're going to do something about the world but is vague about what that might be. She waves her hand over communion wafers she has acquired from Father Vernon and, when the girls swallow them, they find themselves in a state of ecstasy. They throw a huge party for the Estate residents. There are no fights, because there is no alcohol, and party history is truly made as a small crowd of elderly people join the fun. A long extension cable is produced and Pete and his band set up their new equipment. Of course, the neighbours complain. But Theresa gives them some of the wafers and before long they have opened up their houses to the party.

The girls move into the Presbytery at Father Vernon's suggestion. He feels their campaign to do something about the world will be more safely waged where he can keep an eye on them. God has got Himself a job in a chippy to pay His way and his good looks mean there is a long queue of women waiting to be served. God's been a great success in the area. But He urges Father Vernon to direct the girls' campaign more clearly: they need to be noticed, get organised - they need a mission, the Supreme Being opines.

At the girls' first public meeting in Bolton town square, several wheelchair-bound spectators are able to walk again. After two or three similar events, the fame of the *Miracle Girls*, as they come to be known, spreads locally, then nationally. Breakfast TV shows want to interview them, requests flood in for Theresa to open supermarkets and private functions and although she never accepts an invitation, she is said to have appeared everywhere from Sainsbury's to the roof of Liverpool Cathedral .

When Theresa appears in public, the sort of organization

reserved for music festivals is required. If the slightest indication is given of an impending appearance, the motorways of the North West become jammed within hours. Coachloads of physically disabled race against each other to be the first to arrive at the scene.

As well as the Presbytery, the Sunnymeadow Estate is buzzing. Youths in the area leave their jobs to help the organisation. There is food to be distributed; special squads are created to help keep petty crime at bay. In fact, many of the squads are made up of the petty criminals themselves, so they know what they're doing.

It's not long, however, before things begin to go wrong for the group. Donated funds go missing. Theresa agrees with Betty that a miracle here, a miracle there isn't changing the way people are. And Theresa confesses to Betty she hasn't performed a miracle for weeks, hasn't magicked the wafers. She had felt uncomfortable curing some people rather than others. But when she stopped, she was staggered to find the miracles continued: spectators were curing themselves. After a huge meeting on the moors which turns into a stampede and near riot, things are never to be the same again.

God comes to the conclusion that divine powers are wasted on human beings. Things always seem to go wrong. And he is deaf to the pleas of Father Vernon and Canon Drinkwater to give the girls a second chance.

The Police are also planning to end the miracle girls' enterprise which they regard as a threat to public order in violation of the new Criminal Justice Act. Powerful hallucinogenic drugs are planted in the Presbytery and are unfortunately taken accidentally by some of the girls with disastrous consequences before the Police can mount a raid. Although not succeeding in making a drugs bust, the Police do find the money, the goods, the musical equipment. Under interrogation, the group members betray each other. Theresa takes the blame for it all, is charged and remanded in custody. Two days later, she's found hanging in her cell.

Theresa faces God for the first time. He sympathises with her failure to save mankind. She gives him a mouthful. Why create human beings so they only appear to be able to find their own strengths by believing in the power of a being greater than themselves? She knows they don't need this dependence. She saw it when she stopped using supernatural powers herself. Isn't it about time God allowed the human race to grow up? And another thing, when a group like theirs on the estate had triumphed over their circumstances by co-operation and team spirit, why allow forces inside the group like greed and selfishness and outside, like the police threatened by the girls' power, to destroy what is so positive. Surely, God knows how tough it is to be human after his recent trip? God apologizes. Yes – He'd forgotten exactly how difficult it was. What does Theresa think he should do? Not write off the human race so easily, she replies. God smiles. He likes her nerve.

A little elderly man on the Sunnymeadow Estate tells a knot of women outside the parade of shops that a divine airship has landed in his garden. But they aren't interested.

Betty answers the knock on her door. It is Theresa, standing there in the flesh. A scream of joy. Betty dives on her. She has new clothes, eyeliner and lip gloss. She's lost all her powers, though, she tells Betty. Who needs them? asks her mate, hugging Theresa and pulling her inside.

Chapter 9 – Those who can, do…

'Those who can, do; those who can't, teach' and those who can't teach, teach teachers. It was after my year at Coronation Street that I decided my time as a full-time writer was at an end. The era of the stand-alone single drama, my clear strength, was over. Yes – the British feature film industry had been growing through the nineties but getting a movie off the ground was then more difficult than getting a TV drama made. And I had to admit that what a BBC producer had remarked much earlier in my career had some truth (she'd said it to someone else who told me!): 'Andy Armitage – superb dialogue, plotting not so hot'. So that I wasn't really cut out for any genre requiring narrative complexity or length and all TV drama then, as series or serials, had both. (I certainly wouldn't have survived in the contemporary world of streaming: we're currently on the 6th season of the American *House of Cards*, 65 episodes in – how do they do it?).

It's exciting to create drama – but TV drama requires high levels of collaboration – or, looked at another way, there are a lot of people who want to interfere! And unless you're a marquee writer (those who are so successful that they're all powerful – you'll often recognise them because they get to direct and/or executive produce the programmes they've written) you don't have much clout. You're eminently sackable if you're not compliant. And TV executives don't like your failure: because your success is their success.

There was also, for me, a question of values. When Trevor Griffiths had called TV drama the true National Theatre, you did feel you were contributing something that was socially, politically or morally valuable. This is not to undermine current TV drama, much of which is of very high quality. But TV drama, I believe, is now chiefly about entertainment, ratings and cash. I was, then, as the millennium approached, missing the social, political and moral value at the centre of what I was doing. I was also missing, well....people, the buzz of interacting with a range of folk on a daily basis. I'm a hopeless gossip and a nosey bugger, principally because I'm interested in people and their stories and I'd been deprived of this, banged up with my computer all day. Also, as a teacher, I'd got a real thrill at seeing students develop and succeed. I was under no illusion that good teachers are often unappreciated. (When Friends Re-United had burst onto the scene in the 90s, I logged in, in anticipation, to the pages of my previous schools and college to see what my ex-students would say about me. Not a word. But paeans of praise for the teachers I knew were incompetent!). However, this was somehow not important. I'd done some part-time teaching at Canterbury Christ Church for a couple of years and my colleagues there were mithering me to return full-time. So, in 1998, I took a full-time post, some ten years after I'd left.

Like other new staff, I was to have an induction conducted by a senior manager. This took place in the boardroom. The boardroom looked, through large panes of glass, over into the college chapel. Along with several others, I sat across the board room table looking into the chapel. The senior manager sat opposite, his back to the chapel. At the time, there was a severe shortage of teaching space and the chapel was converted into a lecture theatre when services were not taking place. On this particular day, the chapel was bursting with nursing students, listening to a physiology lecture. Today's topic? The anus. These were the days of the overhead projector. Images were projected onto a huge screen, maybe fifteen by fifteen feet. The lecturer was practising a reveal technique whereupon layers of transparencies were peeled back as the description of the anus took us further into the organ. From where we sat, the senior manager's head was at the centre of this anus and appeared to be rising up into it as the transparencies were removed. I could feel the vibrations from the other inductees as we struggled to control ourselves.

Within two years, I'd been promoted from Senior to Principal Lecturer and, three years on, I was Head of the Department of Post-Compulsory Education, training teachers for the Further Education sector. One of my first acts on joining up was to galvanise the department into publishing. And so began twenty years of writing educational textbooks: not as glamorous or exciting as writing TV drama but just as hard and, I think, more rewarding.

We had a Certificate in Education course for in-service staff but there was no suitable text to support students, particularly those in the completion phase, who were working towards graduate level. In 1999, we published *Teaching and Training in Post-Compulsory Education*. As I write, there are probably at least ten competitor texts but ours was the first to support FE trainee teachers working to graduate level and beyond. We didn't dream this would be published in five editions over seventeen years and become one of the key texts in the field for such a long period. I took the role of editor and myself and my colleagues contributed chapters. Susan Wallace, Emeritus Professor at Nottingham Trent University, praised the 5th edition thus:

'This fifth edition of what has surely become a classic text on teaching in further education is everything one would expect it to be: packed with practical advice for teachers, underpinned by clear and accessible discussion of relevant theory. *Teaching in Post-14 Education and Training* encourages the teacher to reflect and to review their own practice. It interrogates current concepts of professionalism and prevalent ideological approaches to vocational education and training. Its exploration of values in relation to recent educational reforms provides the reader with a model of critical analysis essential to the professional educator. This book will provide a valuable resource for teachers and teacher-trainers alike.'

I think I must have fallen in love with Alison when she first walked through my door. It would be another four years before those feelings would come to the surface. Alison had applied for The Postgraduate Certificate in Education to teach in the post-compulsory sector which I'd had validated. This was its first year of operation (the 22nd cohort of this programme has just completed, with over four hundred students trained to teach in the sector. Alison's daughter, my stepdaughter, Lauren, was to complete the programme some fifteen years after her. With distinction.) Because it was new, there were problems with our Admissions department processing applications. Alison had already been interviewed but had not heard whether she had been successful. Her fall back was to do an MA at a London University and she, understandably, needed to know, either way, if she had a PGCE place. We had a strict policy of leaving admissions to Admissions, for a variety of reasons and therefore I couldn't tell her – even though I knew her application and interview performance had been very strong.

Alison did enrol on the PGCE and excelled on it, receiving offers of employment early on while still a student. I have huge admiration for the education route Alison took. As a mother of small children, she returned to study and completed a degree. After her PGCE, she went on to take an MA in Education, paid for by her then employer, became a mentor for other student teachers and is now completing her doctorate. The introduction of undergraduate tuition fees, beginning with the Labour Government in 1998, then up to £3K in 2004 and then, in 2012, to £9000 has meant a collapse in the numbers of mature students in higher education. It is just not feasible for mature students to take on the debt that eighteen-year-olds do (it's not feasible for them either!). The Alisons of today have been disenfranchised.

My University was involved in a trans-national, EU funded education project. This enabled teachers from several countries to visit and share practice. A small group of us travelled several times to Lingen in Lower Saxony where we would observe and work with German further education teachers. I don't think it can have occurred to the project designers that not understanding German might be an insurmountable problem (I'd done A Level German but that was twenty-five years before and all I could remember was the compound verb '*wiederbelebungsversuchenanmachen*' – 'to give artificial respiration', which I'd managed to shoehorn into every essay I wrote). The German dual vocational system had been, and still is, the envy of the world but, following re-unification, the tried and trusted didactic teaching approaches were not working with a much wider range of young people in the system. I could see early on that this job was not going to be easy. I watched one teacher attempting to explain the German social security system to a group of Maler (painters and decorators) most of whom had Russian as their first language, using overhead transparencies which were illegible. Ten minutes into the session, he exclaimed 'Pause' (break) and off the Maler went for a fag. I asked him why the early break. 'They'd riot if I didn't,' he replied.

On another occasion, I watched a teacher conduct a lesson about control technology: he had the most extraordinary board technique. He would start writing at one end of the white board and continue across – it covered the entire length of the front of the room. When he reached the other side, he turned and rubbed out what he'd written as he came back. Why, I couldn't fathom. Save him a trip I suppose. But it meant the students had to have written down what the teacher had written by the end of his first trip. After about an hour of this he walked over to me seated in the corner and looked down on me. 'So, what exactly is your status in the United Kingdom?' Or, in other words, 'Who is this nosey twat spying on me in the corner?'.

The deal was that the Germans would pay our expenses when we visited them and we'd return the gesture when they came back to us. On our first trip, they put us up at the very comfortable Hotel Am Wasserfall, nestling by the River Ems. The Germans came to dinner that first night and the principal of the college sat next to me, keeping a close eye on the proceedings. I'd had a glass of white wine with the first course and changed to red for the main meat course. Half way through dinner he raised an eyebrow. 'So, zwei Farben Wein mit dem Abendessen, Andy?' 'So, two colours of wine with dinner, Andy?' When the Germans came to Canterbury we put them up at a large hotel in the city centre. We went to dinner on their first night but they were gathered grim-faced in the bar. 'Es gibt Silberfischen im Betten,' said the principal 'There are silver fish in the beds.' Even though we hurriedly rebooked them into another hotel, the sleight had been made. On our next trip to Lingen, we found ourselves in a very shabby B and B. My room had a bare lightbulb.

My colleague, John Lea, had a good idea for our next book. In *Working in Post-Compulsory Education*, he would pair colleagues and ask them to write a polemical section which would, if not oppose, then complement the other's section. I knew that my colleague, Dennis Hayes, (Dennis and I were opposed on most educational issues) was going to defend an Enlightenment concept of education. For my part, I wanted, in 'In Defence of Vocationalism', to explore the theoretical underpinning of my view that the introduction of pre-vocational and vocational programmes of learning, from the 1980s onwards, had offered important learning opportunities for young people which a narrow academic curriculum was unable to do. I'd taught on vocational programmes, specifically BTEC programmes, in FE in the early 1980s (as I write, defenders of BTEC are desperately attempting to save it from the present government's cull of vocational qualifications) and I knew that students found that the active role required of learners and the real-life practical situations this learning took place in, to be motivating factors offering a much enhanced learning experience for them than that they'd already had in more traditional academic programmes. My experience of introducing programmes such as the Certificate of Pre-Vocational education (CPVE) and then the Technical and Vocational Education Initiative (TVEI) nationally, convinced me that these had offered much richer experiences for 14+ students. I had, and so had the teachers I was training, witnessed Damascene conversions of alienated, disaffected young people who suddenly saw that these programmes encouraged and developed abilities and talents they had which had been ignored by academic curricula. Most educationists reviled the introduction of these programmes as constituting a narrow, instrumentalist, skills-based curriculum driven by ideological, social, economic and labour market factors. Only a handful of educationists saw the value of attempting to bridge the gap, of integrating academic and vocational education: Professor Richard Pring, Ken Spours among them (Ken Spours was to be a member of Mike Tomlinson's working party which produced the report recommending replacing GCSE and A Level with a diploma. The Blair Government threw this out. 2004 was an election year!).

'In Defence of Vocationalism' traces the origin of my views to Dewey and other theorists. For Dewey, knowledge and truth were to be constructed by learners from their experience: both their own previous personal experience as well as their interaction in a series of social contexts. Dewey's conception of the vocational is extremely broad: 'A vocation is any form of continuous activity which renders service to others and engages personal powers on behalf of the accomplishment of results.' Kolb acknowledges his debt to Dewey in the development of his model of experiential learning. Such learning for Kolb involves a cyclical process where the learner's concrete experience becomes the object of their reflective observation. This, in turn, leads to the development of abstract concepts which are then tested experientially in new situations. For Kolb, experiential learning has certain key features:

'First is the emphasis on the process of adaptation and learning as opposed to content and outcomes. Second is that knowledge is a transformation process, being continuously created and recreated, not as an independent entity to be acquired or transmitted. Third, learning transforms experience in both its objective and subjective forms.'

(Kolb, D.A. Experiential Learning)

Kolb also acknowledges his debt to Kurt Lewin who emphasized the central role of subjective personal perceptions in experiential learning. Lewin's work, in turn, was a stimulus both to the development of the 'reflective practitioner' of Schon and to the notion of the self-directed learner at the centre of Malcolm Knowles's 'andragogy'. Self-directedness, in the sense that effective learning can result only from the individual construing their experience as personally meaningful to them, is at the centre of the work both of Gibbs and Rogers. Key learning strategies for Gibbs include reflection, learning by doing, personal development tasks, group and project work and problem-based learning, all familiar features of vocational programmes. Rogers also puts a premium on the significance of learning to students and their ability to create meaning through their learning. This involves the whole person engaging both with their own experience and their feelings. For Lave and Wenger, situated learning involves the whole person and takes place as part of their active, lived participation in a community of practice. I have already described my discovery of Gardner's work as eye opening for me. His identification of seven distinct types of intelligence implies that students should experience a much wider range of learning opportunities than traditional schooling offers.

The Quality Assurance Agency is the body responsible for monitoring higher education in the UK. It first came into my life in the early Noughties when it carried out a Subject Review of Education. As the head of an Education department, I played a prominent role in the proceedings. And I remember being completely clueless about the whole affair. I just couldn't get a grip of the criteria we were being measured by. It was The Daffodil Competition all over again, fifty years on.

My poor colleague who had written the self-evaluation document, was charged with gathering the evidence supporting our quality. He did this in a logical way by allocating a box file for each assessment point containing relevant supporting documentation. The problem, which we never solved, was that some evidence was relevant to more than one assessment point. So that, when you opened some boxes, there was no documentation, just a slip saying 'Please see Box X, Box Y and Box Z'. The boxes covered an entire wall of the reviewers' base room. I did giggle at the thought of reviewers angrily going from box to box in search of the original documentation as if it was an egg hunt!

The review went from bad to worse. A 'huge' problem arose when the post-compulsory reviewer discovered that some of our students at one college were being taught in a centre which was physically separate from the college itself and had not undergone a resources check which the college had, even though they were being taught by staff who had been checked. It was a 'got you' moment. The reviewers seemed to be operating a total quality management approach in which the discovery of one fault undermined the whole operation. Was the enthusiasm in finding this fault by the post-compulsory reviewer related to his authorship of a competitor volume to *Teaching and Training in Post-Compulsory Education* published two years later? Was this professional jealousy? Who knows? The staff gathered in the board room for the reviewers' verdict. We scored sixteen out of twenty-four. I thought this was a pretty good score – over 60 per cent but apparently it was at the lower end of the scale. I was very angry. I knew our provision was excellent. It would take me over a decade to have this recognised.

Elaine found out about my relationship with Alison before Alison's husband did. Knowing this, Elaine rang him up and told him about it. He told their children, Lauren and Joe, fifteen and thirteen at the time. It was an explosive period. I hadn't simply fallen in love with Alison and out of love with Elaine and so, for the third time in my life, I was in love with two women at the same time. Elaine and I fought a great deal. Physically. She's a strong and very determined woman. I remember, after one bout, I was left with only the collar of my tee-shirt hanging round my neck. The scratch marks she inflicted on my arms still show up white every summer, reminding me of the pain of the time.

Alison and I began to build a life together. Literally and emotionally. We rented an unfurnished property in a village outside Canterbury and found ourselves furnishing and equipping it like newlyweds. The children, of course, took time to adjust, dividing their time between their father and mother. The rent on the village property, together with my continuing payment of the mortgage on what was now Elaine's residence, meant that money was tight so, after a year, we moved into a house back in Canterbury, owned by Alison and her husband as a rental property. However, by 2006, we were ready to house hunt.

On a cold January afternoon, we turned up at a property on the main street of the village where we'd previously rented. The occupants, themselves renting the house, were surprised to see us. This surprise, we were soon to learn, was because the estate agent had mistakenly arranged for us to view a property at the other end of the village where the occupants were waiting for us, not this one which we had wanted to view. And it was perfect. Although it had black bin liners across the windows as temporary curtains, it suited our needs exactly. It was late 18th century, detached, three bedrooms, two bathrooms – even a studio in the back garden – ideal as a den for the teenagers (the house had been a butcher's, the studio a slaughterhouse). Alison noted that I'd marched through the house, quickly, in and out of every room, just as my nephew had done the following year when he came down for our wedding. This was the one.

It took until August to sell the property Alison had acquired as part of her divorce proceedings. Shortly after moving in, we were in our new sitting room, cavernous in comparison with the cramped bungalow, deliriously singing along to *Jerusalem* on the Last Night of The Proms blasting out of our new telly at 70. Spookily, we discovered that the property we'd previously rented actually backed onto our garden. We'd been plagued by renovation noise throughout the year we were there but couldn't actually see the work going on because of the way the bathroom window was hinged. But all that work had, in the end, been for us. And we're still enjoying it.

Les Girls, day trip to France.
Clockwise – Tracy, Carol, Ali D, Nicola, Ali A

As well as becoming step-father to two children, my relationship with Alison meant I became an honorary sister of her small group of female friends, The Girls. Ali D, Tracy, Carol and Nicola terrified me at first. I found them loud and intimidating (I think their menfolk still do as a group!). In the early days, when The Girls were meeting at our place, I would make myself scarce. However, our house became the one it was most convenient for them to congregate at so I couldn't be bothered to go out. Then, I would eat dinner with them before scuttling off to watch TV elsewhere. Finally, full membership – a 'sister', as Tracy calls me. I became one of them and Alison's friends are my friends. I still do absent myself when they dabble with the cards because I find their absolute credulousness scary but I find them very funny and enjoy their company immensely. At a time of life when friendship circles naturally decrease, it's heartening to have access to a group of real friends. And like true friends they support each other. I remember when they came round en masse after Alison's hysterectomy op to do our gardening. It was touching. Mind you, Ali D still managed to uproot the asparagus patch we'd been carefully nurturing for several years.

The QAA came calling again. It had changed its methodology: it was now carrying out 'development engagements' with individual subject areas (like many education processes, it turned out to be the opposite of what it purported to be – this engagement was not developmental). Our senior management, for reasons that still escape me, had selected my area for this engagement. I had no more idea about the rules of engagement than I had in the previous subject review. Another Daffodil Competition. I remember flailing during mock interviews by the then dean, who, irked by my terrible answers to her questions, humiliatingly turned to other members of my department in search of decent answers. I should have been warned of what was to come when the engagement chair complained that the evaluation document I had written prior to the event was not evaluative. The event itself, over three days, is a blur. But it was worse than the subject review since none of the panel was an education subject specialist. We were being assessed by people who knew nothing about our subject. I do remember one moment, when a reviewer complained that our MA assignment assessment sheet didn't indicate assessment of all the learning outcomes of the relevant module. I suggested she turn the page over. Oh – she hadn't read that side! No scores on the doors this time: two judgements of confidence instead.

Life with Joe and Lauren was obviously tricky at first. There was an irony in that a national expert on the education of 14-19-year-olds was now living with two of them for the first time. Lauren (now in her early thirties and herself a teacher) still giggles at how I didn't clock that the coins I piled in a plate by the side of our bed subsidised their bus fares for several years. I wondered why the pile didn't seem to grow! I decided not to try to be an authority figure. Young people of their age rebel against authority anyway let alone that imposed by an alien step-father. So, I became one of them, an honorary adolescent. This meant when they were rude to me, I was rude back to them in the same way. It worked. This stance had been arrived at by a crude form of transactional analysis. It was tough on Alison because it meant that she now had three adolescents to deal with instead of two.

In spite of the trauma of their parents splitting up, we never suffered the challenges from Lauren and Joe often experienced by the parents and step-parents in re-constituted families. Both have flourished as adults. After a degree in Media Studies, Lauren now teaches with husband, Harvey, at a challenging school in the South East (they had both attended Royal Holloway, London at the same time but had never met there). They are proud parents, and we are proud grandparents, of two-year-old Penny. Joe qualified highly as a plumber and works successfully across the South East. He is married to accountant Laura and they occupy a very chic residence in Whitstable (Alison and I were to use both their work roles in our recently published book on apprenticeships).

Ofsted became responsible for inspecting all phases of initial teacher education in the early noughties. So, we had only just waved good bye to the QAA – which changed its methodology yet again and by the mid Noughties was conducting whole institution audits (I managed to dodge ours completely) – when Ofsted came to call. In 2006, our phase was inspected. What was helpful was that the lead inspector came on a pre-inspection visit weeks before the actual inspection itself. So that you had plenty of time to arrange the goods nicely in the shop window – or, as it might turn out – re-arrange the deckchairs on the Titanic! I decided to lead my troops from the front – there were forty or fifty training staff across the consortium who could have been observed – and offered myself up on the sacrificial table of observation. I decided to teach a session on Harvard referencing – God knows why – I guess I thought that if I could make the tedious interesting, I would be demonstrating a feat of pedagogy. And remember, these were practising FE teachers even though they were undertaking an initial qualification – potentially difficult, bolshie and critical of their trainers, teachers can make the worst students. In fact, the most difficult group I have ever taught, more difficult than at the comprehensive I taught at in Liverpool in the seventies, were a group of university teachers following a PGCE in Higher Education. Completely unmanageable! So, there was I, ten minutes before the evening class was to start, before the inspector's arrival, carrying out my pre-flight safety checks. Loose leads across the floor are potential trip hazards and I checked these then double checked the floor plugs. Unfortunately, I caught the skin of my knuckle between the plug and the socket. As anyone who has done so will know, if you cut a knuckle joint, you bleed profusely. Thankfully, I managed to avoid bleeding on my handouts, neatly arranged on the table in front of me and legged it to the bogs, imploring arriving students to locate sticking plasters as I went. In the end, the session went well but I remember the inspector eyeing the dressing on my knuckles, as if I'd had a fist fight in the pub on the way to class. The overall grade for the inspection was 'Good – Grade 2.' We were on the way to restoring our reputation, so badly undermined by the QAA.

Karen Flanagan had been a fellow student and friend of Alison's on the PGCE and after graduation, went off to teach Special Educational Needs students in FE before completing her Master's with us. By 2006, she had joined the Department and would go on to direct the PGCE she had taken seven years earlier. However, she knew that I intended to ask Alison to marry me but that I hadn't had the courage to pop the question. One morning she strode into my study. 'Right, come on then.' Our first stop was Madam Oiseau on Northgate where we bought some very expensive chocs. Flanagan managed to blag a box for herself as well, as I remember. Next stop was an exclusive jeweller's on Sun Street. So exclusive that you had to ring the bell and be scrutinised by the owners before being admitted. 'What kind of price range did you have in mind?' enquired the jeweller. I mentioned a figure. 'Double it,' ordered a growling Flanagan from the corner. We came away with a beautiful ring with a 1930s design which cost twice as much as I'd intended to pay. On the way back, we stopped at the Northgate Florist, where Flanagan managed to secure a bunch for herself, as well as the bouquet I'd bought for Alison. I had to secrete all this in my car boot and was nearly undone later in a row outside Sainsbury's when I wouldn't let Alison open the car boot to put a bag of groceries in. All this was recounted at the wedding later that year by Flanagan in her speech at the reception, by which time she'd managed to abandon her sparkly, red Wizard of Oz bridesmaid's shoes for a pair of red DMs boots.

In 2008, I persuaded Alison to, and she was successful in, applying for the programme directorship of the PGCE 14-19 at Canterbury Christ Church. I had helped establish this in 2002 and managed to convince the Teacher Training Agency, as it was then, as well as those conferring FE teacher qualification status to recognise it as the first ever programme to qualify teachers to teach both in the secondary and FE sectors. (This is now commonplace and, following the Wolf Report, Qualified Teacher Learning and Skills (QTLS) is regarded as equivalent to Qualified Teacher Status (QTS) for the purpose of teaching in schools). I was delighted Alison was going to pick up the mantle. She was to study these students and follow their subsequent careers as part of the doctorate she is just completing.

Four years after the Grade 2 Ofsted inspection, Ofsted were back. This time, they were inspecting the Primary, Secondary, and FE phases as well as employer-based training. As soon as this inspection was confirmed, I broke out in psoriasis which I still suffer from over a decade later. One of my staff, who was medically trained, looked at it and declared it 'Ofsted Psoriasis'.

We heads of department were summoned to the feedback on the inspection. Primary, Secondary, including the 14-19 PGCE and Employment-based Training, had gained eight Grade Ones out of eight for Overall Effectiveness and Capacity to Improve, while FE had Grade One for Capacity to Improve but Grade

Two for Overall Effectiveness. I remember going back to give the news to my staff. FE has been called the Cinderella Sector in contrast to secondary and primary phases. And those of us nationally in FE teacher training, around forty universities at the time, certainly felt it was regarded as the Cinderella Training Sector. 'Wouldn't it be great if, one day, the situation was reversed,' I told them, 'with FE teacher training gaining Outstanding and the other phases only Good?' I invoked an epithet used by my father when describing an unlikely event. 'If X happened', he would say, 'I'd walk bare-arsed to the post office.'

The following year, I responded to an advert placed by Ofsted. They wanted teacher trainers from the university sector to apply to be seconded to Ofsted for a year. They would be trained as Her Majesty's Inspectors and participate in and lead inspections of initial teacher training. I wasn't sure if this was a PR stunt, aimed at cosying up to the sector. Unlike schools and colleges, universities have a history of independence and autonomy, awarding their own qualifications. Many, therefore, were cagy about being inspected by a Government appointed quality watchdog. I was keen to take up this opportunity. Firstly, I thought (and I was right) that working as an inspector, going over to the other side, would give me insights into the process of inspection which might be useful when I went back to being a provider. Secondly, the secondment would afford me access to my colleagues' practice which, hopefully, would enrich my own. This was a double-edged sword. I would be responsible for making judgments about the quality of the practice of providers who were essentially my peers, many of whom I knew professionally and, in some cases, personally. These were judgments which could end up affecting their careers.

So, there I was, in my whistle and flute, with three other colleagues, two secondary and one primary specialist, at Ofsted HQ in Holborn, London being greeted by none other than Her Majesty's Chief Inspector of Schools, Christine Gilbert. She invited us out to dinner that night, which we thought was a good start (and paid, which we reckoned was an outstanding start)! Then we were off to Bristol, HQ Ofsted South, to complete our induction training and meet our mentors. The training itself wasn't very good. I think it was because most HMI, in common with many university teacher educators I'm familiar with, have a history of teaching children or young people, and are not necessarily good adult educators. My mentor, once I was introduced to him, seemed to have had an immediate aversion to me, which I thought was unlikely to support my professional development. This lasted for a couple of months. Then one day, there was a volte face and I couldn't do anything wrong. He was now encouraging and wrote glowing evaluation reports of my work. He did say, some months down the line, that my laugh reminded him of his father's so maybe this was what triggered his immediate repulsion.

We had to shadow a number of inspections before being let loose on the real thing. My first was a school inspection in West London. I stayed with the HMI inspection lead at a hotel near the school where he was to rendezvous with his team. I was soon to be introduced to the black humour most professions possess. We were driving to the school in the HMI's car and his satnav suddenly lost its signal. 'Shit,' he said. 'I've never been to the school before.' 'Why don't we follow those children?' I said, pointing to the hordes of children swarming along the pavement. 'Which ones? I haven't a clue what the uniform looks like.' We finally located the school through trial and error. As we approached the school, he said, 'Right, if there's a parking place it's at least Requires Improvement. If there's a cone reserving it, then it's Good. If somebody's standing there ready to lift the cone, it's definitely Outstanding.' I was very impressed by the lead inspector that day. He was analysing complex information, carrying out inspection activities himself – observing, going on learning walks - he was managing his team, having difficult conversations with senior staff. At the end of the day, he had to draw all the data together and give a series of complex judgements and verdicts. It was a clear demonstration of the challenge I had before me.

My initiation into inspection culture was gradual. I was at my first shadow of an inspection of initial teacher education at a university in the North of England. The HMI on these inspections tend to stay together at the same hotel. So, at dinner on the first night, the waiter went around the table, there were seven or eight of us, asking us what drinks we wanted. I went first. 'Dry white wine please - yes, large, thank you.' As each in turn asked for water, my face reddened. Finally, the lead inspector asked for a couple of jugs of water for the table. 'Tap, please,' he asked. I hadn't remembered taking a vow of temperance at my induction. It turned out that HMI rarely drank alcohol on inspections because there was no point in a sixteen-hour working day when it was advisable.

Part of the challenge of the role was a logistical one. I was slated to carry out an inspection based in Sheffield but at centres throughout Yorkshire and Humberside. Ofsted staff make all the travel and accommodation arrangements for inspectors centrally so I was booked into a hotel in the centre of Sheffield. As I checked in, I asked about the hire car that had supposed to have been delivered to the hotel for me earlier in the day. Eventually, a member of staff was located who knew about this. 'Oh yes,' he said, 'I remember – they tried to leave the car with us but, because we don't have a car park, they couldn't. So, they took it back again.' I was due at a school in Bradford at 9am the following morning so I needed the wheels that night. It was now 7.30pm and the Ofsted staff who had booked the car weren't available. I rang the local office of the car hire firm. No reply. I rang the national HQ of the car hire firm. The person who answered confirmed all their Sheffield offices were now closed but they would try to get the manager of a local office to open up for me. Eventually, I took a call from the manager of one of their hire car centres in Sheffield. But it was on the outskirts of the city. Could I get there?

So, I climbed into a cab and made my way out there. By now, I was starting to feel like Brian Stimson, John Cleese's headmaster character in *Clockwise*. By the time I arrived, the modest saloon which I had been supposed to drive had long ago been allocated to someone else. There was only one vehicle left. Would that do? I looked over at a monster of a vehicle, a 4x4 the size of a Sherman tank. I climbed into the driving seat. The dashboard resembled the instrument panel of a Boeing 757. To say the Satnav was complex would be an understatement. It promised to do everything but make a cup of tea for you. 'Don't worry', said the helpful car hire centre manager, 'I'll enter the hotel postcode and you just put your foot down.' Which I did. But at the first lights I pulled up at, the engine cut out. 'Fuck

– the fucking engine's cut out!' I shouted, now overwhelmed by panic. 'The fucking engine's fucking cut out! No!' This was 2012 and what I didn't realise was that the engine of this vehicle was a first-generation stop-start one allegedly designed to cut fuel use and eliminate idle emissions. By chance, I pressed the accelerator and, lo, the engine leapt into action. My relief was tempered as I reached the hotel which I remembered did not have a car park. So, I spent another half hour circling Sheffield in search of one. I would have a further panic in the morning when I came to pick the car up. 'Fuck - where's the fucking ignition? Where is the fucker?' This was 2012 and what I didn't realise was that this car was a first-generation engine with a start button instead of an ignition key, which I should have realised since the key fob had no key. But no-one had said!

So, I reached the Bradford school in time in the end and cruised into the car park in my tank. As I pulled into a parking space, another car came up behind me and flashed me. I got out. 'Excuse me,' a woman shouted through the driver's window. '…you're in my space.' When I looked, each space had large capital letter initials painted in it. Each member of staff had their own parking space. I moved the car and then went into the school office. 'Sorry,' said the secretary, 'we don't have spaces for guests. But go out of the school and turn right, take the second left and you'll find plenty of parking.' So, I did and made my way back to the school. But I was now locked out. 'Main gate locked from 9am', a notice helpfully informed me.

I liked and admired the inspectors I worked with. There was the odd one who enjoyed the power rather too much but by and large they were a fair, perceptive and knowledgeable bunch. And I enjoyed their company. On the last night of my last inspection, again in Sheffield, we went out for an Italian meal to 'celebrate' my departure. Not sure I appreciated the sentiment here. However, I left my colleagues with an impression of me at my insufferable worst. We were playing a game of 'best places in the world we'd eaten'. The first HMI said. 'Well – my restaurant's in Paris, Montmartre – it's a roof restaurant…' 'Hotel Terrasse,' I shouted, 'overlooking the cemetery!' I went on. The second HMI ventured her preference. 'Mine's in Bologna….,' 'The Diana,' I irritatingly interjected, 'on the way to the station from the main square. Known as the high temple of Bolognese cuisine. I had the most wonderful seafood risotto there, cooked at the table'. This was shaping up like a sketch from The Catherine Tate Show. 'Mine's also in Italy, in Venice…' said the next HMI. 'It has to be Harry's Bar,' quoth I, 'birthplace of the Bellini. I've got a Tosin ashtray copy from Harry's Bar.' 'Mine's also Italian, Sardinia actually, piped up a fourth HMI…' 'I bet it's the Grazia Deledda, Arzachena,' I guessed correctly, 'had the most divine roast goat there.' They'd had enough. We all quietly returned to our plates of pasta.

I'd been back in my head of department role for a year when it was decided that my faculty was to restructure. Why? I really can't remember. Most educational organisations seem to be in a constant state of re-organisation for re-organisation's sake, as far as I could see. But, fortunately, I was a member of the senior management team overseeing the re-structure, so I would have some say in it.

Meanwhile, my department applied for government funding to run a project to train high calibre 'premium' graduates for the FE sector. The organisation 'Teach First' had been phenomenally successful training high flying graduates to teach in challenging schools in areas of social deprivation and this project appeared to be an attempt to emulate that success for the FE sector. Successful graduates would receive a wacking great bursary of £30K for two years while taking a customised PGCE and completing a Master's degree – no fees required for either. The funding available to successful bidders was £1.2M.

And then Ofsted returned. I had been poacher turned game-keeper at Ofsted but had now turned back into a poacher provider. Our department's inspection master plan sprang into action. However, the week began badly with two of our trainees at one college judged as requiring improvement. Fortunately, the college tutor had independently made the same judgment as the inspector which strengthened the inspector's confidence in the robust quality of our assessment of performance. We heads of department would meet each evening to compare notes. The heads of primary and secondary seemed glummer each day. Our phase lead inspector had us sit in on the commentary from his team, who were all over London and the South East, so I knew we were heading for Outstanding – but had to contain my glee for my colleagues' sakes. And then, on the final day, the jury was in, the verdicts pronounced: Primary QTS - four Grade 2 judgements, Secondary QTS - four Grade 2 judgements, Initial Teacher Education for FE – four Grade 1 judgements. I returned to my department's building on a cloud. The journey we had made from the damning QAA assessment over a decade before via two more QAA events and three Ofsted inspections was over. Back at HQ, my delighted staff reminded me I had one more task remaining: walking bare-arsed to the post office.

But it didn't end there. I was sitting quietly at my desk the following morning when the phone rang. It was the director of the premium graduate project. He'd called to give me feedback on our application. I pretended to get a pad and paper even though I had no intention of noting feedback for a project we'd failed to get. I asked him to go ahead. 'Well – you've got the project,' he said. 'That's the feedback.' We were the only university in the country to do so. My staff went wild. Ofsted Outstanding and £1.2M in twenty-four hours.

That term, the restructure was complete. My post had been merged with others! Even though I had been central to the process, it came as a bit of a shock. And, although I was sixty-four that term, I simply hadn't seen myself retiring. I stayed on for a term to carry out an investigation into what the areas of development were for Primary and Secondary coming out of the inspection, irony of ironies, before retiring at Christmas.

Shortly before I left, I was very excited to see pop up in my in-box, an email headed, 'From the Vice-Chancellor'. And it was clearly a personal email from him, not a staff round robin. What parting gift would the institution be bestowing on me prior to my exit? How would it mark my twenty-five years' loyal service (culminating in Ofsted Outstanding and a £1.2M project)? An honorary fellowship, an honorary degree, an emeritus chair? A bonus? 'Dear Andy,' it began, 'as someone who has made a valuable contribution to the University this year, I am pleased to offer you two free tickets to any event of your choice at this year's Canterbury Festival.' Er…well… thank you very much. We attended a very depressing concert by a Russian A cappella choir. The high point of the evening was a chorister on the back row fainting (she went on to make a full recovery).

My dean and my colleague heads of department invited Alison and myself out for a farewell dinner at a Moroccan restaurant in town. I was very touched by this. However, I nipped up to the loo at the end of the meal and when I came down, the dean assured me the bill had been taken care of. It was only when we were on the way home that Alison informed me that she'd had to take care of the bill for the two of us when none of my colleagues came forward! A sheeny lot, educationalists!

Come January, all my ducks turned out to be in a row. My teacher's pension lump sum (more money than I'd had in my life) went into my bank account, as did my voluntary redundancy payment – nearly a year's salary - and the first instalment of my teacher's pension payments. I had been carefully monitoring this while on a month's retirement trip to Hong Kong, Australia and Thailand with Alison. The following June my state pension kicked in.

My retirement has been anything but. It gave me the opportunity to work nationally as I had at Ofsted, rather than provincially. As the only provider who has led Ofsted inspections of initial teacher education, I have been in great demand and have worked with twelve universities to prepare them for inspection. I have in my time been an external examiner/assessor for nine universities and, as I write, am external for two universities. I was, for three years, Chair of the Post 16 Committee of the Universities' Council for the Education of Teachers (UCET) which involved me in various national issues, including apprenticeships for teachers. This role enabled me to travel to Panama as part of a British Government experts panel advising the Panamanian Government on technical and vocational education reform. I have spoken at and chaired education conferences. I have worked in various capacities with the Education and Training Foundation which describes itself as 'the expert body for professional development and standards in Further Education (FE) and Training in England'. I have been a facilitator on their Outstanding Teaching Learning and Assessment Project, advised on professional standards, advanced teacher status and training for the Government's new T Levels. I have co-written a book with Alison on apprentice-ships....this is beginning to sound like a job application. Most of all, I have had the opportunity to be grandad to beautiful Penny, to whom this book is dedicated. It is an opportunity, never having had children of my own, to witness the joy of her growing and blossoming.

THE END